HAPPY 21st POLLY
"TRUST YOU WILL COOK
UP A STORM"
Best wishes
Peter

Cook's
BIBLE

Cook's
BIBLE

THE DEFINITIVE COOK'S GUIDE

First published in 2010
LOVE FOOD is an imprint of Parragon Books Ltd

Parragon
Queen Street House
4 Queen Street
Bath BA1 1HE, UK

ISBN: 978-1-4075-9739-3

Seasonal Food Chart by Christine McFadden

Printed in China

Notes for the Reader

This book uses both metric and imperial measurements. Follow the same units of measurement throughout; do not mix metric and imperial. All spoon measurements are level: teaspoons are assumed to be 5 ml, and tablespoons are assumed to be 15 ml. Unless otherwise stated, milk is assumed to be full fat, eggs and individual vegetables are medium, and pepper is freshly ground black pepper.

The times given are an approximate guide only. Preparation times differ according to the techniques used by different people and the cooking times may also vary from those given. Optional ingredients, variations or serving suggestions have not been included in the calculations.

Recipes using raw or very lightly cooked eggs, fish, meat or poultry should be avoided by infants, the elderly, pregnant women, convalescents and anyone suffering from an illness. Pregnant and breastfeeding women are advised to avoid eating peanuts and peanut products. Sufferers from nut allergies should be aware that some of the ready-made ingredients used in the recipes in this book may contain nuts. Always check the packaging before use.

Picture Acknowledgements

The publisher would like to thank the following for permission to reproduce copyright material on the following pages:

Corbis cover image: Whisk and Wooden Spoon © E.Fenot/photocuisine/Corbis
Getty images: jacket flaps/endpapers: Cutlery on table © Shoula/Getty Images, 2, 4–5, 8–9, 10, 11, 12, 48–49, 74–75, 100–101, 126–127, 152–153, 178–179, 204–205, 230–231, 256–257, 261

Introduction

Seasonal Food Chart

	Spring			Summer			Autumn			Winter		
FISH & SEAFOOD	Early	Mid	Late	Early	Mid	Late	Early	Mid	Late	Early	Mid	Late
Clams	•	•					•	•	•	•	•	•
Cod	•	•	•	•	•	•	•	•	•	•	•	•
Haddock			•	•	•	•	•	•	•	•	•	•
Lobster		•	•	•	•	•	•	•	•	•		
Mackerel			•	•	•	•	•	•				
Mussels	•	•					•	•	•	•	•	•
Plaice			•	•	•	•	•	•	•	•	•	
Prawns*	•	•	•	•	•	•	•	•	•	•	•	•
Salmon		•	•	•	•	•	•					
Sardines			•	•	•	•	•					
Scallops	•					•	•	•	•	•	•	•
Sea bass	•					•	•	•	•	•	•	•
Shrimp	•	•	•	•	•	•	•	•				•
Squid				•	•	•	•	•	•	•	•	
Tuna*	•	•	•	•	•	•	•	•	•	•	•	•
MEAT												
Beef	•	•	•	•	•	•	•	•	•	•	•	•
Lamb (spring)		•	•	•	•	•	•	•	•	•	•	•
Pork	•	•	•	•	•	•	•	•	•	•	•	•
POULTRY & GAME												
Chicken	•	•	•	•	•	•	•	•	•	•	•	•
Duck	•	•	•	•	•	•	•	•	•	•	•	•
Goose							•	•	•	•	•	
Pheasant								•	•	•	•	•
Quail	•	•	•	•	•	•	•	•	•	•	•	•
Turkey	•	•	•				•	•	•	•	•	•
VEGETABLES & SALADS												
Asparagus			•	•								
Aubergines					•	•	•					
Beans, broad				•	•	•	•					
Beans, French				•	•	•	•	•				
Beans, runner				•	•	•	•	•	•			
Beetroot	•				•	•	•	•	•	•	•	•
Brussels sprouts	•							•	•	•	•	•
Butternut squash							•	•	•	•	•	
Cabbage, green	•	•	•	•	•	•	•	•	•	•	•	•
Cabbage, red	•	•	•	•		•	•	•	•	•	•	•
Cabbage, Savoy	•	•					•	•	•	•	•	•
Cabbage, white	•	•	•	•	•	•	•	•	•	•	•	•
Carrots	•	•	•	•	•	•	•	•	•	•	•	•
Celery	•	•	•	•	•	•	•	•	•	•	•	•
Chillies					•	•	•	•				
Courgettes				•	•	•	•	•				
Cucumber	•	•	•	•	•	•	•	•	•	•		
Fennel				•	•	•	•	•				

This is an approximate guide to availability since weather conditions vary from region to region.

With the exception of items marked as imported, with an asterisk, the chart shows the seasons for produce grown in the UK and northern Europe.

The seasons for fish and shellfish apply to wild rather than farmed food.

	Spring			Summer			Autumn			Winter		
	Early	Mid	Late	Early	Mid	Late	Early	Mid	Late	Early	Mid	Late
Garlic (fresh)			•	•	•							
Globe artichokes				•	•	•	•	•	•			
Jerusalem artichokes	•							•	•	•	•	•
Leeks	•	•				•	•	•	•	•	•	•
Lettuce			•	•	•	•	•	•				
Mushrooms (wild)			•				•	•	•			
Onions, main crop	•			•	•	•	•	•	•	•	•	•
Onions, pickling				•	•	•						
Onions, spring	•	•	•	•	•	•	•	•	•	•		
Parsnips	•						•	•	•	•	•	•
Peas				•	•	•	•					
Peppers					•	•	•	•				
Potatoes	•	•	•	•	•	•	•	•	•	•	•	•
Pumpkin							•	•	•			
Rocket		•	•	•	•	•	•	•	•	•	•	•
Shallots	•						•	•	•	•	•	•
Spinach	•	•	•	•	•	•	•	•	•	•	•	•
Swede	•						•	•	•	•	•	•
Sweetcorn					•	•	•	•				
Sweet potato*	•	•	•					•	•	•	•	•
Tomatoes					•	•	•	•				
Turnip (baby)			•	•				•	•	•	•	•
Watercress	•	•	•	•	•	•	•	•	•	•	•	•
HERBS												
Basil			•	•	•	•	•					
Chives		•	•	•	•	•	•	•	•			
Coriander		•	•	•	•	•	•	•	•			
Dill			•	•	•	•	•					
Mint		•	•	•	•	•	•	•	•			
Oregano		•	•	•	•	•	•	•	•	•	•	•
Parsley (curly)	•	•	•	•	•	•	•	•	•	•	•	•
Parsley (flat leaf)		•	•	•	•	•	•	•	•			
Rosemary	•	•	•	•	•	•	•	•	•	•	•	•
Sage	•	•	•	•	•	•	•	•	•	•	•	•
Tarragon			•	•	•	•	•	•				
Thyme		•	•	•	•	•	•	•	•	•		
FRUIT & NUTS												
Apples	•						•	•	•	•	•	•
Apricots*				•	•	•	•					
Almonds*									•	•	•	•
Blackberries					•	•	•	•				
Blueberries					•	•	•					
Cherries				•	•	•						
Cranberries*								•	•	•		
Grapes*	•	•	•	•	•	•	•	•	•	•	•	•
Oranges*	•	•	•	•	•	•	•	•	•	•	•	•
Pears							•	•	•	•	•	
Raspberries			•	•	•	•	•	•				
Rhubarb	•	•	•	•	•	•	•				•	•
Strawberries				•	•	•	•					

Healthy Eating

The American writer Marjorie Rawlings once said that food imaginatively and lovingly prepared, eaten in good company, warms the soul with something more than mere calories. While this is true, it is also true that the human body needs a regular and balanced intake of over 70 nutrients – vitamins and minerals – in order to keep it working properly and protect it from disease.

The five food groups

A healthy and balanced diet needs to contain adequate amounts of five major food groups: protein, carbohydrates, fat, minerals and vitamins.

Protein

Protein provides the building blocks for the body. Everyone's requirement differs, depending on health, age and size, but as a rough guide, the average minimum requirement is around 50 g/1¾ oz per day. There are two types of protein: complete protein, found in foods of animal origin, such as meat, poultry, fish, eggs, milk and cheese, and in certain plants, such as buckwheat and quinoa; and incomplete protein, found in foods of non-animal origin, such as nuts, seeds, grains, beans and pulses. Complete proteins provide the proper balance of amino acids necessary to build body tissues; incomplete proteins need to be mixed with small amounts of complete protein in order to provide adequate nutrition.

Carbohydrates

The main source of the body's energy is carbohydrates. No official daily requirement exists, but a minimum of 50 g/1¾ oz daily is recommended to avoid an acid condition of the blood called 'ketosis'. This condition occurs when your body has to use fat instead of carbohydrates to provide its energy.

Carbohydrates are therefore an essential part of a healthy human diet. They can be found in starchy and sugary foods. There are two types of carbohydrate: complex carbohydrates, which can be found in bread, pasta, rice, cereals, beans, pulses, fruit and vegetables; and simple carbohydrates, which can be found in many desserts, puddings, cakes, chocolate, sweets and fizzy drinks.

Complex carbohydrates take longer to be broken down in the body, which means they release energy into the body more slowly and gradually. These are the best carbohydrates to eat. The sugary, simple type of carbohydrate will provide a quick boost of energy, but this surge of energy is quickly used up; such 'highs and lows' of energy are not good for maintaining good health and vitality.

Fats

These days we are encouraged to eat a low-fat diet, but to cut fat out completely would be very unhealthy. What we should be doing is eating the types of fat that are good for us, and reducing our intake of the potentially harmful kinds. Saturated fat is potentially harmful in excessive amounts: it can raise our blood cholesterol levels and blood pressure.

A good way to remember which foods are high in saturated fat is to think of those fats that stay solid at room temperature, such as lard and butter. It is these kinds of solid fats that clog our arteries and can lead to heart disease. The healthier kinds of fat are polyunsaturated fats, such as sunflower oil and soya oil, and monounsaturated fats, such as olive oil and groundnut oil. We also need a regular intake of essential fatty acids (EFAs): these actually help the body to burn off excess fat. Good sources of EFAs include oily fish, sunflower seeds, pumpkin seeds and avocados. So it is not true to say that all fat is bad for you. Restrict saturated fat in your diet by all means, but not the other kinds. Remember also that a low-fat diet is unsuitable for children under five years of age.

Minerals

There are about 18 minerals required for healthy body function, and the six best-known minerals are: calcium (found in milk, cheese and beans), iodine (found in seafood, kelp and onions), iron (found in red meat, egg yolks, oysters, nuts and beans), magnesium (found in figs, lemons, nuts, seeds and apples), phosphorus (found in meat, poultry, fish, whole grains, eggs, nuts and seeds) and zinc (found in steak, wheatgerm, brewer's yeast, eggs and pumpkin seeds). Minerals are essential for maintaining good health. For example, a deficiency of calcium can lead to rickets or osteoporosis, and a deficiency of iron can cause anaemia.

Vitamins

This food group comprises organic substances that can be found within the foods we eat. We need only minuscule amounts of these substances in order to be healthy, but a deficiency of even one type of vitamin can cause us to be unhealthy. Vitamins range from the 'fat-soluble' kind, such as A (found in green leafy vegetables, liver and dairy products), D (found in fish liver oils, sardines, tuna and dairy products) and E (found in soya beans, whole wheat and grains, and eggs), to the 'water-soluble' kind, such as C (found in citrus fruits, green leafy vegetables and tomatoes). Some people think that it is possible to live on vitamins only, but this concept is a myth: vitamins are only one of the five main nutrients necessary for a healthy body. It is always preferable to get your vitamins naturally from the foods you eat, rather than from synthetic materials such as tablets, because synthetic vitamins can sometimes cause toxic reactions. Natural vitamins are much safer.

Making the right choices

It is vital to make good food choices and eat sensibly. Did you know, for example, that a diet high in salt and saturated fat can increase the risk of heart disease, while eating other foods, such as beans, can help to reduce cholesterol and prevent heart disease? The message here is that what you absorb into your body plays a crucial role in your health and overall wellbeing. Eating more of the right foods, and reducing your intake of the potentially harmful ones, can contribute enormously to how well you feel and the state of your physical health.

So which are the right foods to eat and which are the wrong ones? It is not always easy to decide. For example, too much salt can lead to higher blood pressure and depleted adrenal glands, but to cut it out completely would be very unwise because we need a certain amount each day in order to stay healthy. Salt actually helps to keep our fluid levels in balance and our muscles healthy. The amount we need, however, is very low – less than 5 g/1 teaspoon per day. Since many foods we buy have salt added already – for example, cheese or ready-prepared foods such as pizzas – we can usually get the amount we need without having to add extra salt to our meals. It is the habit of adding extra salt to our food that tends to push us over the healthy limit. Basically, a balanced diet should consist of plenty of fruit, vegetables, whole grains and cereals, dairy products, and smaller quantities of protein foods from animal sources (such as meat, fish, eggs, or dairy products) as well as from non-animal sources (such as beans, peas, nuts and seeds). A vegetarian diet is also perfectly healthy, as long as it is balanced and contains all the essential nutrients.

DOS AND DON'TS FOR A HEALTHY DIET

Here are some tips to help keep your diet healthy and your body in peak physical condition:

DO eat regular meals – never skip them, especially breakfast. Skipping meals will encourage your body to go into 'starvation mode' and store up fat.

DO eat at least five portions of fruit and vegetables each day. They can be fresh, frozen or canned, but vary them as much as possible. Not all fruits and vegetables contain the same amount of health-giving nutrients, but when you are in any doubt, you can estimate that one portion is equal to about 85 g/3 oz. Any of the following foods also equal one portion:

- one 150 ml/5 fl oz glass of fruit juice
- one orange, apple, nectarine, peach or banana
- half a grapefruit
- two plums
- a quarter of a cucumber
- one pepper or tomato
- an 85 g/3 oz portion of cauliflower or broccoli
- three heaped tablespoons of any vegetable, for example peas, carrots, sweetcorn, beans or pulses.

DO eat more whole grains, such as oats, barley, rye and corn. Choose wholemeal bread and pasta instead of white varieties, and wholegrain brown rice instead of polished white rice.

DO eat oily fish regularly, at least three times a week if you can.

DO choose organic produce wherever possible: organic foods are free from artificial additives and pesticides, and are a much healthier choice.

DO drink at least eight 225 ml/8 fl oz glasses of water a day. This means consumption of at least 1.8 litres/3 pints daily. You need a regular and adequate intake of water to flush toxins from the body and replace water lost through urine and sweat. Inadequate water consumption leads to dehydration, with symptoms such as headaches, tiredness and loss of concentration. Prolonged dehydration can lead to constipation and kidney stones.

DON'T eat too much saturated fat. Reduce your intake of greasy fried foods and fatty red meat.

DON'T eat too many sugary foods, such as sweets, chocolate, puddings, desserts and fizzy drinks.

DON'T buy processed foods. Processed foods are often full of artificial additives, such as preservatives, colours and sweeteners – even packaged salad leaves have undergone chemical processing before they reach the retailers' shelves. Instead choose foods that are fresh and in their natural state. The benefits in terms of better flavour and more health-giving nutrients far outweigh the convenience of ready-prepared, packaged foods.

DON'T drink too much caffeine. It is a powerful stimulant and can make you feel lively, but in excess it can lead to health problems. Too much caffeine can lead to irritability, insomnia and feverish symptoms. Very high doses can cause more serious problems. The British Medical Journal reported that people who drink five or more cups of coffee a day have a 50 per cent higher risk of a heart attack than people who do not drink coffee. The main sources of caffeine are coffee, tea, cola drinks and cocoa, so avoid these drinks as much as possible. Switch to herbal teas and fruit juices instead. Some medicines also contain caffeine, so check the ingredients before you take them, and use an alternative if possible.

DON'T consume too much alcohol. Women should drink no more than 2 units a day, and men should drink no more than 3 units a day. A unit is equal to one small glass of 9% proof wine (125 ml/4 fl oz), a half-pint of lager or one pub measure of spirits (30 ml/1 fl oz). Try to keep at least two days a week alcohol free, and don't save up your weekly unit allowance for consumption on a single occasion.

DON'T add salt to your food. Alternatively, taste the food before you add salt, then keep the added salt to a minimum.

Health & Safety

The kitchen is often the focal point of the home. However, it is also the riskiest area: fires are much more likely to break out in the kitchen than in any other part of the home, and there is a risk of infestation by pests or potentially harmful bacteria. Adopting good hygiene habits and taking sensible precautions will protect your household from unnecessary accidents and illnesses.

Kitchen hygiene

Cleanliness is essential in the kitchen. Keep all kitchen surfaces scrupulously clean, and wash your hands thoroughly with soap and water when preparing food. Use a separate towel to dry your hands, not a tea towel. Whenever you leave the kitchen or touch a surface, such as a door handle or a curtain, even if it is only for a few moments, remember that your hands will quickly pick up bacteria, even if you think your home is scrupulously clean, so always wash your hands again before resuming any food preparation.

Make sure you use different chopping boards and utensils for cooked and raw foods to prevent cross-contamination of bacteria, especially when you are preparing meat or poultry. If you can afford it and have the room to store them, it is a good idea to have several different-coloured chopping boards for different purposes. You can keep one for raw meat, one for cooked meat, one for vegetables, one for a pet's food, and so on. Wash chopping boards and utensils well in hot, soapy water before and after each use. Glass and polypropylene chopping boards can be washed at relatively high temperatures in the dishwasher.

Change and wash dish cloths and tea towels regularly. Use a covered rubbish bin and disinfect it frequently.

Food preparation

Make sure that you thoroughly wash any foods that need cleaning, such as soil-covered vegetables, and pat dry with kitchen paper. You should also thoroughly defrost any frozen food that requires it, especially meat and poultry, and do not refreeze once it has thawed. The best place to defrost food is in the refrigerator. However, if you are short of time, you can defrost it in a cool room as long as it is well covered to prevent any potentially harmful bacteria from contaminating it.

Throw away any thawed juices from meat and poultry – do not use them in your dishes. And remember never to reuse a marinade, especially if it has been used for meat or poultry.

When reheating cooked meat dishes, remember that they may be reheated once only, and must reach a temperature of at least 75°C/167°F.

Do not leave cooked rice uncovered at room temperature for any length of time. Potentially harmful bacteria can multiply quickly on cooked rice, so if you have to store it, leave it to cool, cover it with clingfilm as soon as possible and keep it in the refrigerator. Use it within two days. The same goes for any cooked meats or poultry.

Safe storage

Always buy food as fresh as possible, and from a reputable supplier. Check any 'use by' or 'best before' dates, because sometimes out-of-date items languish on retailers' shelves and are bought by the unwary. Cover all exposed foods with clingfilm before refrigerating. If you buy a whole bird, remove any giblets from the cavity, cover with clingfilm and refrigerate separately from the bird. Store raw and cooked meat and poultry separately in different parts of your refrigerator.

Store your potatoes in a dark place, away from sunlight, or they will turn green – even fluorescent lighting can make them turn green. Green patches in potatoes contain a chemical called solanine. Solanine tastes bitter, and in large concentrations it can give you an upset stomach, so do not buy any potatoes with green patches. If, despite your best efforts, a potato you have bought or grown has developed a small green patch, cut the patch out, then use the rest of the potato. If the green covers a large area, you should discard the whole potato.

Kitchen first aid

Every kitchen should have a basic first-aid kit. Your standard kit should include rubber gloves, antiseptic wipes, burn cream, eye pads, safety pins, different-sized dressings, and triangular bandages. Catering establishments use blue plasters in order to make them easier to spot should they fall off. Although you don't have to use this type at home, their deep-blue colouring makes them ideal for home use too.

A fire blanket is also a good precaution in a kitchen. It can be a very useful item to have on hand in case a fire breaks out, and it can also be used to help keep a shock victim comfortable until help arrives.

FIRE SAFETY

As an absolute minimum, fit a battery-operated smoke alarm outside your kitchen, and check the battery regularly. Do not position it in the kitchen itself or over a direct source of smoke or heat, or it may be set off accidentally. Even better, ask a qualified electrician to install smoke and heat detectors throughout your home – for reliability they should be wired up to your mains electricity supply.

It is also a good idea to keep a fire extinguisher in the kitchen. Here are some other tips for kitchen fire safety:

- Keep electrical leads, oven gloves and tea towels away from the cooker.
- Keep your cooker clean, especially the grill and oven. A build-up of fat can catch fire.
- Do not let your sleeves or other loose clothing hang over the stove while you are cooking.
- Never leave pans on the cooker unattended. If you have to leave them, even for a few seconds, perhaps to answer the telephone, remove them from the heat.
- When you've finished cooking, make sure the cooker or oven is turned off.
- If a pan catches fire and you can't put it out easily and quickly, don't take any risks with your safety. Leave the house at once (making sure that you close all doors behind you as you go), and call the fire brigade immediately. If the fire is small and you are confident you can handle it, put a fire blanket over it, or alternatively run a cloth under the tap, wring it out and then cover the pan with it. Do not throw water into the pan because this action could exacerbate the problem. Turn off the heat as soon as you can get to it safely.

Equipment

A selection of carefully chosen tools is essential in the kitchen. If you are a beginner, you can make do with a few multi-purpose utensils, then add to them as your confidence grows. If you are an experienced cook, you may want to add some more sophisticated items, such as a pasta machine, to your range of tools.

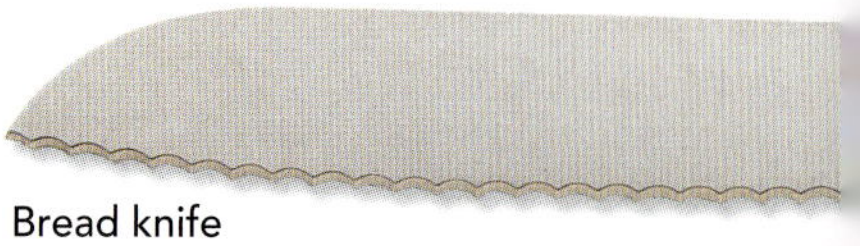

Bread knife

Carving knife

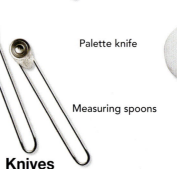

Palette knife

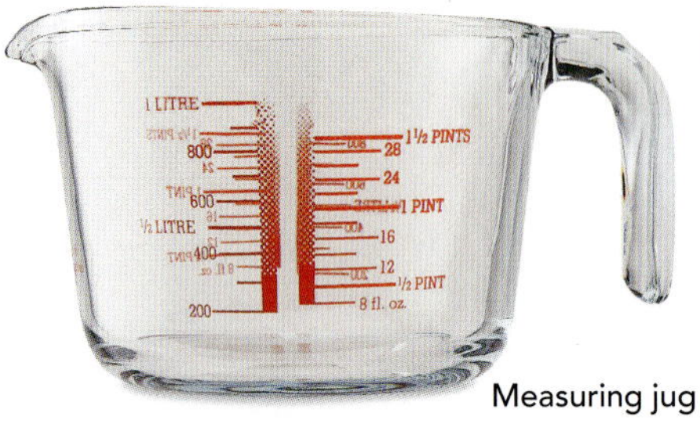

Measuring jug

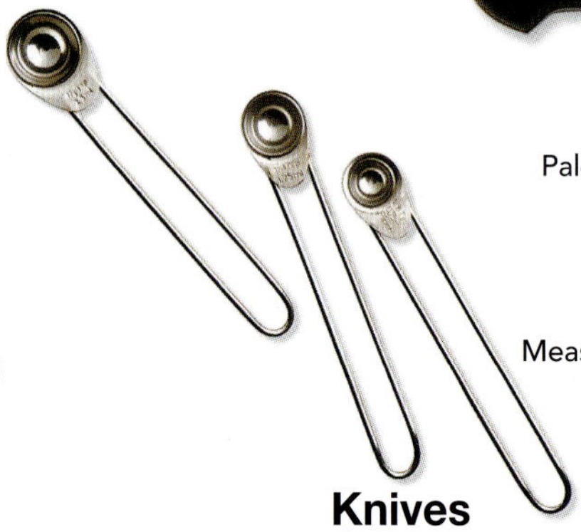

Measuring spoons

Measuring equipment

The items listed here are useful for measuring liquids and solid foods. If you have scales, jugs and spoons with both metric and imperial measurements, you should stick to just one unit of measurement.

Kitchen scales

Scales come in manual and electric versions. It is best to buy scales that show both metric and imperial measurements.

Measuring jug

Jugs (usually available in both 600-ml/1-pint and 1.2-litre/2-pint sizes) are useful for measuring liquid ingredients. Choose ones in transparent materials that show both metric and imperial measurements.

Measuring spoons

These spoons are ideal for measuring both liquid and dry ingredients accurately.

Measuring cups

Unless you intend to use American recipes, you will not need measuring cups. American cooks use measuring cups instead of kitchen scales. The cups usually come in a nesting set of four different sizes: ¼, ⅓, ½ and 1 cup. They are available in stainless steel or plastic.

Knives

Buy the best quality knives you can afford because they will last longer, and keep them sharp. The first three listed here are the essential knives; the rest can be added later.

Small paring knife

A paring knife is invaluable for cutting vegetables, fruit, meat and cheese. It is 6–9 cm/2½–3½ inches in length.

Cook's knife

This good multi-purpose knife is 15–30 cm/6–12 inches long, and is essential for slicing and chopping.

Bread knife

This long serrated knife is ideal for slicing bread.

Small serrated knife

This knife is most often used for cutting vegetables and fruit. It is usually about 13 cm/5 inches long.

Cleaver

Its flat, rectangular blade is ideal for cutting meat joints.

Filleting knife

This knife has a flexible blade of about 20 cm/8 inches in length, and is used for vegetables, fruit and raw fish.

Carving knife

This knife has a blade about 30 cm/12 inches long, with a point for easy carving around the bones of joints. It usually comes with a carving fork, which has two long prongs and sometimes a guard to protect against accidents.

Cook's knife

Small paring knife

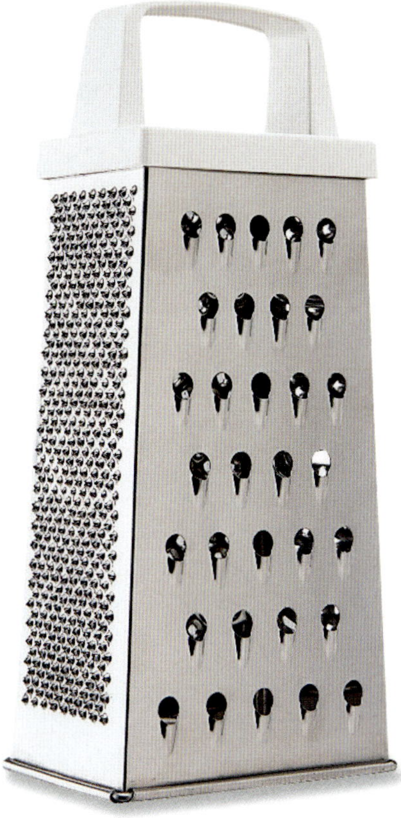

Grater

Other cutting tools and equipment

In addition to a basic set of knives, you will need some other cutting tools. Some of these tools are very specific, such as the zester, while others are for more general use.

Mezzaluna
The mezzaluna has two handles and a curved blade, and is used for chopping herbs and vegetables.

Palette knife
This knife is used for spreading rather than cutting, and it has many uses in the kitchen. It is ideal for icing cakes.

Knife sharpener
Although this has a handle like a knife, instead of a blade it has a long rod of roughened steel. When the edge of a knife is run along the rod at a 45° angle, it sharpens the blade.

Can opener
This everyday tool comes in many varieties, from hand-operated ones to wall-mounted automatic devices.

Zester
A citrus zester has a rectangular metal head with holes along the top edge. The holes are there to help remove fine shavings of zest without picking up the white pith.

Vegetable peeler
You can buy a swivel-bladed version or one that has a slicing blade in the middle and a sharp tip for coring.

Grater
There are different graters for different purposes, but a good, multi-purpose version to buy is a hollow box-shaped grater with a handle at the top and different cutting holes on each side.

Apple corer
This hollow, cylindrical tool is essential for removing cores from apples and pears quickly and easily.

Pastry cutters
These round circles are available in metal or plastic and are useful for cutting pastry circles. They are also ideal for shaping biscuits.

Kitchen scissors
Choose stainless-steel all-purpose scissors and keep them especially for use in the kitchen.

Zester

Vegetable peeler

Pots and pans

When you are buying pots and pans, choose the best quality you can afford. If cared for properly, they will more than repay the extra cost because they will last for many years.

Saucepans

You will need a small, preferably non-stick, milk pan for making sauces and scrambled eggs, and at least three other different-sized saucepans – small, medium and large. Choose saucepans that have secure lids. A large casserole dish with a lid is useful for casseroles, stews and whole birds.

Frying pans

You will need a small omelette pan, and a larger frying pan for more substantial foods. Non-stick varieties are ideal for cooking low-fat meals, but are not essential. A ridged griddle pan imparts a lovely stripy effect to food and is ideal for chargrilling beef and tuna steaks.

Steamer

Steamers come in different varieties. For example, you can buy a folding metal steamer that adjusts to any size of saucepan. You can also buy metal and bamboo steamers that are placed on top of the saucepan – some have more than one tier so that you can steam more than one food at a time. In addition, there are electric steamers, which are useful if you want to save space on the hob.

Wok

A wok is a deep, rounded, bowl-shaped pan with a handle. It is ideal for cooking stir-fries.

Large saucepan with lid

Ovenware and bakeware

Non-stick baking equipment will help you to slide out your culinary creations with ease. Take care not to scour it, however, or you will scratch the non-stick coating. Silicone bakeware needs little or no greasing or oiling.

Baking sheets and trays

Some of these rectangular and square metal sheets are flat and others have a lip around the edges. They are essential for baking a variety of foods, from oven-roasted vegetables and pizzas to meringues and biscuits.

Cake tins

To start with, a couple of round 20-cm/8-inch diameter shallow tins will come in handy for making sponges, and a deeper 23-cm/9-inch diameter springform cake tin will be useful for making larger cakes. A large square tin with removable section dividers will enable you to make different-sized square and rectangular cakes.

Flan/tart tins and dishes

These are usually round, and often have a fluted edge. They are ideal for baking quiches, flans and tarts, and come in a variety of sizes. The loose-based, stainless steel variety conducts heat better than ceramic ones and enables food to be lifted out easily.

Pie tins and dishes

These tins come in a variety of shapes and sizes, and are usually fairly deep with a protruding rim for pastry edging.

Roasting tins

These metal tins are deeper than baking trays, and are ideal for roasting meat and poultry.

Muffin tins

These rectangular tins usually come with 12 large, round indentations, which are ideal for making savoury or sweet muffins, individual fruit pies or Yorkshire puddings.

Loaf tins

These rectangular tins have deep sides and come in different sizes. They are useful for baking bread or savoury nut roasts.

Ramekins

These small, round dishes have many uses in the kitchen. They are very handy for making individual soufflés and crème caramels. They also double up nicely as serving dishes for butter, olives and nuts.

Frying pan

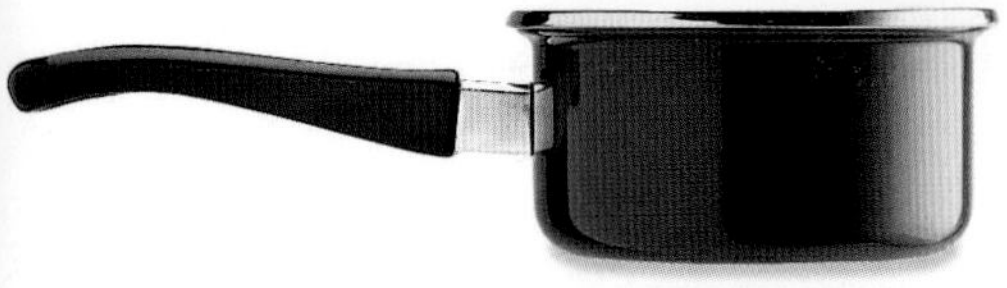

Saucepan

Ramekins

Sieves and strainers

The following items are useful in any kitchen. In particular, a sieve is essential for sifting dry ingredients such as flour, while a colander will make light work of draining a variety of foods.

Sieves

These come in metal or nylon, and are useful for sifting flour and straining liquid ingredients. Always use the nylon variety for acidic ingredients, such as berries.

Colander

A colander is a metal or plastic perforated bowl that is used for draining liquid from foods. They are available in different sizes and may have one or two handles and a flat base so that they can sit steadily on a work surface.

Egg separator

Although this small, round, slotted spoon is not essential, new cooks in particular will find it helpful for separating egg yolks from whites.

Dredger

This mesh-covered container is especially useful for sprinkling icing sugar or cocoa powder on to cakes and desserts.

Bowls and basins

You can buy bowls and basins in a variety of different materials and sizes, but metal will react with acid ingredients such as lime juice, so do not use metal bowls for acid-based marinades.

Mixing bowls

Mixing bowls are available in a variety of materials, including ceramic, glass, plastic and stainless steel. At least one large mixing bowl is essential, although several bowls of different sizes are even better. For example, you will need a smaller bowl to whip cream. You can also buy bowls that are sufficiently decorative to double up as serving bowls at the table.

Pudding basins

These come in different sizes and materials, including metal, ceramic, plastic and glass. A large pudding basin is ideal for making a substantial summer pudding or Christmas pudding for a large household, while a set of smaller basins is useful for making individual chilled or steamed puddings. It is often worth recycling basins from shop-bought puddings too.

Sieve

Colander

Pudding basin

Large mixing bowl

Spoons and spatulas

Spoons and spatulas are very helpful for lifting, turning, shaping, draining and serving a variety of foods. Here are some of the utensils you will find most useful.

Fish slice
This slotted lifting tool is essential when lifting floppy food, such as omelettes, fried eggs or fish fillets, from frying pans.

Draining spoon
This large, slotted spoon is ideal for lifting solid foods out of liquids so that the liquid drains away, and for skimming foam from the surface of simmering liquids, such as stock, and from jams and marmalade.

Serving/basting spoon
This large spoon is useful for serving food on to plates. It often has a groove on one side to direct the flow of juices and sauces.

Ladle
This is helpful for ladling soups into bowls or punch into glasses.

Tongs
A set of tongs is handy for turning hot food on a griddle pan or a barbecue.

Wooden spoon
This type of spoon is available in different sizes and is handy for mixing ingredients evenly, without scratching the delicate surfaces of pans and bowls.

Spatula
This utensil is available in wood, rubber or silicone, and is used for folding mixtures such as egg whites. The rubber and silicone types are also ideal for scraping down the sides of mixing bowls to get all the mixture out.

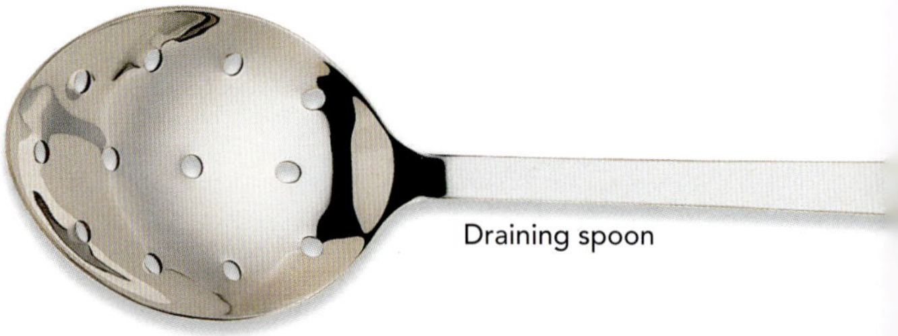

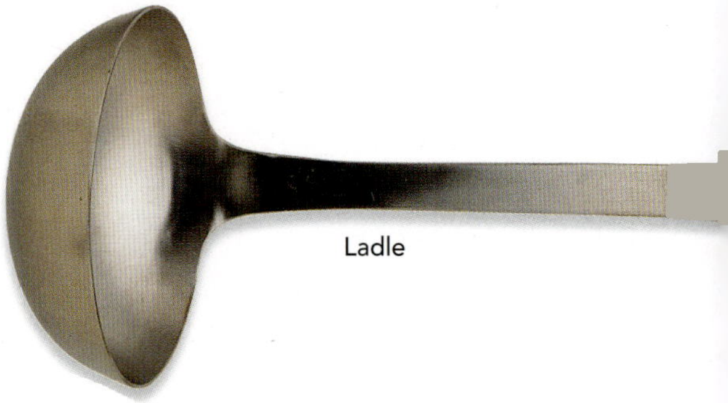

HOT HANDLES

Do not leave spoons and spatulas with metal handles to stand in the pan while cooking on a hot stove. Metal handles can get very hot, and are likely to cause burns.

Other useful utensils

You can add to your cooking utensils as and when you need them. Here are some of the items you are likely to find most useful and will want to buy sooner rather than later.

Citrus squeezer

These usually come in plastic or glass. They have a strainer to catch any pips, and a bowl underneath to catch the juice.

Corkscrew and bottle opener

You can buy these individually or combined into one utensil. The lever-action corkscrew is the easiest kind to use.

Pastry brush

Brushes are useful for sealing pies with water and for glazing.

Garlic press

A garlic press is not essential but is handy for crushing garlic cloves cleanly and efficiently. Some have a detachable grille for easy cleaning.

Hand whisks

Whisks are available in a variety of shapes and sizes. The most common is the balloon whisk, used for whisking egg whites and cream. Whisks with silicone-coated wires can be used in conjunction with non-stick saucepans.

Rolling pin

This long, cylindrical utensil usually comes in wood, glass or ceramic, and is essential for rolling out pastry.

Potato masher

This utensil is essential for mashing potatoes and other vegetables such as swede.

Pestle and mortar

These two utensils come as a pair in a variety of sizes and materials, such as marble and porcelain. They are used for crushing herbs and spices.

Chopping boards

Buy several different-coloured boards so that you can keep one for raw meat and poultry, one for cooked meats, one for vegetables, and so on.

Wire cooling racks

These metal racks can be round or rectangular, and are ideal for cooling cakes, biscuits and bread. It is often useful to have two racks to accommodate larger batches.

Skewers

Long stainless-steel skewers are a good choice, although other materials, such as wood, are also available. Skewers are essential for cooking kebabs. They are also useful for inserting into cakes and joints of meat to test if they are cooked all the way through.

Pie funnel

This is available in a variety of shapes and materials, and is used to hold up the pastry in pies. It prevents pastry becoming soggy by allowing the steam to escape.

Ice cream scoop

This tool is useful for scooping neat domes of ice cream or mashed potato on to plates.

Decorative moulds

These moulds are available in many shapes and sizes, and in plastic, metal or silicone. They can be used for shaping mousses, ice creams, jellies and creamy desserts.

Piping bags and nozzles

These piping tools come in various sizes and shapes and are useful for creating piped decorations in icing or cream on cakes and desserts.

Thermometers

Use a thermometer to test the temperature of your refrigerator and oven, in the preparation of meat and sugar, and when deep-frying.

Kitchen timers

Timers are available in different designs and sizes, and are useful for monitoring the cooking times of dishes.

Citrus squeezer

Garlic press

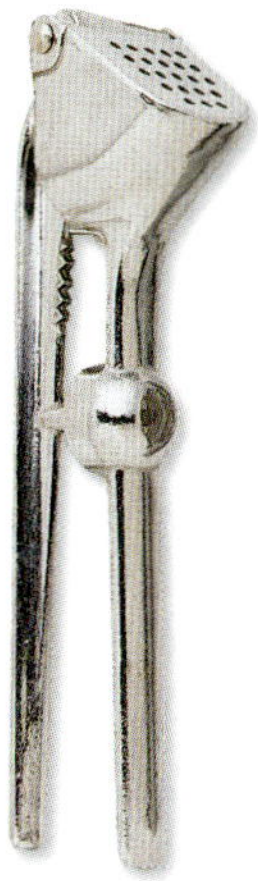

Potato masher

Pastry brushes

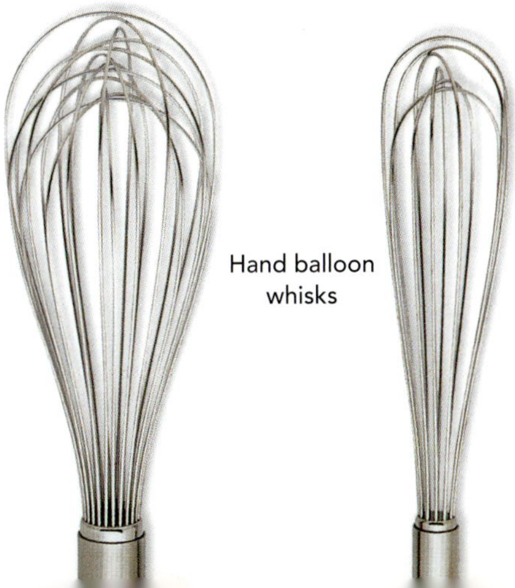

Hand balloon whisks

Machines and electric utensils

There is a wide variety of machines and electrical devices for the kitchen, and these make quick and easy work of preparing food – especially useful when catering for families or parties.

Free-standing mixer

Pasta machine

Food processor
This multi-purpose machine has metal blades that chop, shred and grate foods. Usually, it also comes with a selection of other attachments that mix and knead ingredients, such as sponge mixes and pastry dough.

Mini chopper
This compact machine is handy for chopping small quantities of nuts, garlic and herbs.

Blender
A blender is useful for puréeing foods, such as soups, batters, milk shakes and smoothies. It is also known as a liquidizer. The hand-held version allows you to purée food in a saucepan while it is cooking on the hob.

Pasta machine
If you prefer to make your own fresh pasta, you will find this machine indispensable for rolling and cutting pasta into noodles, ribbons and various decorative shapes.

Grinder
This very useful machine is essential for grinding nuts and coffee beans. It is also ideal for making fresh breadcrumbs, as are food processors and blenders.

Free-standing mixer
This machine, which is also called a food mixer, has a large bowl and a selection of mixing tools, such as a whisk and a dough kneader. It enables you to beat and whisk foods much faster than you can by hand.

Hand-held mixer
This tool, which you can hold over a bowl or saucepan, is more portable than a free-standing mixer. It is suitable for light mixtures, such as eggs and cream, but for more substantial mixtures you will find a free-standing mixer easier to use.

Deep-fat fryer
This heavy-based machine usually comes with a wire basket that can be hooked on to the side of the machine for easy draining of the cooking oil.

Pressure cooker
This deep, heavy electric saucepan is not essential, but it is useful for steaming food such as rice in about half the normal cooking time.

Slow cooker
This small appliance is very useful for cooking stews and casseroles slowly, and saves you having to use the oven. It also uses less electricity than an oven does. Simply add the food, cover, plug it in and wait for the lovely aromas to emerge.

CONVERSION CHARTS

OVEN TEMPERATURES

Celsius	Fahrenheit	Gas mark	Oven heat
110°	225°	¼	very cool
120°	250°	½	very cool
140°	275°	1	cool
150°	300°	2	cool
160°	325°	3	moderate
180°	350°	4	moderate
190°	375°	5	moderately hot
200°	400°	6	moderately hot
220°	425°	7	hot
230°	450°	8	very hot
240°	475°	9	very hot

SPOON MEASUREMENTS

1 teaspoon of liquid = 5 ml

1 tablespoon of liquid = 15 ml

OTHER MEASUREMENTS

Liquid volume		Weight		Linear	
Metric	Imperial	Metric	Imperial	Metric	Imperial
50 ml	2 fl oz	5 g	⅛ oz	2 mm	¹⁄₁₆ inch
100 ml	3½ fl oz	10 g	¼ oz	3 mm	⅛ inch
150 ml	5 fl oz	25 g	1 oz	5 mm	¼ inch
200 ml	7 fl oz	50 g	1¾ oz	8 mm	⅜ inch
300 ml	10 fl oz	75 g	2¾ oz	1 cm	½ inch
450 ml	16 fl oz	85 g	3 oz	2 cm	¾ inch
500 ml	18 fl oz	100 g	3½ oz	2.5 cm	1 inch
600 ml	1 pint	150 g	5½ oz	5 cm	2 inches
700 ml	1¼ pints	225 g	8 oz	7.5 cm	3 inches
850 ml	1½ pints	300 g	10½ oz	10 cm	4 inches
1 litre	1¾ pints	450 g	1 lb	20 cm	8 inches
1.5 litres	2¾ pints	500 g	1 lb 2 oz	30 cm	12 inches/1 foot
2.8 litres	5 pints	1 kg	2 lb 4 oz	46 cm	18 inches/1½ feet
3 litres	5¼ pints	1.5 kg	3 lb 5 oz	50 cm	20 inches/1⅔ feet

Preparation Techniques

You will find this section a valuable source of reference for all the basic preparation techniques you are likely to need in everyday cooking. There are also some advanced techniques for the more experienced cook.

> Grind

> Crush

> Fold

Grind
To crush food, such as nuts or coffee beans, to a powder or into very small pieces. For this job, you can use a coffee grinder, food processor, or a pestle and mortar for a coarser result.

Infuse
To steep flavourful ingredients, such as herbs or spices, in a liquid in order to flavour it.

Bard
This means to wrap pieces of fat, such as bacon, around lean cuts of meat and poultry to keep them moist and impart more flavour. For example, you can wrap chicken or turkey breasts with rashers of bacon before baking. You can also wrap a meat loaf with bacon rashers to keep it moist during baking.

Crush
This technique is useful for bringing out the flavour of garlic and herbs, and can be done by pressing the flat side of a knife blade down on to the garlic or herbs. You can also adapt this technique to make biscuit crumbs for cheesecakes. Simply place the biscuits in a polythene bag, tie the end securely, then use a rolling pin to crush the biscuits inside the bag.

Baste
When you spoon juices or fat over food during cooking, this is known as 'basting'. It helps to keep the food moist and seal in the flavour.

Fold
This technique involves mixing a light mixture into a heavier one using a spoon or spatula in a figure-of-eight movement. This is done to keep the air within the mixture.

Marinate
This term means to soak food in a marinade for a few hours or days to tenderize it and give it more flavour. You can marinate meat, poultry, fish and vegetables. Marinades usually consist of oil and vinegar, and are flavoured with different mixtures of herbs and spices.

> Beat

> Rub in

> Shred

Beat
This technique involves using a fork, spoon or electric mixer in a vigorous stirring motion to remove any lumps from sauces and incorporate air into omelettes and cake mixtures.

Deglaze
This technique is used after sautéeing food (normally meat). After the food and excess fat have been removed from the pan, a small amount of liquid – such as stock or wine – is stirred in to loosen browned bits of food in the pan. This mixture often forms the base for a sauce to accompany the food.

Knock back
This entails knocking the air out of bread dough after it has risen.

Rub in
This technique is mainly used when making pastry. Using the fingertips, rub the fat into the flour, lifting it high over the basin in order to trap air in the mixture, making it lighter and giving a better result.

Marble
This technique is used to combine two different-coloured ingredients in order to create a marbled effect. For example, you can lightly mix melted white chocolate into melted plain dark chocolate to create a marbled pattern.

Clarify
You can clarify butter or a liquid. To clarify butter, heat it slowly to separate the milk solids, which sink to the bottom of the pan, skimming any foam off the top. Clarified butter, such as Indian ghee, has a higher smoke point than ordinary butter so you can cook with it at higher temperatures. To clarify a liquid, such as a stock, add egg whites and/or egg shells to it and simmer for 10 minutes, then cool and strain it. The egg whites or shells draw out the impurities.

Shred
This technique involves using a small, sharp knife or grater to cut food into very thin lengths.

Line
To line a tin with something to prevent food sticking to it during cooking. The most common method is to rub butter or oil over the surface of the tin, then cover with baking parchment before adding the food. You can also use bacon rashers as a lining for savoury non-vegetarian dishes.

> Butterfly

> Whisk

> Chiffonade

Butterfly
To butterfly a leg of lamb, insert the knife into the cavity of the leg bone and cut to one side to open out the meat, then make a shallow surface cut down the centre to keep the meat open flat. You can also butterfly other foods, such as chicken breasts or large prawns.

Knead
This technique uses the heel of the hand to pull and stretch bread dough in order to develop the gluten in the flour so that the bread will keep its shape when it has risen. You can also knead dough in a food processor or food mixer that has a dough hook attachment.

Whisk
Whisking involves beating a light mixture, such as cream and eggs, vigorously with a whisk to incorporate more air. You can use a balloon whisk (but it takes a lot of effort), an electric hand mixer, a free-standing mixer or a food processor with a whisk attachment.

Skim
This term means to remove foam or fat from the surface of a simmering liquid with a large slotted spoon or a ladle.

Zest
This means to remove the outer layer of citrus fruit. A zester shaves off the zest without picking up the bitter white pith underneath.

Chiffonade
A French term meaning 'made of rags', it refers to the effect you get when you roll leafy vegetables together, then slice them crossways into ribbons with a sharp knife.

Enrich
This means adding a rich ingredient to a dish in order to create a richer texture or flavour. For example, you could add butter to a dough, or cream to a sauce.

Glaze
This involves brushing water, beaten egg, or sugar and water on to pastry before baking to give it a glossy shine (and make it crunchy if sugar is added). To glaze a ham, remove the skin from the partly cooked meat then coat the outer surface with some sugar

> Emulsify

> Tenderize

> Mash

and mustard and continue cooking. You can also glaze sweet dishes with melted jam or chocolate.

Emulsify
Emulsification happens when one liquid is slowly added to another in a gradual stream while stirring or blending rapidly. For example, mayonnaise is made by adding oil in a slow stream to a beaten egg mixture while whisking or blending vigorously.

Lard
To lard means to insert strips of pork fat into a lean cut of meat to flavour it and keep it moist.

Julienne
This technique involves cutting food, such as carrots and celery, into fine batons or strips.

Tenderize
This involves pounding meat, such as a beef steak, with a mallet in order to break down the tough fibres. You can also tenderize meat by marinating it.

Grease or oil
This is to rub a little butter or oil over the surface of a pan or tin to prevent food sticking to it during cooking.

Steep
Steeping means to soak an ingredient in hot liquid in order to release its flavour into the liquid.

Cut
This method means to use a sharp knife to make an incision or separate a food into smaller pieces.

Mash
Mashing means to reduce food, usually cooked potatoes and other root vegetables such as swede, to a pulp using a potato masher or a free-standing mixer.

Chop
This means to cut food into small pieces using a sharp knife. For example, to chop a herb, hold the tip of the knife blade down with one hand, then use your other hand to raise the handle of the knife up and down as you chop the herb. You can chop food roughly or finely, depending on your requirements. Roughly chopped means that the food will be left in larger pieces than when finely chopped.

Dress
This can mean to add a dressing to a salad, to decorate a dish before serving or to pluck and truss poultry.

> Truss

> Purée

> Crimp

Truss
This means to pull a poultry or game bird into shape then secure with string or skewers before cooking. This technique is particularly useful for preventing stuffing falling out of a bird.

Cream
Creaming is similar to beating, in that you use a fork, spoon or electric mixer to beat ingredients together until they are smooth. This technique is usually associated with something rich and creamy, such as butter.

Purée
This describes reducing food to a smooth pulp. You can do this by pushing food through a sieve or using a blender.

Macerate
To macerate means to soak a food in a liquid, often alcohol, to soften it.

Open freeze
This technique means to freeze foods, uncovered, in a single layer. For example, you can cut fruit, such as mango, into small pieces, spread them out on a tray and freeze them uncovered. Then transfer the pieces individually to a freezer bag and use as required. This technique is also useful for freezing small individual fruits, such as summer berries.

Crimp
For this technique, use the finger and thumb of one hand and the index finger of the other hand to 'pinch' pastry together around the edge of a pie or pasty. This gives it a decorative effect.

Cure
Curing means to preserve a food by salting or smoking it.

Degorge
This is soaking meat, poultry or fish in a solution of cold water and salt to remove impurities. It also means salting aubergines to remove their bitter juices.

Dredge
Dredging means to sprinkle flour on to a surface when rolling out pastry, or icing sugar or cocoa powder over desserts.

> Sift

> Cross-hatch

> Sieve

Sift
This technique involves shaking dry ingredients, such as flour, through a sieve to remove lumps and introduce more air into the mixture.

Mince
This is to grind food, such as meat, into small pieces using a knife or mincer.

Spatchcock
This means to remove the backbone from a bird and secure it so that it can be cooked flat and therefore more rapidly. To remove the backbone, first tuck under the wings and remove the wishbone. Then turn the bird over and cut along each side of the backbone to remove it. Use your hands to push down on the bird's breast and flatten it. Finally, push a metal skewer through the thighs and another through the wings and breast to secure the bird.

Cross-hatch
To cross-hatch means to score criss-cross patterns on the surface of foods to allow them to absorb marinades or be removed from their skins. You can cross-hatch the outer layer of fat on a pork joint before cooking to allow the fat to drain and create a decorative effect.

Grate
This means to shred food into small pieces. You can use a box grater or food processor.

Shuck
This is how we remove the husks from corn and the shells from peas.

Peel
Peeling involves removing the outer skin or rind from foods such as oranges, avocados or potatoes. Depending on the food, you can use your hands, a sharp knife or a vegetable peeler

Sieve
This involves pushing food through a sieve in order to create a purée.

Snip
This means using kitchen scissors to cut green leafy vegetables or herbs into very small pieces.

Cooking Methods

In this section you will find all the traditional cooking techniques, from boiling to roasting, as well as the popular health-conscious methods, such as steaming and stir-frying.

> Fry

> Deep-fry

> Dry-fry

Fry

This method involves cooking food in hot fat, usually oil, in a frying pan. Frying food gives it a delicious flavour. You can shallow-fry or deep-fry food. Deep-frying needs a lot more oil and can be dangerous, so it is always better to shallow-fry food if possible. However, for some foods, such as tempura (a Japanese dish of batter-coated pieces of fish and vegetables) and Scotch eggs, deep-frying is unavoidable. You can also stir-fry food: this method needs only a little oil and is a very healthy way to cook.

Deep-fry

This technique involves immersing food completely in very hot oil and cooking it at a very high temperature. It is important to choose the correct oil: groundnut and soya oil have the highest smoke points (the temperature at which the oil begins to emit smoke) and are therefore the most suitable for deep-frying. Rapeseed and corn oil have the next highest, and are also suitable. Sunflower oil has a lower smoke point and should not be used for deep-frying. Deep-frying food can be dangerous because it is possible to spill the hot oil or the pan can catch fire, so great care must be taken and the pan should never be left unattended. A thermostatically controlled deep-fat fryer is a safer and easier option, but still needs care and attention during use. The oil should be heated to a high temperature in order to allow rapid cooking; the high temperature will also help to seal the food and prevent it absorbing too much oil. Add the food to be cooked in small quantities – adding too much at the same time will reduce the temperature of the oil and the cooked food will be soggy rather than crisp. When the food is cooked, lift it out carefully using a fish slice or slotted spoon, or the wire basket if using a deep-fat fryer. Allow any excess oil to drain away from the food on to kitchen paper.

Dry-fry

This method involves cooking food or spices in a frying pan without using fat or oil. For example, you can cook Indian spices, flat breads or Mexican tortillas in a dry frying pan. You can also dry-fry pumpkin seeds or pine kernels until they are golden and lightly toasted, but watch these carefully while cooking, as they can burn very easily.

> Pan-fry

> Shallow-fry

> Stir-fry

Pan-fry

This is another quick and healthy way of cooking food. It involves cooking food quickly in a frying pan with either no fat at all (as in dry-frying) or with the absolute minimum amount of fat necessary. Some foods, such as bacon rashers, have enough fat content of their own, and therefore do not need any added fat. In fact, the fat they emit during cooking can be enough to pan-fry other foods at the same time – in this way, the dish has a minimum amount of fat and maximum flavour.

Shallow-fry

This method of cooking is suitable for foods that will not burn easily – for example, foods that are protected in some way, such as foods coated with flour, breadcrumbs or batter. You will need to add enough oil so that the food will not stick to the pan or burn. Take care to heat the oil to a high temperature because this will help to seal the food when it is added and prevent it absorbing too much oil. (Food cooked in oil that has not reached the right temperature will be soggy and laden with oil.) Cook the food in the oil for the required time, then turn it over and cook on the other side. Use a fish slice to lift out the food, and let any excess oil drain away from the hot food on kitchen paper. Where this method differs from sautéing is that the food is not moved around the pan, and generally a little more oil is used.

Stir-fry

This method comes from Asia and is another very healthy way to cook because of the small amount of oil needed. Foods such as meat, poultry and vegetables are cut into small, similar-sized pieces and cooked rapidly, while being tossed constantly, in a wok. You can also use a large frying pan for stir-frying, but a wok is better because the food cooks more rapidly as it comes into contact with the hot sides of the wok. Chinese cooking distinguishes between four or five different methods of stir-frying, but two are the most common. The first is a very rapid technique, where the food is fried in a little oil at the highest heat while being tossed constantly. Foods cooked in this way are often marinated first. The other technique is less vigorous and more moist: the food is cooked in a little liquid, such as a stock, and constantly turned and moved around the pan. Noodles and sauce are often added towards the end of the cooking time. It is important not to overfill the wok, or the food will steam instead of fry.

> Boil

> Simmer

> Reduce

Boil

To boil means to cook food in a liquid (usually water, milk or stock) in a saucepan at boiling point (100°C/212°F). Not all foods are boiled continually: sometimes they are 'brought to the boil', then the temperature is reduced and the food is left to simmer (bubble gently). You can cook many foods in this way, including vegetables, rice, pasta, meat and eggs. You can also boil a liquid rapidly for a period of time in order to evaporate excess (see Reduce).

Simmer

To simmer means to cook food in liquid that is just below boiling point; there will be very gentle bubbles on the surface of the liquid. This method is often combined with the boiling technique (see Boil), where a food is first brought to the boil, then the heat is reduced and the food is allowed to simmer for a period of time.

Reduce

This is not really a complete cooking method in its own right, but it is a useful technique, especially for sauces. To reduce a liquid, simply boil it down rapidly in an uncovered pan. This evaporates the liquid and makes the sauce thicker.

Blanch

Blanching is a useful technique for loosening skins on foods such as tomatoes, preserving the colour of vegetables, reducing any bitterness in ingredients and preparing foods for freezing. Blanching also helps to reduce the salt content in cured meats. To blanch a food, simply immerse it in boiling water for a few seconds, then plunge it into cold water to prevent further cooking.

> Steam

> Sauté

> Caramelize

Steam

Steaming is a very healthy way to cook, because the food does not come into direct contact with the liquid and therefore more of the nutrients are preserved. Steaming is suitable for a wide range of foods, from poultry and fish to vegetables and puddings. If you use a folding metal steamer, simply bring a small amount of water to the boil in the base of the pan, place the steamer inside, add the food, cover the pan and steam until cooked to your taste. Bamboo steamers are used in a similar way. You can also steam puddings: bring enough water to the boil to come halfway up the side of the pudding basin, then place the basin inside the pan and steam the pudding for the recommended time (taking care to top up with boiling water if necessary during cooking).

Sauté

This is similar to frying, but involves moving the food around the frying pan to prevent it browning too rapidly. Usually a small amount of oil or butter is used to oil or grease the pan and prevent the food burning.

Caramelize

This term most often refers to the method of caramelizing sugar or onions. To caramelize sugar, heat it until it melts into a syrup. The colour varies from light golden to dark brown, depending on the cooking time. A sugar thermometer is useful here, to get the sugar to the required temperature. When the sugar is removed from the heat, it quickly sets and becomes brittle, but retains its caramelized appearance. You can also sprinkle sugar over a food and caramelize it under a preheated hot grill or by heating its surface with a kitchen blow torch. To caramelize onions, cook them gently in butter for 30 minutes, or until they turn a rich golden brown.

> Sear

> Poach

> Sweat

Sear

To sear means to brown meat, poultry and fish rapidly over a high heat. This process helps to seal in the juices and keeps the centre of the food moist.

Braise

This is a long, slow way to cook food. It is especially useful for tough cuts of meat, and for poultry and vegetables. To braise foods, first brown them in oil, then cook them very slowly in a small amount of flavoured liquid, such as stock or wine, in a dish with a tight-fitting lid. You can cook them on a hob or in an oven.

Poach

To poach means to cook food in a liquid at just below boiling point and it is a very gentle method of cooking. The liquids commonly used for poaching are water and alcohol. You can poach poultry, fish, eggs (as long as they are very fresh) and fruit.

Poaching fruit

Pour enough wine or sugar syrup into a pan to cover the fruit. Bring to a simmer, add the stoned fruit and simmer for 15 minutes, or until tender. Lift out the fruit, reduce the liquid by boiling it down, then pour it over the fruit.

Sweat

This means to cook food (often vegetables such as onions) gently in water or fat until they are softened but not brown.

Toast

This process uses dry heat to cook foods. For example, you can toast nuts by baking them dry in the oven or cooking them under a preheated hot grill. You can also toast bread under the grill, or you can spear marshmallows on forks and toast them over a fire.

> Flambé

> Bake blind

> Roast

Flambé

Strictly speaking, to flambé is more to do with food presentation than it is a cooking method, but since it involves warming an ingredient it is included here. Flambé is a French word meaning 'flamed'. It involves sprinkling liqueur over a food, such as a Christmas pudding, then setting the alcohol alight just before serving. It makes a dramatic spectacle at the table, and also burns off the alcohol content.

Bake

To bake means to cook food in an oven using dry heat. For example, you can bake potatoes, cakes, biscuits, breads and custards.

Bake blind

This means to bake a pastry case without a filling. To bake blind, first line a greased pie tin or flan dish with rolled-out pastry, prick it with a fork, place a layer of baking paper over the pastry and weight it with ceramic or metal baking beans. Then place it in a preheated oven and bake it. Remove from the oven and leave to cool slightly before removing the beans and paper (if you remove them too soon, the pastry will stick to the paper). If you haven't got any baking beans, you can use dried beans or pulses instead. Baking blind helps to ensure that the pastry stays crisp after the filling is added, and is especially necessary if the filling does not need to be cooked, or needs only a very short cooking time.

Roast

Roasting is similar to baking, in that food is cooked in the oven using dry heat. In this case, however, the process is often used for meat, poultry and vegetables. It is usually necessary to add a little fat when roasting foods to keep them moist. Roasting can really bring out the flavour of a food: for example, peppers that have been roasted are extra sweet and flavourful. You can roast a wide variety of vegetables – potatoes and parsnips, garlic, onions, carrots, fennel, sweet potatoes, aubergines and swede.

> Stew

> Pot-roast

> Griddle

Stew

Stewing is a very slow method of cooking. It is similar to braising, except that the food is cut into smaller pieces and more liquid is used. This technique is suitable for meat (especially tough cuts because the long cooking process helps to tenderize the meat), poultry, fish, vegetables, grains such as barley, and certain fruits such as apples, pears, peaches and nectarines.

Casserole

This cooking method is similar to braising: you should use a large, heavy-based casserole dish with a tight-fitting lid. First brown the food in oil, add a small amount of flavoured liquid, cover with the lid, then cook very slowly in the oven. Sometimes a casserole is likened to a stew (see Stew), where the food is cut into smaller pieces and more cooking liquid is added. After cooking, you can serve the food directly from the casserole dish.

Pot-roast

This technique is very similar to braising in that it involves cooking food (usually meat, especially beef) very slowly in a covered pot in the oven. Very little liquid is used.

Blow torch

One of the cook's best-kept secrets is blow-torching food. This method of cooking is simple, quick and effective. You can buy a kitchen blow torch from any reputable kitchen equipment store, and you will find it inexpensive and convenient. It has a variety of uses. For example, to make a crunchy, caramelized topping for crème brûlées, simply sprinkle them generously with white sugar until the surfaces are completely covered.

Griddle

Traditionally, a griddle is a flat, usually rimless, pan, which is used to cook pancakes and drop scones with the minimum of oil. Griddles usually have a long handle and are often made of a heavy metal that conducts heat well, such as cast iron. The term 'griddle' is often confused with chargrill (see below).

> Chargrill

> Barbecue

> Grill

Chargrill

Chargrilling enables you to cook food in the minimum amount of fat and it gives the food attractive charred stripes. You can cook meat, poultry, fish and vegetables in this way. Simply heat a ridged griddle pan on the hob, brush the food with a little oil (never brush the oil on to the pan directly), then place the food on the heated pan. Cook according to the recipe, turning the food over once to cook on the other side. You can also chargrill food on a metal grid set over hot coals.

Barbecue

With this method the food is usually cooked on a mesh over hot coals. The barbecue apparatus can range from a simple portable tray consisting of a mesh with flammable, slow-burning paper underneath, to an elaborate electric barbecue. Foods are often marinated first, in order to give them more flavour and to aid the cooking process. Also, in order to prevent burns, use long-handled utensils to lift and turn the food.

Grill

Grilling is a quick and healthy way to cook food. Modern cookers usually have an integral grill; they also come with a grill pan with a wire mesh to allow excess fat to drain away. A grill should always be preheated before use. Grilling is a very versatile method of cooking: you can cook meat, poultry, fish and vegetables under a grill, and toast other foods such as bread and cheese. Grilling food involves cooking it directly under the heat source, which ensures that the outside of the food is browned quickly, while the inside stays moist.

Storecupboards

A good store of non-perishable foodstuffs is an essential part of every cook's kitchen. Well-stocked kitchen cupboards, and perhaps a larder, ensure that you always have a good selection of staple items on hand for every occasion. Make sure you check the use-by dates of your stored items regularly, and discard any that are out of date.

Olive oil

Extra virgin olive oil

Sunflower oil

Nut oil

Corn oil

Oils

There are many different varieties of oil available these days, but it is not necessary to buy them all. You simply need oil that is suitable for drizzling and for cooking at high temperatures.

Olive oil
This mildly fruity oil is ideal for drizzling over salads. It can range from a champagne colour to bright green. The best oils are cold-pressed – this is a chemical-free process that uses only pressure and produces a low level of acidity. You can also flavour it with different ingredients. For example, try adding some herbs, such as basil leaves, or some garlic to it – after a day or two the oil will become infused with their flavour. Its smoke point (the temperature at which it begins to smoke) is 210°C/410°F.

Extra virgin olive oil
Produced from the first cold-pressing of the olives, this oil has a very low acid level. It is the most expensive type of olive oil, and has a peppery, fruity flavour. You can use it for drizzling over salads and hot dishes such as pizzas. Its smoke point is 210°C/410°F.

Corn oil
This oil is economical to buy, and therefore is a good choice for cooking. However, it has a strong, distinctive flavour that makes it unsuitable for dressings and drizzling over dishes. Its smoke point is 210°C/410°F.

Sunflower oil
This is a good multi-purpose oil that can be used for most cooking purposes. However, it is not recommended for deep-frying because this method needs an oil with a higher smoke point. The smoke point of sunflower oil is 199°C/390°F. Sunflower oil has a very light flavour and is therefore ideal in dressings.

Sesame oil
This oil comes in two varieties: one has a light colour and a nutty flavour, the other is darker and has a stronger flavour. The darker one is most often used in Asian dishes. This oil is excellent for frying and stir-frying. Its smoke point is 210°C/410°F.

Vegetable oil
A blend of various oils, mainly rapeseed, soya, coconut and palm. It is best used for frying rather than in salads because it is quite greasy.

Soya oil
This economical oil is extracted from soya beans and has a light yellow colour. Like rapeseed oil, its popularity is growing because it is low in saturated fat. Its smoke point is 232°C/450°F, which makes it ideal for all types of cooking, including deep-frying. However, it has a strong taste and is therefore not suitable for dressings or for drizzling over finished dishes.

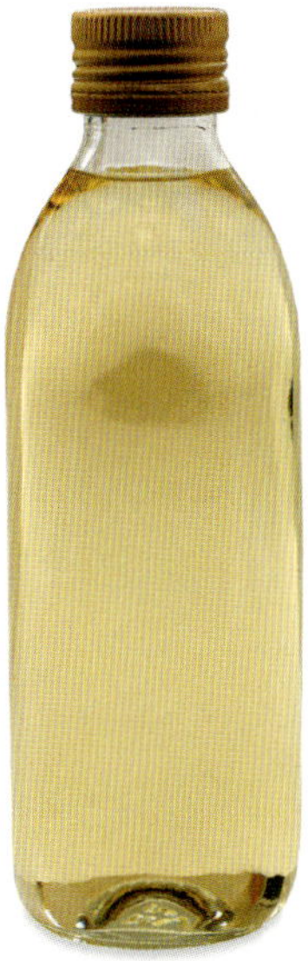

Vegetable oil

Basil-flavoured olive oil

Malt vinegar

Red wine vinegar

Balsamic vinegar

Rapeseed oil

This oil is gaining in popularity because it is lower in saturated fat than other oils. It also contains the omega-3 essential fatty acid, which is now widely believed to help reduce cholesterol levels. It has a mild flavour and so is suitable for salad dressings as well as for cooking. Its smoke point is 229°C/444°F.

Groundnut oil

A combination of a very mild flavour and a high smoke point of 232°C/450°F makes groundnut oil extremely versatile. It is therefore suitable for dressings and mayonnaise, and for drizzling over dishes, as well as for all forms of cooking, including deep-frying.

Vinegars

Vinegar adds a lovely, pungent kick to dressings, marinades, sauces and a wide range of dishes. It is available in different varieties, and here are some of the most popular types.

Malt vinegar

This is made from malted barley and is available in two varieties: a colourless form, which is very strong and is used for pickling, and a dark brown variety, which is used in chutneys and on traditional British fish and chips. This vinegar is not suitable for dressings.

Cider vinegar

This vinegar is made from apples and has a strong, sharp taste. It is best used with meats and in pickles and chutneys.

Wine vinegars

These are available in different varieties, mainly red, white and sherry. They can be used in dressings, marinades and sauces, and can be sprinkled over food.

Balsamic vinegar

This delicious vinegar is thick, dark and slightly sweet. It is made from grape juice that is aged in barrels over a period of years.

Speciality vinegars

Some vinegars are infused with fruits such as berries, nuts or a wide variety of herbs. Other popular favourites are rice vinegar (used in Asian cooking) and cane vinegar, which has a rich, slightly sweet taste.

Flour

Keep your flour fresh by storing it in an airtight container with a tight-fitting lid in a cool, dry place. You can store white flours for 6–8 months, and wholemeal flours for up to 2 months.

Cornflour

This powdery flour is made from corn kernels and is used for thickening sauces, soups and desserts. It is usually mixed with a small quantity of cold liquid to make a smooth paste before being added to hot dishes.

Plain flour

This flour is used for thickening sauces as well as for making batters and pastry.

Self-raising flour

Plain flour that has had baking powder and salt added is known as self-raising flour. It is used for making cakes and biscuits.

Rice flour

This powdery flour is made from white rice, and is used mainly in baked foods and to make Asian rice-flour noodles.

Strong bread flour

This flour is used for making bread. It contains a high level of gluten, which helps to give the bread dough its elasticity. If you are using a wholemeal variety, keep it in an airtight container in the refrigerator.

Malted brown flour

This is a brown flour that has had malted wheat grains added for a distinctive nutty flavour.

Wholemeal flour

This flour has a stronger flavour than white flour and contains wheatgerm, which means it has a higher fibre, fat and nutrient content. However, since it has a higher fat content, it should be stored in the refrigerator to prevent it from going rancid.

Pasta, noodles and grains

All these different dried pasta shapes, noodles and grains keep well in the storecupboard. They are ideal for cooking quick, satisfying meals at short notice.

Long-shaped pasta

There are different varieties of dried long-shaped pastas, including spaghetti, fettuccine (narrow ribbons), tagliatelle (slightly wider ribbons) and vermicelli (very fine, hair-like lengths). These pastas are usually made with durum wheat or wholewheat flour, and may be coloured using ingredients such as spinach (green), beetroot juice (red), tomatoes (orange-red) or even squid ink (black).

Short-shaped pasta

Dried short shapes of pasta include conchiglie (shells), fusilli (spirals), farfalle (bows) and tubular varieties such as penne and macaroni. These shapes are particularly good for holding chunky sauces.

Other shapes of dried pasta

Other favourite shapes to keep in your storecupboard include lasagne (rectangular sheets) and cannelloni (large tubes).

Dried noodles

Most noodles are associated with Asian cooking. The main difference between noodles and long-shaped pasta is that noodles usually have egg added, such as Chinese egg noodles. Alternatively, sometimes they are made from rice flour. Noodles are very popular in stir-fries and soups. Many varieties need no cooking – you simply soak them in hot water for a few minutes before adding them to the dish of your choice.

Long-grain rice

You can buy white and brown varieties of long-grain rice. When cooked, the grains stay dry and separate and do not clump together. This rice is used in savoury dishes.

Medium-grain rice

These grains are a little shorter than long-grain rice, and more moist. They tend to clump together when cooked. This rice is used in savoury dishes such as Spanish paella and Japanese sushi.

Short-grain rice

This rice has short grains that are more starchy and moist than medium- and long-grain rice. There are different varieties, including pearl rice (used in Asian cooking) and arborio and carnaroli rice (used in risottos).

Easy-cook rice

The grains in easy-cook rice are polished and partly boiled so that they are quick and easy to cook and stay fluffy and separate. Easy-cook rice is a convenient alternative to white or brown rice, but does not have as much flavour.

Wild rice

This is a marsh grass that is cultivated in the United States and Canada. The grains are long and black and have a nutty flavour. Wild rice is expensive, so for economy reasons it is often mixed with less-expensive brown long-grain rice.

Bulgar wheat

This comprises wheat kernels that have had the bran removed. They are then steamed, dried and ground into different degrees of coarseness. The result is a golden-brown grain that has a nutty flavour. It can be cooked like rice and is also excellent in salads.

Couscous

This is not a true grain, but pieces of semolina dough that have been rolled, dampened and coated with a fine wheat flour. It makes a fine accompaniment to savoury dishes.

Polenta

This yellow grain is made from cornmeal and is very popular in Italian cooking. It can be eaten hot or cold. It can also be cooked in a slab then cut into squares and grilled or fried.

Noodles

Spaghetti

Long-grain brown rice

Assorted dried pasta shapes

Pulses

All pulses except lentils and split peas need soaking for at least 8 hours, then boiling rapidly for 10 minutes before cooking for around 45 minutes. Soya beans need even longer cooking.

Cannellini beans

Red kidney beans

Red lentils

Chickpeas

Aduki beans

Cannellini beans
A type of haricot bean, these long, creamy white beans are excellent in soups and salads.

Red kidney beans
These red, kidney-shaped beans can be added to soups, salads, stews and other savoury dishes such as chilli con carne. They can cause food poisoning if not boiled rapidly for at least 10 minutes.

Aduki beans
These small red beans are popular in Japanese cooking, especially coated with sugar. They are also good in soups and salads.

Butter beans
These white, kidney-shaped beans are excellent in soups and salads.

Soya beans
Although most soya beans are yellow, they can also be black, brown or green. They are much richer in nutrients than the other pulses, and are particularly full of protein, as well as iron and calcium. Soya beans are used to make cooking oils and margarine, flour, soya milk and cheeses, soy sauce, tofu, miso and textured vegetable protein. They are good in soups and other savoury dishes, particularly curries. They should be soaked for at least 12 hours, drained and rinsed, then covered with fresh water and brought to the boil. Boil them for the first hour of cooking, then simmer them for the remaining 2–3 hours that it takes to cook them.

Chickpeas
These round, beige pulses have a nutty flavour and are excellent in soups, stews and salads, as well as ground up in dips such as hummus. Like soya beans, they need a longer soaking and cooking time than many pulses, so it is good to keep some canned chickpeas on hand for when you are short of time.

Lentils
These tiny, disc-shaped pulses are available in different varieties and colours. Red and orange lentils become mushy when cooked, and are therefore ideal puréed and used in soups and sauces. The green and continental brown varieties (Puy lentils) keep their shape when cooked and are ideal in warm winter salads, sauces, stews and other savoury dishes.

Split peas
These small peas are disc-shaped and split along a natural seam. They can be yellow or green, and are excellent cooked and puréed. They are also good in soups, bakes and other savoury dishes.

Black-eyed beans
These small beige beans have a circular black 'eye'. They are commonly found in Chinese cooking, and are very popular in sauces, stir-fries and soups.

Borlotti beans
These oval-shaped beans have pale pink to maroon streaked skin. They are creamy when cooked and are excellent in soups, dips and other savoury dishes.

Nuts and seeds

Nuts and seeds have a high oil content, and can quickly go rancid. If they have shells, store them in a cool, dry place. If they do not have shells, refrigerate them in airtight containers.

Peanuts

Pistachio nuts

Almonds

Pine kernels

Hazelnuts

Cashew nuts

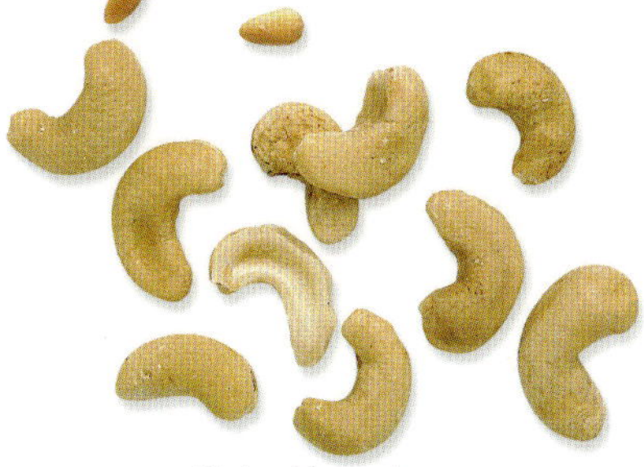

Walnuts

Almonds

These lozenge-shaped nuts have a thin brown covering and a cream centre. They come in two types, sweet and bitter, but it is the sweet variety that is normally used. Available whole, blanched, chopped and crystallized, they are excellent in both savoury and sweet dishes, from salads and savoury bakes to cakes, biscuits and marzipan.

Hazelnuts

These small, round nuts have a brown covering and a cream interior, and a rich, sweet flavour. They are especially popular in muesli and cereals, savoury dishes and bakes, such as nut loaf, as well as sweet dishes including cakes and biscuits.

Walnuts

These nuts have a large, round, wrinkled shell and two double lobes inside. The nuts have a delicious creamy taste and are good in salads and savoury bakes, as well as sweet dishes and cakes. They also make a very flavourful oil.

Pecan nuts

These nuts are golden brown with a beige interior. They have a very high fat content. They are used in a variety of savoury dishes and desserts such as pecan pie.

Cashew nuts

These creamy, butter-flavoured kidney-shaped nuts have a high fat content and are delicious roasted and added to stir-fries and bakes.

Pistachio nuts

These pale green nuts have a delicate flavour. They are often used in stuffings and also to decorate desserts.

Pine kernels

These small, oval nuts are creamy in colour and in flavour. They are excellent toasted or dry-fried, and are used in salads and rice dishes, sauces such as pesto, and a variety of savoury and sweet dishes.

Peanuts

Despite their name, peanuts are not actually nuts, they are legumes and very versatile. They are used to make oil and also peanut butter, which in turn makes a delicious satay sauce. They are also good in salads, side dishes and stir-fries.

Seeds

A selection of seeds can be very useful in your storecupboard. Sunflower seeds, for example, are rich in essential fatty acids and are delicious sprinkled into muesli and salads. Pumpkin seeds are also nutritious and make a good snack. Sesame seeds are popular in Asian cooking and are delicious toasted and in stir-fries. Dill seeds have an aniseed flavour and are good with fish and vegetables. Caraway seeds have a pungent flavour and are used in soups, stews, vegetable dishes and in bread. Poppy seeds are slightly sweet and make an attractive decoration sprinkled over salads and bread rolls.

Spices and seasonings

A selection of spices in your storecupboard is extremely useful for enhancing the flavour of dishes. Some spices, such as ginger and turmeric, are also said to aid digestion.

Ginger
This hot, pungent spice has a lemony flavour when fresh, but a sweeter flavour when dried. It is popular in Indian cooking, as well as in chutneys, desserts and baked goods such as cakes, notably gingerbread, and biscuits.

Turmeric
A peppery spice with a distinctive yellow colour. Turmeric is often used instead of the more expensive saffron. It is especially good in curries and in rice dishes such as paella.

Saffron
This yellow spice has a slightly bitter flavour and a pungent aroma. It is sold in strands and is used in dishes to colour and flavour them.

Coriander
The aromatic flavour of this spice is excellent with meat, poultry and vegetables.

Cumin
This spice has a strong, slightly bitter flavour, and is particularly good with poultry and vegetables.

Cloves
A sweet spice with a strong flavour. Use whole cloves to stud hams and fruits, and ground cloves to add flavour to desserts.

Nutmeg
This sweet-flavoured spice is used in savoury and sweet dishes.

Mace
This spice has a sweet flavour and is excellent in soups and sauces.

Cinnamon
A very popular spice. Cinnamon is sweet and fragrant and is used in desserts and baked foods such as cakes, sweet pies and biscuits.

Curry powder
This is a blend of spices, and the flavour varies from mild to hot. It adds a distinctive flavour to sauces and savoury dishes.

Mixed spice
A mixture of sweet spices, such as cinnamon, cloves, mace and nutmeg, plus one or two others. It gives a delicious flavour to desserts, cakes, biscuits and drinks.

Chilli powder
This is a blend of dried chillies. It adds a kick to sauces and savoury dishes.

Five-spice powder
This blend of five spices usually contains cinnamon, cloves, fennel seeds, Szechuan peppercorns and star anise. It is very popular in Chinese cooking, and gives a wonderful flavour to stir-fries.

Paprika
This has a hot flavour and an attractive red colour. It is ideal as a garnish.

Dried herbs

It is always worthwhile having a collection of dried herbs on hand. They are especially useful for dishes that require a long cooking time, such as casseroles. Use half the recommended fresh quantity.

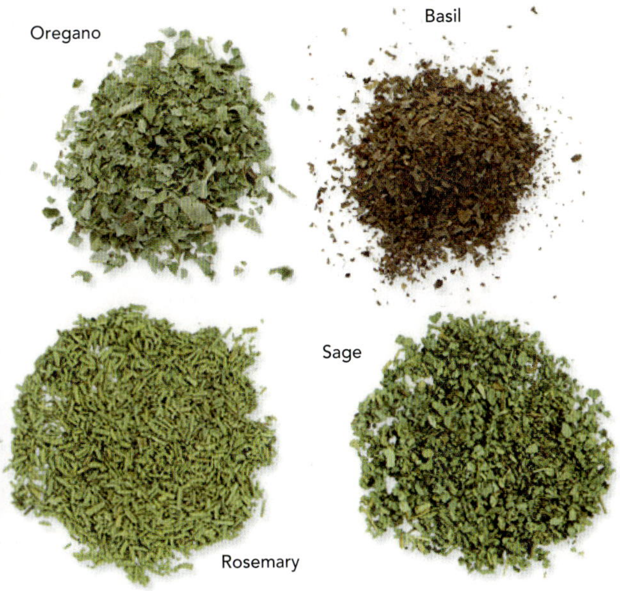

Peppercorns

These come in different varieties. Ground black or white peppercorns are an extremely popular seasoning for a wide variety of savoury foods and also some sweet dishes such as balsamic strawberries. You can also buy green peppercorns.

Salt

This is a great favourite as a seasoning, but care must be taken not to overuse it or it will overpower the food, and be bad for health.

Oregano

This herb has a strong flavour and is perfect sprinkled on pizzas and in pasta sauces.

Basil

This popular herb is delicious in sauces and is particularly good with tomatoes.

Sage

This herb is good in egg, cheese, poultry and meat dishes.

Dill

This is an excellent herb with vegetables and fish.

Rosemary

A pungent herb that goes well with poultry and meat, and also root vegetables, especially potatoes.

Mixed herbs

This combination usually consists of oregano, rosemary and thyme, plus one or two other herbs. Mixed herbs can be used in a variety of savoury dishes, including sauces and Italian dishes such as pizza and pasta.

Sugars and syrups

Store your sugar in a dry place at room temperature. Syrups should be kept in tightly sealed containers at room temperature or in the refrigerator.

Granulated sugar

This basic, cheap sugar is essential in your storecupboard. Use it to sweeten drinks and cereals and to sprinkle on desserts. This coarse sugar is also essential in jam and marmalade making.

Caster sugar

This sugar is finer than granulated sugar and dissolves quickly, so it is ideal for meringues and cakes.

Icing sugar

This very fine sugar is ideal for making icing and for dusting cakes and desserts.

Soft brown sugar

This stronger-flavoured sugar comes in various shades from light to dark and is used in cake and biscuit making.

Demerara sugar

This crunchy brown sugar is delicious sprinkled over desserts and cakes before grilling or baking.

Honey

This comes in a variety of flavours and colours, as either clear, liquid honey or opaque, set honey. It has many uses, from glazing ham and flavouring vegetables to sweetening desserts and drinks.

Golden syrup

This clear, golden syrup is made from evaporated sugar-cane juice. It is used in a variety of dishes, and to top pancakes and ice cream.

Maple syrup

This delicious sweet syrup is used in a wide variety of savoury and sweet dishes, including pancakes.

Sauces, pastes and condiments

A good selection of sauces and condiments is invaluable in the kitchen, and will ensure you always have the right ingredients on hand to add exciting and interesting flavours to your dishes.

Tomato ketchup
This sauce is popular in British cooking and is eaten with cooked foods such as chips and hamburgers. It is also good as an ingredient in dressings and relishes.

Brown sauce
This strongly flavoured sauce is a traditional British accompaniment to a fried breakfast.

Soy sauce
This popular sauce is essential for stir-fries and other Asian dishes. You can buy the Chinese version, which is salty, or the Japanese type, which is slightly sweeter.

Hoisin sauce
This sweet soya-based sauce with a sticky texture is very popular in Chinese cooking. It is known by various names such as Peking sauce.

Worcestershire sauce
This strongly flavoured sauce is made with onions, molasses and anchovies, and is used to season meats, gravies and soups, and occasionally cocktails. A vegetarian version is available.

Pesto sauce
Made from basil, garlic, pine kernels, Parmesan cheese and olive oil, pesto is good with pasta.

Tabasco sauce
This very hot chilli sauce is used in dishes to give them a kick, such as Mexican salsas. It is also used to season certain cocktails.

Thai fish sauce (nam pla)
This salty sauce is made from fermented fish and has a very strong taste and smell. It is used to flavour Thai dishes and as a table condiment.

Horseradish sauce
Horseradish is a root with a very hot flavour. It makes an excellent creamy white sauce, which is very good with meat, poultry, fish and egg dishes.

Plum sauce
This fruity sauce is popular in Chinese cooking and is traditionally served with spring rolls and also Peking duck.

Harissa
This North African condiment is made from oil, garlic, herbs and spices, and is served with soups and couscous.

Tahini
A thick paste made from finely ground sesame seeds. It is used to flavour Middle Eastern dishes.

Thai curry paste
This is available in different varieties: green is the hottest, yellow is the mildest and red varies in the amount of heat. It is a popular ingredient in Thai dishes.

Miso
A paste made from fermented soya beans. It is used in Japanese cooking to thicken and flavour soups and other dishes.

Tomato purée
This is a tomato paste that is useful in sauces and soups because of its intense flavour.

Passata
This is simply sieved tomatoes. It is ideal for soups and sauces, and for spreading over pizzas.

Mustards
You can buy different types of mustard. Dijon mustard has a strong flavour and is used in dips and dressings. English mustard is very hot and useful in dips and dressings. Coarse-grain mustard is usually milder, and is good with a variety of savoury dishes, especially meats.

Canned and bottled foods

Keep your storecupboard stocked with a selection of canned and bottled foods, such as pulses, fish, vegetables and pickled items, and you will never be short of ingredients for delicious meals at short notice.

Canned pulses
You can buy a wide variety of canned beans, such as red kidney beans and chickpeas, which will save you time because you do not have to soak them or cook them. Tins of baked beans in tomato sauce are also indispensable for quick meals.

Canned fish
Canned fish, such as tuna, salmon, crab, anchovies, sardines and pilchards, are versatile items to have in the storecupboard. They are particularly useful when added to pastas and salads.

Canned tomatoes
Canned tomatoes can be used in a wide variety of dishes, from sauces and soups to stews and casseroles.

Coconut milk
Canned coconut milk is very useful for cooking Thai dishes, particularly creamy curries and desserts.

Sweetcorn
Canned sweetcorn is deliciously sweet and ideal in salads, soups, bakes and casseroles.

Water chestnuts
These are popular in Chinese cooking, and are particularly good in stir-fries.

Olives
It is always useful to keep a tin or bottle of olives on hand. They make ideal tapas for unexpected guests and are delicious in salads and pastas and on pizzas.

Sun-dried tomatoes
These are very good in Italian recipes, particularly salads, pastas and bread.

Pickled foods
Onions, gherkins and capers make perfect accompaniments and garnishes for meat and vegetable dishes.

Dried fruits and berries

A selection of dried fruits and berries is very useful to keep on hand. They make ideal snacks and can be used in a wide variety of savoury and sweet dishes, from muesli, vegetable curries and meat dishes to desserts and sweet pies. Dried fruits and berries include currants, raisins, sultanas, apricots, prunes, figs, dates, mangoes, pears, apples, bananas, cranberries and blueberries.

Other items

Here is a selection of other items you will find useful to keep in your storecupboard.

Stock cubes
These are very convenient for soups, casseroles and other dishes, particularly if you do not have enough time to make fresh stock.

Gelatine
You will need gelatine to set mousses and jellies. You can also buy a vegetarian equivalent, such as agar agar.

Chocolate and cocoa powder
These are useful for desserts and baked goods, and also for some savoury dishes.

Vanilla
You can buy vanilla in pod or liquid form (extract) as a flavouring. It is particularly delicious in desserts.

Alcohol
White wine, red wine, sherry and Marsala are handy for a variety of savoury and sweet dishes. Although not essential, flavoured liqueurs are also useful, such as orange, coffee and almond.

Refrigerator and freezer essentials

Your chilled essentials should include eggs, milk, yogurt and créme fraîche. You should also keep some butter, including an unsalted variety, for baking and desserts. Bread is another essential, not just as an accompaniment, but for making breadcrumbs and recipes such as crostini. Cheeses should include an all-purpose firm variety, such as Cheddar, and also Parmesan, as well as cream cheese. You may find bacon rashers useful. Tofu is full of protein: it is good in stir-fries and is useful for vegetarian meals. In the freezer, you might like to keep frozen prawns and fish fillets, vegetables and ice cream.

Chapter 1
Eggs & Dairy

Introduction

Nowadays we can buy a wide range of delicious eggs, from white and brown, organic and free-range, to more exotic types, such as the distinctive blue eggs from the Oakham Blue hen. Likewise, more dairy products are available than before, and we can choose from an ever-increasing array of milk, yogurt, cream, butter and cheese, which are full of protein and very easy to prepare and cook.

Coll duck egg

Goose egg

Quail egg

Free-range hen egg

Khaki Campbell duck egg

Aylesbury duck egg

Buying and storing eggs

Always buy your eggs from a reputable supplier, and do not buy any with cracked shells. Ensure the eggs are as fresh as possible by checking the 'best before' date on the carton. In many cases the 'best before' date is also printed on the eggshells themselves. You can also check an egg's freshness by floating it in water: if it sinks to the bottom of the bowl horizontally, it is very fresh; if it stays vertical with its tip on the bottom, it is less fresh; if it floats to the top it is stale and should be discarded. Store your eggs, pointed ends down, in their carton at the back of a low shelf in the refrigerator. They should not be stored in the refrigerator door, where they will be subject to fluctuations in temperature each time the door is opened. Separated egg whites will keep in the refrigerator in a lidded container for a week, and in the freezer for three months. Egg yolks or whole beaten eggs will keep in the refrigerator for up to 2 days, or in the freezer for up to 3 months (add a little salt to them before freezing). Always label the container with the date of freezing and what it contains. Eggs are best cooked at room temperature, so remember to take them out of the refrigerator about an hour before they are needed.

Whisking egg whites

Eggs that are 3–5 days old are best for whisking. Make sure that everything is clean and that your bowl is free of grease. Put the egg whites in a large bowl. If whisking by hand, use a large balloon whisk in an upward, circular movement. Alternatively, use a hand-held electric whisk or free-standing food mixer. If the recipe calls for a 'soft peaks' consistency, the mixture should form peaks that are soft and will flop over when the whisk is removed. If you need 'firm peaks', the peaks should stand rigid.

Scrambling eggs

Allow 2 eggs and 1 tablespoon of milk per person. Whisk together the eggs and milk in a bowl, then season with salt and pepper. Melt 1 tablespoon of butter in a non-stick pan, then pour in the egg mixture. Stir constantly over a low heat for 5–7 minutes until almost set, then remove from the heat. Stir for 1 more minute, then serve.

Boiling eggs

To boil eggs, bring a small saucepan of water to the boil. Reduce the heat to a simmer, add a pinch of salt, then

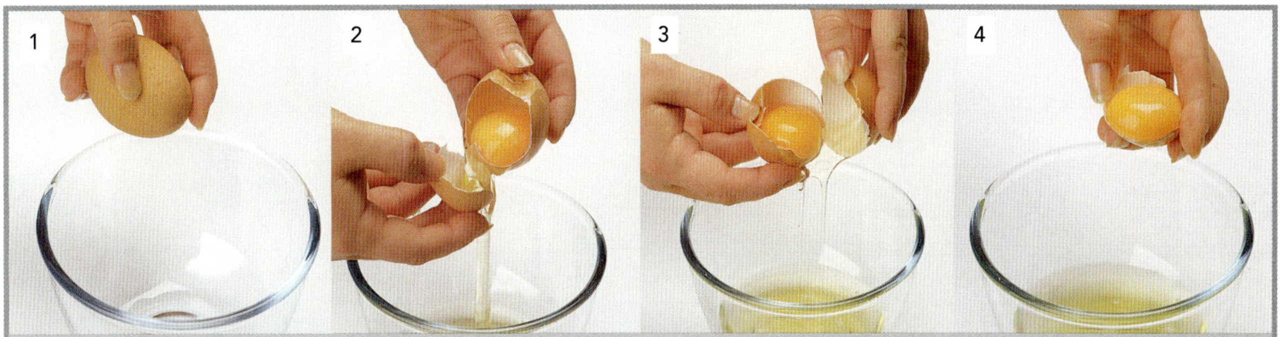

Separating eggs

There are some clever devices available for separating yolks from egg whites, but if you don't have a separating gadget, you can use the shell method (using cold eggs makes this method easier). **1** Crack the egg shell gently on the edge of a bowl. **2** Open the shell slowly, allowing the white to drip into the bowl. **3** Taking care not to break the yolk, pass it from one shell half to the other. **4** Repeat until the yolk and white are fully separated. Alternatively, open the egg into your hand, cradling the yolk gently, and let the white drip through your fingers to separate.

carefully add the eggs. Simmer gently for 4–5 minutes for soft-boiled, and 9–10 minutes for hard-boiled (no longer, or a dark ring will appear around the yolk). Remove with a slotted spoon and plunge into cold water to prevent further cooking. Serve as required.

Frying eggs

Heat 1–2 tablespoons of oil in a frying pan until hot (but not smoking). Break the eggs carefully into the pan so that the yolks remain intact. Cook over a medium heat, occasionally basting with the hot oil to help the yolk set, for 3–4 minutes. Use a fish slice to lift out the eggs and allow the oil to drain away. Serve immediately.

Poaching eggs

Eggs need to be very fresh for poaching or they will break up in the water. You can use a non-stick egg poacher or silicone poaching pods for this, or alternatively you can use the following method.

Fill a small frying pan with enough water to cover an egg. Bring to the boil, then reduce the heat to a simmer. Break the egg carefully into a cup, then pour it gently into the boiling water so that the yolk does not break. Cook for 3–4 minutes; you can baste the egg with a little of the cooking liquid to ensure it is cooked. Lift it out with a slotted spoon and serve.

Coddling eggs

An egg coddler is a porcelain cup with a lid. Grease the coddler with butter, break an egg into it, season wth salt and pepper and loosely screw on the lid. Meanwhile, bring a saucepan of water to the boil, stand the coddler in the water up to the bottom of its lid and simmer for 7–8 minutes. Eat straight from the coddler.

SAFETY

Eggs can carry harmful bacteria and may cause food poisoning if not thoroughly cooked, so do not give dishes with raw or lightly cooked eggs to people who may be particularly vulnerable, such as pregnant or breastfeeding women, babies and toddlers, the elderly, people who are ill or convalescents.

Fresh milk

Clotted cream

Yogurt

Butter

Buying and storing milk

Milk is a good source of protein and calcium. The most commonly available is fresh cow's milk, which comes in full-fat (4% fat), semi-skimmed (less than 2% fat) and skimmed (less than 1% fat). Other varieties include homogenized, which has the fat spread throughout the milk so that there is no creamy layer on top, and long-life (UHT) milk, which has been heated quickly to around 149°C/300°F, then cooled and vacuum-packed to ensure a shelf-life without refrigeration of around six months. You can also buy condensed milk, which is very thick and sweet; evaporated milk, which is sterilized in tins and often used to replace full-fat milk; buttermilk, which tastes like yogurt or thickened low-fat milk; and powdered milk, which you can reconstitute with water and use in place of fresh milk. If you are sensitive to cow's milk, you can buy goat's milk or sheep's milk, or milk made from soya or rice instead.

Most fresh milk is pasteurized (heated then quickly cooled) in order to kill off any harmful bacteria, although some unpasteurized milk is available, often straight from the farm (see Safety box, opposite). Always check the 'best before' date on milk before you buy it, and store fresh milk, covered, in the refrigerator. Semi-skimmed and skimmed milk can be frozen for up to 3 weeks.

Buying and storing yogurt

Yogurt is made by fermenting milk with healthy bacteria. It has a slightly tangy taste and is a healthy choice because it is thick and creamy yet low in fat. Greek-style yogurt is the thickest and has the creamiest consistency. You can also freeze yogurt for a healthy low-fat alternative to ice cream. Check the 'best before' date before buying, and store it in the refrigerator. Keep it covered when not in use.

Buying and storing butter

Butter is made by churning cream until it separates into semi-solids. It comprises at least 80% fat and the other 20% is made up of milk solids and water. Sometimes it is coloured with annatto (a natural colour made from the paste of seeds). Butter is available in salted and unsalted varieties: unsalted is essential for sweet dishes. You can also buy 'spreadable' butter: this has been blended with oil so that it will stay soft and can be spread more easily. Make sure your butter is always tightly wrapped to prevent it absorbing odours. Check the 'best before' date on the packaging. Butter also freezes well, for up to 6 months in the freezer.

Cheddar

Parmesan

Curd cheese

Stilton

Buying and storing cream

Cream is made from the fattiest part of milk. It therefore has a higher fat content than milk, and a milder flavour. Half-fat and single cream have the lowest fat content: the former is useful for pouring into drinks such as coffee, and the latter is ideal for sauces and soups. Soured cream (around 18–20% fat) has a slightly tangy taste and is ideal in savoury dishes, as is the higher fat crème fraîche (up to 50% fat). Whipping cream has a high fat content (30–35%) and is ideal for whipping and piping into decorative shapes. Double cream has a very high fat content (over 40%) and should therefore be used sparingly. It is a delicious luxury for special occasions, perhaps to enrich a sauce or accompany a dessert. Clotted cream has the highest fat content of all (around 60%) and is very thick. It is ideal on scones or as an accompaniment for special desserts. All cream should be kept covered, stored in the refrigerator and used by the 'best before' date on the carton. Double cream can be frozen for up to 3 weeks.

Buying and storing cheese

Cheese is made from milk that is allowed to thicken and then separate into curds (semi-solids) and whey (a liquid). Fresh cheeses are rindless and vary in consistency. Typical cheeses in this category are cream cheese and cottage cheese. Soft and semi-hard cheeses are firmer, and range from creamy soft cheeses with rinds, such as Brie, to firmer cheeses such as Port Salut. Generally, the harder the cheese, the higher the fat content, and hard cheeses have the highest fat of all. They are often easy to grate, and range from Cheddar cheese to Parmesan. Blue cheeses are also available: these have blue veins running through them and a strong flavour and aroma (the veins are made by a friendly bacteria). Blue cheese varieties include Gorgonzola and Stilton. You can also buy cheese made from goat's milk and sheep's milk.

Keep your cheese tightly wrapped. Store fresh cheese in the coldest part of the refrigerator, and the other cheeses in the warmest part. Hard cheeses can be grated ready for use and kept in the refrigerator for up to one week. Use cheeses by the 'best before' date. You can also freeze hard cheeses, but they will have a crumblier texture when they are defrosted. Grated cheese also freezes well but is only suitable for cooking, not for adding to salads.

SAFETY

Unpasteurized milk is available from specialist suppliers, but there is still a risk of disease and therefore this milk should not be given to vulnerable people, especially pregnant or breastfeeding women, babies and toddlers, the elderly, people who are ill or convalescents.

Spinach & Mozzarella Omelette

Serves 4

ingredients

- 1 tbsp butter
- 4 eggs, beaten lightly
- 40 g/1½ oz mozzarella cheese, thinly sliced and cut into bite-sized pieces
- small handful baby spinach, stalks removed
- salt and pepper
- 1 oil-cured red pepper, sliced into strips, to garnish

1 Heat a 25-cm/10-inch non-stick pan over medium–high heat. Add the butter and when it sizzles, pour in the eggs. Season with salt and pepper, then stir gently with the back of a fork until large flakes form. Leave to cook for a few seconds then tilt the pan and lift the edges of the mixture with a spatula, so that uncooked egg flows underneath to cook evenly.

2 Scatter the cheese and spinach over the top, and leave to cook for a few seconds. Once the surface starts to solidify, carefully fold the omelette in half. Cook for a few seconds, pressing the surface with a spatula. Turn the omelette over and cook for another few seconds, until the cheese is soft and the spinach wilted.

3 Slide the omelette onto a warm serving dish and slice into segments. Garnish with strips of red pepper before serving.

Asparagus with Poached Eggs & Parmesan

Serves 4

ingredients

- 300 g/10½ oz asparagus, trimmed
- 4 large eggs
- 85 g/3 oz Parmesan cheese
- pepper

1 Bring 2 saucepans of water to the boil. Add the asparagus to 1 saucepan, return to a simmer and cook for 5 minutes, or until just tender.

2 Meanwhile, reduce the heat of the second saucepan to a simmer and carefully crack the eggs into a cup, then slide them gently into the water, one at a time. Poach for 3 minutes, or until the whites are just set but the yolks are still soft. Remove with a slotted spoon.

3 Drain the asparagus and divide between 4 warmed plates. Top each plate of asparagus with an egg and shave over the cheese. Season to taste with pepper and serve immediately.

Quiche Lorraine

Makes 1 23-cm/9-inch quiche

ingredients

for the pastry

- 175 g/6 oz plain flour, plus extra for dusting
- pinch of salt
- 115 g/4 oz butter, diced
- 25 g/1 oz pecorino cheese, grated
- 4–6 tbsp iced water

for the filling

- 115 g/4 oz Gruyère cheese, thinly sliced
- 55 g/2 oz Roquefort cheese, crumbled
- 175 g/6 oz rindless lean bacon, grilled until crisp
- 3 eggs
- 150 ml/5 fl oz double cream
- salt and pepper

1 To make the pastry, sift the flour with the salt into a bowl. Add the butter and rub it in with your fingertips until the mixture resembles breadcrumbs. Stir in the grated cheese, then stir in enough of the water to bind. Shape the dough into a ball, wrap in clingfilm and chill in the refrigerator for 15 minutes.

2 Preheat the oven to 190°C/375°F/Gas Mark 5. Unwrap and roll out the dough on a lightly floured work surface. Use to line a 23-cm/9-inch quiche tin. Place the tin on a baking sheet. Prick the base of the pastry case all over with a fork, line with foil or baking paper and fill with baking beans. Bake in the preheated oven for 15 minutes until the edges are set and dry. Remove the beans and lining and bake the pastry case for a further 5–7 minutes, or until golden. Leave to cool slightly.

3 For the filling, arrange the cheeses over the base of the pastry case, then crumble the bacon evenly on top. Place the eggs and cream in a bowl and beat together until thoroughly combined. Add salt and pepper to taste. Pour the mixture into the pastry case and return to the oven for 20 minutes, or until the filling is golden and set.

4 Remove from the oven and cool the quiche in the tin for 10 minutes. Transfer to a wire rack to cool completely. Cover and store in the refrigerator, but return to room temperature before serving.

Chive Scrambled Eggs with Brioche

Serves 2

ingredients

- 4 eggs
- 100 ml/3½ fl oz single cream
- 2 tbsp snipped fresh chives, plus 4 whole fresh chives to garnish
- 25 g/1 oz butter
- 4 slices brioche loaf, lightly toasted
- salt and pepper

1 Break the eggs into a medium bowl and whisk gently with the cream. Season to taste with salt and pepper and add the snipped chives.

2 Melt the butter in a sauté pan and pour in the egg mixture. Leave to set slightly, then move the mixture towards the centre of the pan using a wooden spoon as the eggs begin to cook. Continue in this way until the eggs are cooked but still creamy.

3 Place the toasted brioche slices in the centre of 2 plates and spoon over the scrambled eggs. Serve immediately, garnished with whole chives.

Deep-fried Mozzarella

Serves 4

ingredients

- 8 slices bread, preferably slightly stale, crusts removed
- 100 g/3½ oz mozzarella, thickly sliced
- 50 g/1¾ oz black olives, chopped
- 8 canned anchovy fillets, drained and chopped
- 16 fresh basil leaves
- 4 eggs, beaten
- 150 ml/5 fl oz milk
- oil, for deep-frying
- salt and pepper

1 Cut each slice of bread into 2 triangles. Top 8 of the bread triangles with equal amounts of the mozzarella slices, olives and anchovies.

2 Place the basil leaves on top and season with salt and pepper to taste. Lay the other 8 triangles of bread over the top and press down round the edges to seal.

3 Mix the eggs and milk together and pour into a dish. Add the sandwiches and leave to soak for about 5 minutes.

4 Heat the oil in a large saucepan to 180–190°C/350–375°F, or until a cube of bread browns in 30 seconds.

5 Before cooking the sandwiches, squeeze the edges together again.

6 Carefully place the sandwiches in the oil and deep-fry for 2 minutes, or until golden, turning once. (You will have to cook them in batches.) Remove the sandwiches with a slotted spoon and drain on kitchen paper. Serve immediately while still hot.

Double Cheese Soufflés

Makes 6

ingredients

- 25 g/1 oz butter, plus extra for greasing
- 2 tbsp finely grated Parmesan cheese
- 175 ml/6 fl oz milk
- 25 g/1 oz self-raising flour
- whole nutmeg, for grating
- 100 g/3½ oz soft goat's cheese
- 70 g/2½ oz mature Cheddar cheese, grated
- 2 large eggs, separated
- salt and pepper

1 Preheat the oven to 200°C/400°F/Gas Mark 6. Put a baking sheet in the oven to warm. Generously grease the inside of 6 small ramekins with butter, add half the Parmesan cheese and shake to coat the butter.

2 Warm the milk in a small saucepan. Melt the remaining butter in a separate saucepan over a medium heat. Add the flour, stir well to combine and cook, stirring, for 2 minutes until smooth. Add a little of the warmed milk and stir until absorbed. Continue to add the milk a little at a time, stirring constantly, until you have a rich, smooth sauce. Season to taste with salt and pepper, and grate in a little nutmeg. Add the cheeses to the sauce and stir until well combined and melted.

3 Remove from the heat and leave the sauce to cool a little, then add the egg yolks and stir to combine. In a separate bowl, whisk the egg whites until stiff. Fold a tablespoonful of the egg whites into the cheese sauce, then gradually fold in the remaining egg whites. Spoon into the prepared ramekins and scatter over the remaining Parmesan cheese.

4 Place the ramekins on the hot baking sheet and bake in the preheated oven for 15 minutes until puffed up and brown. Remove from the oven and serve immediately. The soufflés will collapse quite quickly when taken from the oven, so have your serving plates ready to take the soufflés to the table.

Courgette, Goat's Cheese & Red Onion Pizza

Serves 4–6

ingredients

- 55 g/2 oz butter, plus extra for greasing
- 400 g/14 oz can chopped tomatoes with chopped herbs
- 1 tbsp olive oil
- 1 small red onion, sliced
- 2 small courgettes, sliced (about 225 g/8 oz total weight)
- 225 g/8 oz plain white flour
- 2 tsp baking powder
- about 115 ml/4 fl oz milk
- 55 g/2 oz mozzarella cheese, grated
- 1 large vine-ripened tomato, thinly sliced
- 100 g/3½ oz soft (dry) goat's cheese, crumbled
- salt and pepper

1 Preheat the oven to 220°C/425°F/Gas Mark 7. Grease a baking sheet and set aside. Open the can of tomatoes and pour the entire contents into a sieve placed over a bowl. Set aside, stirring occasionally, until most of the juice has drained away to leave a thick tomato pulp. Reserve the tomato pulp and discard the juice.

2 Heat the olive oil in a saucepan, add the onion and courgettes and cook for about 5 minutes or until softened, stirring occasionally. Remove from the heat and set aside.

3 Sift the flour and baking powder into a bowl, add a pinch of salt, then lightly rub in the butter until the mixture resembles breadcrumbs. Stir in enough milk to form a fairly soft dough. Knead lightly.

4 Lightly roll out the dough on a lightly floured surface to form a 25-cm/10-inch round and place it on the prepared baking sheet. Spread the strained tomato pulp evenly over the dough, season with salt and pepper, then sprinkle over the mozzarella. Top with the courgette mixture. Arrange the tomato slices on top, then scatter the goat's cheese over the tomatoes.

5 Bake in the oven for about 25 minutes or until cooked and deep golden brown around the edges. Remove from the oven and serve.

Spaghetti alla Carbonara

Serves 4

ingredients

- 450 g/1 lb dried spaghetti
- 1 tbsp olive oil
- 225 g/8 oz rindless pancetta or streaky bacon, chopped
- 4 eggs
- 5 tbsp single cream
- 2 tbsp freshly grated Parmesan cheese
- salt and pepper

1 Bring a large heavy-based saucepan of lightly salted water to the boil. Add the pasta, return to the boil and cook for 8–10 minutes, or until tender but still firm to the bite.

2 Meanwhile, heat the oil in a heavy-based frying pan. Add the pancetta and cook over a medium heat, stirring frequently, for 8–10 minutes.

3 Beat the eggs with the cream in a small bowl and season to taste with salt and pepper. Drain the pasta and return it to the saucepan.

4 Tip in the contents of the frying pan, then add the egg mixture and half the Parmesan cheese. Stir well, then transfer to a warmed serving dish. Serve immediately, sprinkled with the remaining cheese.

Ricotta Cheesecake

Serves 6–8

ingredients

for the pastry

- 175 g/6 oz plain flour, plus extra for dusting
- 3 tbsp caster sugar
- pinch of salt
- 115 g/4 oz unsalted butter, diced and chilled
- 1 egg yolk
- water, for sealing

for the filling

- 450 g/1 lb ricotta cheese
- 125 ml/4 fl oz double cream
- 2 eggs, plus 1 egg yolk
- 85 g/3 oz caster sugar
- finely grated rind of 1 lemon
- finely grated rind of 1 orange

1 To make the pastry, sift the flour, sugar and salt onto a work surface and make a well in the centre. Add the butter and egg yolk to the well. Using your fingertips, gradually work in the flour mixture until fully incorporated.

2 Gather up the dough and knead very lightly. Cut off about one-quarter, wrap in clingfilm and chill in the refrigerator. Press the remaining dough into the base of a 23-cm/9-inch loose-based flan tin. Chill in the refrigerator for 30 minutes.

3 To make the filling, beat all the ingredients together in a bowl. Cover with clingfilm and chill in the refrigerator until required.

4 Preheat the oven to 190°C/375°F/Gas Mark 5. Prick the base of the pastry case all over with a fork. Line with baking paper, fill with baking beans and bake blind in the preheated oven for 15 minutes.

5 Remove the baking paper and beans and leave the tin to cool on a wire rack.

6 Spoon the ricotta mixture into the pastry case and smooth the surface. Roll out the reserved pastry on a lightly dusted work surface and cut into strips. Arrange the strips over the filling in a lattice pattern, brushing the overlapping ends with water so that they stick.

7 Bake in the oven for 30–35 minutes until the top of the cheesecake is golden and the filling has set. Leave to cool on a wire rack before removing the side of the tin. Cut into wedges to serve.

Lemon Meringue Pie

Serves 4

ingredients

for the pastry

- 200 g/7 oz plain flour, plus extra for dusting
- 100 g/3½ oz butter, diced, plus extra for greasing
- 50 g/1¾ oz icing sugar, sifted
- finely grated rind of 1 lemon
- 1 egg yolk, beaten
- 3 tbsp milk

for the filling

- 3 tbsp cornflour
- 300 ml/10 fl oz cold water
- juice and grated rind of 2 lemons
- 175 g/6 oz caster sugar
- 2 eggs, separated
- single cream, to serve

1 To make the pastry, sift the flour into a large bowl. Add the butter and rub it in until the mixture resembles breadcrumbs. Mix in the remaining ingredients. Knead briefly on a lightly floured work surface. Leave to rest for 30 minutes.

2 Preheat the oven to 180°C/350°F/Gas Mark 4. Grease a 20-cm/8-inch ovenproof flan dish with butter.

3 Roll out the pastry to a thickness of 5 mm/¼ inch and line the dish with it. Prick with a fork, then line with baking paper and fill with baking beans. Bake blind in the preheated oven for 15 minutes. Remove the baking paper and beans and leave the dish to cool on a wire rack. Reduce the oven temperature to 150°C/300°F/Gas Mark 2.

4 To make the filling, mix the cornflour with a little water to form a paste. Pour the remaining water into a saucepan. Stir in the lemon juice and rind and the cornflour paste. Bring to the boil, while stirring, and cook for 2 minutes. Cool slightly, then stir in 5 tablespoons of the sugar and the egg yolks and pour into the pastry case. Whisk the egg whites in a separate bowl until stiff. Gradually whisk in the remaining sugar and spread over the pie. Bake in the oven for 40 minutes, or until the meringue is light brown. Remove from the oven and serve with single cream.

Rich Vanilla Ice Cream

Serves 4–6

ingredients

- 300 ml/10 fl oz single cream
- 300 ml/10 fl oz double cream or 600 ml/1 pint whipping cream
- 1 vanilla pod
- 4 large egg yolks
- 115 g/4 oz caster sugar

1 Pour the single cream and double cream into a large heavy-based saucepan. Split open the vanilla pod and scrape out the seeds into the cream, then add the whole vanilla pod. Bring almost to the boil, then remove the pan from the heat and leave to infuse for 30 minutes.

2 Place the egg yolks and sugar in a large bowl and whisk together until pale and the mixture leaves a trail when the whisk is lifted. Remove the vanilla pod from the cream, then slowly add the cream to the egg mixture, stirring constantly with a wooden spoon. Strain the mixture into the rinsed-out saucepan or a double boiler and cook over a low heat for 10–15 minutes, stirring constantly, until the mixture thickens enough to coat the back of the spoon. Do not allow the mixture to boil or it will curdle. Remove the custard from the heat and leave to cool for at least 1 hour, stirring occasionally to prevent a skin forming.

3 If using an ice cream machine, churn the cold custard in the machine following the manufacturer's instructions. Alternatively, freeze the custard in a freezerproof container, uncovered, for 1–2 hours, or until it begins to set around the edges. Turn the custard into a bowl and stir with a fork or beat in a food processor until smooth. Return to the freezer and freeze for a further 2–3 hours, or until firm or required. Cover the container with a lid for storing.

Chocolate Fudge Brownies

Makes 16

ingredients

- 85 g/3 oz butter, plus extra for greasing
- 200 g/7 oz low-fat soft cheese
- ½ tsp vanilla essence
- 225 g/8 oz caster sugar
- 2 eggs
- 3 tbsp cocoa powder
- 100 g/3½ oz self-raising flour, sifted
- 50 g/1¾ oz pecan nuts, chopped

for the fudge icing

- 4 tbsp butter
- 1 tbsp milk
- 75 g/2¾ oz icing sugar
- 2 tbsp cocoa powder
- pecan nuts, to decorate (optional)

1 Preheat the oven to 180°C/350°F/Gas Mark 4. Lightly grease and line a 20-cm/8-inch square, shallow cake pan.

2 Beat together the cheese, vanilla essence and 5 teaspoons of caster sugar until smooth, then set aside.

3 Beat the eggs and remaining caster sugar together until light and fluffy. Place the butter and cocoa powder in a small pan and heat gently, stirring until the butter melts and the mixture combines, then stir it into the egg mixture. Fold in the flour and nuts.

4 Pour half of the cake batter into the prepared pan and smooth the top. Carefully spread the cheese mixture over it, then cover it with the remaining cake batter. Bake in the preheated oven for 40–45 minutes. Leave to cool in the pan.

5 To make the icing, melt the butter in the milk. Stir in the icing sugar and cocoa powder. Spread the icing over the brownies and decorate with pecan nuts, if using. Let the icing set, then cut into rectangles or squares to serve.

Chocolate Mousse Pots

Makes 6

ingredients

- 100 g/3½ oz plain chocolate (minimum 70% cocoa solids), chopped
- 1 tbsp butter
- 2 large eggs, separated
- 1 tbsp maple syrup
- 2 tbsp Greek-style yogurt
- 100 g/3½ oz blueberries
- 1 tbsp water
- 25 g/1 oz white chocolate, grated

1 Put the chocolate and butter in a heatproof bowl, set the bowl over a saucepan of barely simmering water and heat until melted. Leave to cool slightly, then stir in the egg yolks, maple syrup and yogurt.

2 Whisk the egg whites in a large, grease-free bowl until stiff, then fold into the chocolate mixture. Divide between 6 small ramekins and chill for 4 hours.

3 Meanwhile, put the blueberries in a small saucepan with the water and cook until the berries begin to pop and turn glossy. Leave to cool, then chill.

4 To serve, top each mousse with blueberries and the grated white chocolate.

Crème Brûlée

Serves 4–6

ingredients

- 225–300 g/8–10½ oz mixed soft fruits, such as blueberries and stoned fresh cherries
- 1½–2 tbsp orange liqueur or orange flower water
- 250 g/9 oz mascarpone cheese
- 200 ml/7 fl oz crème fraîche
- 2–3 tbsp dark muscovado sugar

1 Prepare the fruit, if necessary, and lightly rinse, then place in the bases of 4–6 x 150-ml/5-fl oz ramekin dishes. Sprinkle the fruit with the liqueur.

2 Cream the mascarpone cheese in a bowl until soft, then gradually beat in the crème fraîche.

3 Spoon the cheese mixture over the fruit, smoothing the surface and ensuring that the tops are level. Chill in the refrigerator for at least 2 hours.

4 Sprinkle the tops with the sugar. Using a chef's blow torch, grill the tops until caramelized (about 2–3 minutes). Alternatively, cook under a preheated grill, turning the dishes, for 3–4 minutes, or until the tops are lightly caramelized all over.

5 Serve immediately or chill in the refrigerator for 15–20 minutes before serving.

Tiramisu

Serves 4

ingredients

- 200 ml/7 fl oz strong black coffee, cooled to room temperature
- 4 tbsp orange liqueur, such as Cointreau
- 3 tbsp orange juice
- 16 Italian sponge fingers
- 250 g/9 oz mascarpone cheese
- 300 ml/10 fl oz double cream, lightly whipped
- 3 tbsp icing sugar
- grated rind of 1 orange
- 60 g/2¼ oz plain dark chocolate, grated

to decorate

- chopped toasted almonds
- crystallized orange peel
- chocolate shavings

1 Pour the cooled coffee into a jug and stir in the orange liqueur and orange juice. Place 8 of the sponge fingers in the base of a serving dish, then pour over half of the coffee mixture.

2 Place the mascarpone in a separate bowl together with the cream, icing sugar and orange rind and mix well. Spread half of the mascarpone mixture over the coffee-soaked sponge fingers, then arrange the remaining sponge fingers on top.

3 Pour over the remaining coffee mixture then spread over the remaining mascarpone mixture. Scatter over the grated chocolate and leave to chill in the refrigerator for at least 2 hours.

4 Serve decorated with chopped toasted almonds, crystallized orange peel and chocolate shavings.

Chapter 2
Fish & Seafood

INTRODUCTION

Fish and shellfish are very good for you: they are full of protein, iodine and magnesium, which are essential for building tissue, regulating the metabolism and keeping the bowel healthy. Oily fish in particular are rich in essential fatty acids, which help to lower cholesterol and support the immune system.

Dover sole

Brown trout

Buying and storing fresh fish

Nowadays there is a wide variety of fish available. You can buy fresh flat fish, such as plaice, sole or halibut, or round fish, such as cod, haddock, salmon or trout. You can also buy preserved fish, which have been smoked, dried or salted. When buying fresh whole fish, choose those that smell fresh or that smell of the sea. Avoid any that smell of ammonia. They should have moist, clear eyes and shiny, firm bodies. You can ask your fishmonger to skin, gut and fillet whole larger fish for you. Refrigerate the fish as soon as you get home. Fresh fish is best eaten on the day of purchase, but it will keep for a day or two if necessary. Frozen fish will keep for up to six months in the freezer, but will need thawing in the refrigerator for at least 8 hours before use. Oily fish, such as mackerel, should be wrapped well in clean damp cloths and stored in the refrigerator. Lower-fat white fish, such as cod and haddock, can be covered with clingfilm. Use it by the 'best before' date on the packaging.

Smoked fish

You can buy a wide variety of smoked fish. Smoked salmon is very popular and is usually served cold with slices of lemon. Smoked trout has a mild flavour and is best partnered with horseradish or slices of lemon. Smoked mackerel has a rich flavour and needs a sharp sauce, such as dill or mustard. Smoked haddock is delicious served with a creamy sauce or in kedgerees, while smoked cod is popular in pies. Kippers are best grilled or poached. Fresh smoked fish should be wrapped well in clingfilm and stored in the refrigerator. Smoked fish is often bought vacuum-packed. Store it in the refrigerator and use by the 'best before' date.

Preparing and cooking fresh fish

There is a wide range of white fish available these days. Some, such as cod and haddock, are low in fat, while other types of fish, such as sardines, are rich in healthy essential fatty acids.

Herring

Mackerel

Cod

This round fish has firm, white, flaky flesh and a mild flavour. It can be baked, grilled, poached, pan-fried or deep-fried in batter or breadcrumbs.

Haddock

Like cod, this round fish has firm, white flesh and a mild flavour. It can be baked, grilled, poached, pan-fried or deep-fried, and in many recipes is interchangeable with cod.

Hake

Milder-flavoured than cod, this round fish can be fried, baked or steamed and is also useful in soups.

Pollack

This is a close, though smaller relative of cod. It is cooked in the same way as cod or haddock and is often used in mixed fish soups.

Trout

Like salmon, this round fish is available farmed or wild, but the wild variety is rare. It can be pan-fried, grilled, poached, steamed, barbecued or baked. This is an oily fish, which means that it is rich in essential fatty acids.

Halibut and turbot

These large flat fish both have firm flesh and an excellent flavour and are interchangeable in many recipes. You can fry, poach, steam, grill or bake both these fish.

Mackerel

This is a round fish with a delicious flavour. It is at its best when simply grilled, but can also be fried or barbecued. It is another oily fish that is good for your health.

Sole

This flat fish comes in two varieties – lemon sole and Dover sole – and in different sizes. Dover sole has an excellent flavour and needs little added flavouring to bring out its best qualities. Lemon sole has less flavour, but is improved with the addition of other flavourings. You can pan-fry, deep-fry, bake, steam or grill both types.

Herrings, sardines, sprats and whitebait

These small fish have lots of bones, so it is best to ask your fishmonger to remove the innards and as many bones as possible. They can be barbecued, deep-fried, baked or grilled. They are also oily fish, and therefore rich in essential fatty acids.

Plaice

This flat fish needs extra flavouring but is very good when pan-fried or deep-fried, baked, grilled, poached or steamed.

Salmon

This round fish is available farmed or wild. A popular fish, it can be pan-fried, grilled, poached, steamed, barbecued or baked. Salmon en croûte or en papillote (salmon baked in pastry or in parchment) are particularly popular dishes. Salmon is another oily fish.

Tuna

This is a round oily fish with firm, 'meaty' flesh that makes wonderful steaks with only a very mild fish flavour. The steaks are excellent chargrilled for 2–3 minutes each side (do not overcook). You can also bake, barbecue, grill, braise or stew fresh tuna.

Fresh and frozen shellfish

You can buy fresh shellfish from fishmongers and many shops and supermarkets. In some cases, prawns for example, you can also buy them ready prepared, cooked and frozen.

Lobster

Oyster

Buying and storing shellfish

Shellfish can cause food poisoning, so always buy them as fresh as possible from a reputable supplier. Shellfish should smell fresh or sweet – avoid any that smell of chlorine or sulphur.

If you are buying mussels, clams or oysters, the shells should be tightly closed and not cracked or damaged. Refrigerate shellfish in a covered container as soon as you get home and use on the day of purchase. If you buy live lobster or crabs, place something heavy on top of the container to stop them escaping. Handle shellfish as little as possible and prepare with thoroughly clean equipment and hands.

Squid

Preparation and cooking techniques

Preparation techniques vary enormously depending on the type of shellfish you are using. If you are in any doubt, your local fishmonger will be able to give you advice. Shellfish does not need to cook for long periods of time so stick to the recommended cooking times. Do not overcook it or you could impair the texture and/or taste. Squid, for example, becomes unpleasantly rubbery if cooked for too long.

Prawns

Crab and lobster

You can buy crabs and lobsters alive or cooked. If you buy them live, make sure the claws are tied with string. Put them in the freezer for 1 hour before cooking to desensitize. To cook, take a large saucepan and pour in enough water or stock to cover the crab or lobster. Bring it to the boil, add the crab or lobster, cover the pan and boil until it turns red. Allow 5 minutes of cooking for every 450 g/1 lb of crab. For a lobster, allow 5 minutes for the first 450 g/1 lb, plus an extra 3 minutes for each further 450 g/1 lb. To remove the cooked meat from the crab, crack the claws and remove and reserve the white meat. Snap off the tail, then use your hands to break the shell. Lift out the body, cut it in half lengthways and scoop out the meat. Then lift out the brown meat from the shell. The edible parts of a lobster are the meat in the tail and claws, the liver, and the roe if the lobster is female. Cooking a lobster and removing the meat can be fiddly, however, so it is usually best to ask your fishmonger to do this for you.

Mussels

You should use fresh mussels on the day of purchase and keep them in lightly salted water until you are ready to use them. To clean and debeard them, use a small knife to scrape off any barnacles from the shells, then pull out and discard any clumps of hair (these are called 'beards'). Use a stiff brush to scrub the shells under cold running water, then tap each mussel sharply with the handle of the knife and discard any that do not close tightly. To steam them, heat a little liquid (water, stock or wine) in a large saucepan, add the cleaned mussels, cover the pan and steam them, shaking the pan occasionally, for 5–6 minutes. Remove from the heat and discard any mussels that remain closed. You can also grill or bake them half-shelled, or stew them shelled.

Oysters

These shellfish are usually eaten raw. Use a stiff brush to scrub the shells under cold running water, and discard any that are open. To open an oyster, insert a knife blade between the two shell halves and twist it to prise them open. Use a spoon to lift out the oyster inside (you will need to cut it from the muscle underneath). Serve it on a half-shell. You can also bake or grill oysters in their half-shells, or stew them shelled.

Prawns

These come in different sizes and you can buy them peeled or unpeeled, cooked or raw. Cooked, peeled prawns are also available frozen. To peel and devein a raw prawn, carefully peel off the shell (you can remove the tail or leave it on for decorative effect). Using a small knife, make a shallow cut along the dark vein to reveal it, then remove it with the knife's tip. Discard the vein, then rinse the prawn under cold running water and pat dry with kitchen paper. Prawns require very little cooking – for example, you need to stir-fry them for only 2–3 minutes until they turn pink. You can pan-fry, stir-fry, grill, bake, barbecue or steam them.

Scallops

These have a delicate flavour and are becoming increasingly popular. They should be creamy-white with pink corals. They need a minimal amount of cooking, usually 1–2 minutes on each side if you are pan-frying them shelled. You can also grill or bake them in their half-shells.

Squid

You can buy squid whole or already prepared. The edible parts are the tentacles, fins, pouch and the ink. Sauté the squid for 2–3 minutes only – do not overcook it or it will go rubbery. You can also deep-fry, bake, poach and stew it.

Clams

Use a stiff brush to scrub the shells under cold running water, and discard any that stay open when tapped. To open a clam, insert a knife blade between the two shell halves and twist it to prise them open. Use a spoon to lift out the soft flesh inside. You can eat clams raw, or you can steam them in their shells for 4 minutes or until they have opened. You can also bake or grill them in their half-shells, or stew them shelled.

Mussels

Seafood Chowder

Serves 6

ingredients

- 1 kg/2 lb 4 oz live mussels
- 350 g/12 oz skinless white fish fillets, such as cod, sole or haddock
- 4 tbsp plain flour
- 1.5 litres/2¾ pints fish stock
- 1 tbsp butter
- 1 large onion, finely chopped
- 200 g/7 oz cooked or raw peeled prawns
- 300 ml/10 fl oz whipping cream or double cream
- salt and pepper
- snipped fresh dill, to garnish

1 Discard any mussels with broken shells or any that refuse to close when tapped. Rinse and pull off any beards. Put the mussels in a large, heavy-based saucepan. Cover tightly and cook over a high heat for about 4 minutes, or until the mussels open, shaking the pan occasionally. Discard any that remain closed. When they are cool enough to handle, remove the mussels from their shells and set aside.

2 Meanwhile, lightly poach the fish fillets in a saucepan of gently simmering water for 4–5 minutes (if in one piece), or until just cooked but still moist. Using a fork, flake the flesh into a bowl.

3 Melt the butter in a heavy-based saucepan over a medium–low heat. Add the onion, cover and cook for 3 minutes, stirring frequently, until it softens.

4 Add the fish stock and bring to the boil. Slowly whisk in the flour until well combined and bring back to the boil, whisking constantly. Season with salt, if needed, and pepper. Reduce the heat and simmer, partially covered, for 15 minutes.

5 Add the poached fish and mussels and stir to combine. Stir in the prawns and cream.

6 Taste and adjust the seasoning. Simmer for a few minutes longer to heat through. Ladle into warmed bowls, sprinkle with dill and serve.

Creamy Salmon Baked Potatoes

Serves 4

ingredients

- 4 baking potatoes, about 275 g/9¾ oz each, scrubbed
- 250 g/9 oz skinless salmon fillet
- 200 g/7 oz reduced-fat soft cheese
- 2–3 tbsp skimmed milk
- 2 tbsp chopped/snipped fresh herbs, such as dill or chives
- 60 g/2½ oz mature Cheddar cheese, grated
- salt and pepper

1 Preheat the oven to 200°C/400°F/Gas Mark 6. Prick the skins of the potatoes and put on the top shelf of the preheated oven. Bake for 50–60 minutes until the skins are crisp and the centres are soft when pierced with a sharp knife or skewer.

2 Meanwhile, lightly poach the salmon fillet in a saucepan of gently simmering water for 4–5 minutes (if in one piece), or until just cooked but still moist. Alternatively, cut into 2–3 evenly sized pieces and cook in a microwave oven on Medium for 2 minutes, then turn the pieces around so that the cooked parts are in the centre, and cook for a further 1 minute, or until just cooked but still moist. Using a fork, flake the flesh into a bowl.

3 In a separate bowl, blend the soft cheese with just enough of the milk to loosen, then stir in the herbs and a little salt and pepper.

4 When the potatoes are cooked, preheat the grill to high. Cut the potatoes in half lengthways. Carefully scoop the potato flesh out of the skins, reserving the skins, add to the soft cheese mixture and mash together. Lightly stir in the salmon flakes.

5 Spoon the filling into the potato skins and top with the Cheddar cheese. Cook under the preheated grill for 1–2 minutes until the cheese is bubbling and turning golden. Serve immediately.

Smoked Fish Pie

Serves 6

ingredients

- 2 tbsp olive oil
- 1 onion, finely chopped
- 1 leek, thinly sliced
- 1 carrot, diced
- 1 celery stick, diced
- 115 g/4 oz button mushrooms, halved
- grated rind of 1 lemon
- 350 g/12 oz skinless, boneless smoked cod or haddock fillet, cubed
- 350 g/12 oz skinless, boneless white fish, cubed
- 225 g/8 oz cooked peeled prawns
- 2 tbsp chopped fresh parsley
- 1 tbsp chopped fresh dill, plus sprigs to garnish
- salt and pepper

for the sauce

- 4 tbsp butter
- 4 tbsp plain flour
- 1 tsp mustard powder
- 600 ml/1 pint milk
- 85 g/3 oz Gruyère cheese, grated

for the topping

- 675 g/1 lb 8 oz potatoes, unpeeled
- 4 tbsp butter, melted
- 25 g/1 oz Gruyère cheese, grated

1 For the sauce, heat the butter in a large saucepan and, when melted, add the flour and mustard powder. Stir until smooth and cook over a very low heat for 2 minutes without colouring. Slowly beat in the milk until smooth. Simmer gently for 2 minutes then stir in the cheese until smooth. Remove from the heat and place some clingfilm over the surface of the sauce to prevent a skin forming. Reserve.

2 Meanwhile, for the topping, boil the whole potatoes in plenty of salted water for 15 minutes. Drain well and leave until the potatoes are cool enough to handle.

3 Preheat the oven to 200°C/400°F/Gas Mark 6. Heat the oil in a clean saucepan. Add the onion and cook for 5 minutes until softened. Add the leek, carrot, celery and mushrooms and cook for a further 10 minutes, or until the vegetables have softened. Stir in the lemon rind and cook briefly.

4 Add the softened vegetables with the fish, prawns, parsley and dill to the sauce. Season to taste with salt and pepper and transfer to a greased 1.7-litre/3-pint casserole dish.

5 Peel the cooled potatoes and grate them coarsely. Mix with the melted butter. Cover the filling with the grated potato and sprinkle with the grated Gruyère cheese.

6 Cover loosely with foil and bake in the preheated oven for 30 minutes. Remove the foil and bake for a further 30 minutes, or until the topping is tender and golden and the filling is bubbling. Garnish with dill sprigs and serve.

Sweet Potato & Tuna Fish Cakes

Serves 4

ingredients

- 175 g/6 oz sweet potatoes, peeled and chopped
- 175 g/6 oz canned tuna in brine, drained
- 4 spring onions, trimmed and chopped
- 1 tbsp grated lemon rind
- 1 tbsp chopped fresh coriander
- pepper
- lemon wedges, to garnish
- freshly cooked green beans, to serve

1 Cook the sweet potatoes in a saucepan of boiling water for 10–12 minutes, or until tender when pierced with a fork. Drain and mash.

2 Flake the tuna then add to the mashed potatoes together with the chopped spring onions, lemon rind, chopped coriander and pepper to taste.

3 Mix the ingredients lightly together then, using slightly dampened hands, shape into 4 rounds. Place on a plate, cover loosely and leave to chill in the refrigerator for at least 30 minutes, longer if time permits.

4 Preheat the oven to 190°C/375°F/Gas Mark 5. Place the fish cakes on a large non-stick baking sheet and cook for 20 minutes, or until piping hot. Transfer to serving plates, garnish with lemon wedges and serve with freshly cooked green beans.

Baked Salmon with Wild Rice

Serves 4

ingredients

- 250 g/9 oz wild rice, rinsed and drained
- 75 g/2½ oz butter
- 1 tbsp olive oil, plus extra for greasing
- 400 g/14 oz button mushrooms, wiped and thinly sliced
- 1 tbsp chopped fresh tarragon, or ½ tbsp dried tarragon
- 300 g/10½ oz leeks, trimmed and thinly sliced
- 12 thin lemon slices
- 4 salmon fillets, any small bones removed
- 4 tbsp dry white vermouth
- 125 g/4½ oz crème fraîche
- salt and pepper

1 Bring 1.2 litres/2 pints water to the boil in a large saucepan. Add the rice and 1½ teaspoons of salt and return the water to the boil. Cover the pan, reduce the heat to low and simmer for 45–50 minutes until all the liquid has been absorbed and the rice is tender. Add 30 g/1 oz of the butter and fluff with a fork.

2 Meanwhile, preheat the oven to 220°C/425°F/Gas Mark 7. Cut 4 circles of greaseproof paper large enough to hold a salmon fillet with some mushrooms and leeks spooned on top. Fold the circles in half and brush the bottom halves with oil.

3 Melt 30 g/1 oz of the remaining butter with the oil in a large frying pan over a high heat. Add the mushrooms and cook, stirring, for about 6 minutes until they start to give off their liquid. Add the tarragon and salt and pepper to taste and stir. Tip the mushrooms out of the pan and set aside. Melt the remaining butter in the wiped-out pan. Add the leeks with salt and pepper to taste and cook, stirring, for 6 minutes, or until tender.

4 Arrange 3 lemon slices in a row along the fold on each of the paper circles. Place a salmon fillet on top, top with one quarter of the mushrooms and the leeks and add a tablespoon of vermouth, 2 tablespoons of crème fraîche and some salt and pepper. Fold over the circles and crimp the edges so the parcels are sealed and none of the juices can escape. Transfer to a baking tray, place in the oven and bake for 12 minutes or until the flesh flakes.

5 Place the salmon on a bed of wild rice and serve.

Cod & Chips

Serves 4

ingredients

- 900 g/2 lb potatoes
- four 175-g/6-oz thick pieces cod fillet, preferably from the head end
- vegetable oil, for deep-frying
- salt and pepper
- lemon wedges, to serve

for the batter

- 15 g/½ oz fresh yeast
- 300 ml/10 fl oz beer
- 225 g/8 oz plain flour
- 2 tsp salt

for the mayonnaise

- 1 egg yolk
- 1 tsp wholegrain mustard
- 1 tbsp lemon juice
- 200 ml/7 fl oz light olive oil
- salt and pepper

1 For the batter, cream the yeast with a little beer to a smooth paste. Gradually stir in the remaining beer. Sift the flour and salt into a bowl, make a well in the centre, add the yeast and whisk to a smooth batter. Cover and leave at room temperature for 1 hour.

2 For the mayonnaise, process all the ingredients except the oil in a food processor for 30 seconds until frothy. With the machine still running, gradually add the oil, drop by drop, until the mixture begins to thicken. Continue adding in a steady stream until it has been incorporated. Adjust the seasoning. Thin with a little hot water if too thick, and chill.

3 Cut the potatoes into chips about 1.5 cm/⅝ inch thick. Heat a large saucepan half filled with vegetable oil to 140°C/275°F, or until a cube of bread browns in 1 minute. Cook the chips in 2 batches for 5 minutes, or until cooked through but not browned. Drain on kitchen paper and reserve.

4 Increase the heat to 160°C/325°F, or until a cube of bread browns in 45 seconds. Season the fish, then dip into the batter. Deep-fry 2 pieces at a time for 7–8 minutes until golden brown and cooked through. Drain on kitchen paper and keep warm while you cook the remaining fish and the chips.

5 Increase the heat to 190°C/375°F, or until a cube of bread browns in 30 seconds. Deep-fry the chips again, in 2 batches, for 2–3 minutes until crisp and golden. Drain on kitchen paper and sprinkle with salt. Serve the fish with the chips, mayonnaise and lemon wedges.

Baked Sea Bass with White Bean Purée

Serves 4

ingredients

- 2 tbsp olive oil
- 1 tbsp fresh thyme leaves
- 4 large sea bass fillets, about 175 g/6 oz each
- cherry tomatoes on the vine, to serve
- salt and pepper

for the White Bean Purée

- 3 tbsp olive oil
- 2 garlic cloves, chopped
- 800 g/1 lb 12 oz canned cannellini or butter beans, drained and rinsed
- juice of 1 lemon
- 2–3 tbsp water
- 4 tbsp chopped fresh flat-leaf parsley

1 Preheat the oven to 200°C/400°F/ Gas Mark 6. Mix the oil, thyme and a little salt and pepper to taste together in a small bowl or jug. Arrange the sea bass fillets on a baking tray, pour over the oil mixture and carefully turn to coat well. Put the tray on the top shelf of the preheated oven and bake for 15 minutes.

2 Meanwhile, make the bean purée. Heat the oil in a saucepan over a medium heat, add the garlic and cook, stirring, for 1 minute. Add the beans and heat through for 3–4 minutes, then add the lemon juice and a little salt and pepper to taste. Transfer to a blender or food processor, add the water and blend lightly until you have a purée. Alternatively, mash thoroughly with a fork. Stir the parsley into the purée.

3 Serve the sea bass fillets on top of the warm bean purée with a drizzle of any pan juices. Serve with vine tomatoes.

Mediterranean Fish Casserole

Serves 6

ingredients

- 2 tbsp olive oil
- 1 red onion, peeled and sliced
- 2 garlic cloves, peeled and chopped
- 2 red peppers
- 400 g/14 oz canned chopped tomatoes
- 1 tsp chopped fresh oregano or marjoram
- a few saffron strands soaked in 1 tbsp warm water for 2 minutes
- 450 g/1 lb white fish (cod, haddock or hake), skinned and boned
- 450 g/1 lb prepared squid, cut into rings
- 300 ml/10 fl oz fish or vegetable stock
- 115 g/4 oz cooked shelled prawns
- 6 cooked whole prawns in their shells, to garnish
- 2 tbsp chopped fresh flat-leaf parsley, to garnish
- salt and pepper
- crusty bread, to serve

1 Heat the oil in a frying pan and fry the onion and garlic over a medium heat for 2–3 minutes until beginning to soften.

2 Deseed and thinly slice the peppers and add to the pan. Continue to cook over a low heat for a further 5 minutes. Add the tomatoes with the herbs and saffron and stir well.

3 Preheat the oven to 200°C/400°F/Gas 6. Cut the white fish into 3-cm/1¼-inch pieces and place with the squid in a casserole dish. Pour in the fried vegetable mixture and the stock, stir well and season to taste.

4 Cover and cook in the centre of the preheated oven for about 30 minutes, until the fish is tender and cooked. Add the prawns at the last minute and just heat through.

5 Transfer to warmed bowls, garnish with the whole prawns and chopped parsley and serve with crusty bread.

Paella

Serves 4

ingredients

- 3 tbsp olive oil
- 2 tbsp butter
- 2 garlic cloves, chopped
- 1 onion, chopped
- 2 large tomatoes, deseeded and diced
- 85 g/3 oz frozen peas
- 1 red pepper, deseeded and chopped
- 150 g/5½ oz arborio rice
- 2 tsp dried mixed herbs
- 1 tsp saffron powder
- 425 ml/15 fl oz chicken stock
- 4 skinless, boneless chicken breasts
- 150 g/5½ oz lean chorizo, skinned
- 200 g/7 oz cooked lobster meat
- 200 g/7 oz prawns, peeled and deveined
- 1 tbsp chopped fresh flat-leaf parsley, plus extra to garnish
- salt and pepper

1 Heat the oil and butter in a large frying pan over a medium heat. Add the garlic and onion and cook, stirring, for 3 minutes, or until slightly softened.

2 Add the tomatoes, peas, red pepper, rice, mixed herbs and saffron and cook, stirring, for 2 minutes. Pour in the stock and bring to the boil. Reduce the heat to low and cook, stirring, for 10 minutes.

3 Chop the chicken into bite-sized pieces and add to the frying pan. Cook, stirring occasionally, for 5 minutes. Chop up the chorizo, add to the frying pan and cook for 3 minutes. Chop up the lobster meat and add to the pan with the prawns and parsley. Season with salt and pepper and cook, stirring, for a further 2 minutes.

4 Remove the frying pan from the heat, transfer the paella to a large serving dish or individual plates, garnish with the chopped parsley, and serve.

Seafood Gratin

Serves 4

ingredients

- 450 g/1 lb cod fillets
- 225 g/8 oz prawns, peeled and deveined
- 225 g/8 oz scallops
- 3 tbsp extra virgin olive oil
- 1 garlic clove, chopped
- 4 spring onions, chopped
- 1 courgette, sliced
- 425 g/15 oz canned plum tomatoes
- 2 tbsp chopped fresh basil
- 50 g/1¾ oz fresh breadcrumbs
- 75 g/2¾ oz Cheddar cheese, grated
- salt and pepper

1 Preheat the oven to 190ºC/375ºF/Gas Mark 5. Bring a large saucepan of water to the boil, then reduce the heat to medium. Rinse the cod, pat dry with kitchen paper and add to the pan. Cook for 5 minutes. Add the prawns and cook for 3 minutes, then add the scallops and cook for 2 minutes. Drain, refresh under cold running water and drain again.

2 Heat 2 tablespoons of the oil in a frying pan over a low heat. Add the garlic and spring onions and cook, stirring, for 3 minutes. Add the courgette and cook for 3 minutes, then add the tomatoes with their can juices, and the basil. Season to taste with salt and pepper and leave to simmer for 10 minutes.

3 Brush a shallow baking dish with the remaining oil and arrange the seafood in it. Remove the saucepan from the heat and pour the sauce over the fish. Scatter over the breadcrumbs and top with cheese. Bake in the oven for 30 minutes until golden. Transfer to warmed plates and serve.

Warm Tuna & Kidney Bean Salad

Serves 4

ingredients

- 4 fresh tuna steaks, about 175 g/6 oz each
- 1 tbsp olive oil
- 200 g/7 oz canned kidney beans, rinsed and drained
- 100 g/3½ oz canned sweetcorn, rinsed and drained
- 2 spring onions, trimmed and thinly sliced
- salt and pepper
- lime wedges, to garnish

for the dressing

- 5 tbsp extra virgin olive oil
- 3 tbsp balsamic vinegar
- 1 tbsp lime juice
- 1 garlic clove, chopped
- 1 tbsp chopped fresh coriander
- salt and pepper

1 Preheat a ridged griddle pan. While the pan is heating, brush the tuna steaks with olive oil, then season with salt and pepper. Cook the steaks for 2 minutes, then turn them over and cook on the other side for a further 2 minutes, or according to your taste, but do not overcook. Remove from the heat and allow to cool slightly.

2 While the tuna is cooling, heat the kidney beans and sweetcorn according to the instructions on the cans, then drain.

3 To make the dressing, put all the ingredients into a small bowl and stir together well.

4 Put the kidney beans, sweetcorn and spring onions into a large bowl, pour over half of the dressing and mix together well. Divide the bean and sweetcorn salad between individual serving plates, then place a tuna steak on each one. Drizzle over the remaining dressing, garnish with the lime wedges, and serve.

Pan-fried Prawns

Serves 4

ingredients

- 4 garlic cloves
- 20–24 unshelled large raw prawns
- 125 g/4½ oz butter
- 4 tbsp olive oil
- 6 tbsp brandy
- salt and pepper
- 2 tbsp chopped fresh flat-leaf parsley, to garnish
- lemon wedges, to serve

1 Using a sharp knife, peel and slice the garlic.

2 Wash the prawns and pat dry using kitchen paper.

3 Melt the butter with the oil in a large frying pan, add the garlic and prawns, and fry over a high heat, stirring, for 3–4 minutes, until the prawns are pink.

4 Drizzle with brandy and season with salt and pepper to taste. Sprinkle with the chopped parsley and serve immediately with lemon wedges.

Goujons of Plaice

Serves 2

ingredients

- 2 plaice fillets, about 175 g/6 oz each, skinned
- 2 tbsp plain flour
- 1 egg, beaten
- 115 g/4 oz white or wholemeal breadcrumbs, made from one-day-old bread
- 1 tbsp finely chopped fresh flat-leaf parsley
- 1 garlic clove, peeled and crushed (optional)
- 225 ml/8 fl oz vegetable oil, for frying
- salt and pepper
- lemon wedges, to serve
- aïoli, to serve

1 Cut the fillets across diagonally into thin strips, about 1 cm/½ inch wide.

2 Season the flour well and put on to a plate. Roll the strips of fish in the flour until well covered.

3 Place the beaten egg in a shallow dish and then dip the fish into it.

4 Mix the breadcrumbs with the parsley, and garlic if using, and season well. Put the mixture into a plastic bag, add the goujons and toss to coat thoroughly. Chill in the refrigerator for at least half an hour.

5 Heat the oil in a frying pan and fry half the goujons over a medium heat for 2–3 minutes, turning them with a slotted spoon. Remove from the pan and drain on kitchen paper. Keep warm. Repeat using the remaining fish.

6 Serve at once with lemon wedges and a bowl of aioli.

Linguine with Clams

Serves 4

ingredients

- 200 g/7 oz dried linguine pasta
- 3 tbsp extra virgin olive oil
- 4 garlic cloves, finely chopped
- 2 shallots, finely chopped
- ½ fresh red chilli, finely chopped
- 125 ml/4 fl oz white wine
- 1 kg/2 lb 4 oz fresh clams, tellines or cockles, cleaned
- 1 tbsp fresh chopped flat-leaf parsley
- zest of 1 lemon
- salt and pepper

1 Cook the linguine according to the instructions on the packet, drain and toss with a splash of olive oil. Cover and keep warm.

2 Add half the olive oil to a large saucepan with a lid and place over a high heat. Add the garlic, shallots and chilli and cook gently for 8–10 minutes until soft. Add the wine, bring to the boil and cook for 2 minutes. Add the clams, cover and cook for a further 2–5 minutes, or until all the clams have opened. Discard any clams which remain closed. Add the drained linguine, parsley, lemon zest, the remaining olive oil and some salt and pepper and mix through.

3 Serve in warmed bowls, with another bowl for discarded shells.

Chapter 3
Meat

01 0183

Introduction

Meat is rich in protein and easy to cook. It makes an excellent centrepiece to any meal, and you can choose from a wide range of joints and cuts, from the economical to the indulgent, to suit any occasion.

Beef

Lamb

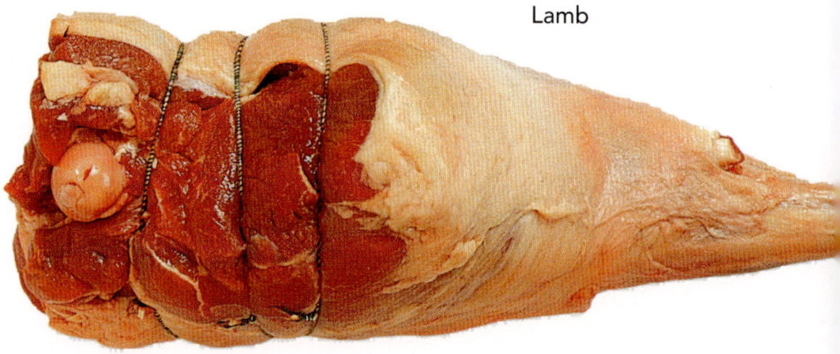

Buying and storing meat

Always buy your fresh meat from a reputable supplier. For lamb, choose firm, pinkish, marbled meat; avoid any that looks dark and soggy. The fat should be cream-coloured, not yellow. For pork, choose moist, pinkish meat with white fat. Avoid any meat that looks oily or that has yellow fat. For beef, look for meat that is deep burgundy red, not bright red; the fat should be cream-coloured, not yellow. Choose beef that has a marbling of fat through it – this will ensure that the meat stays moist during cooking. For veal, the flesh should be a very pale pink and the fat white. If it is turning red, it means that the meat is older than it should be.

If you are buying a joint of meat, allow 175–350 g/ 6–12 oz per person, depending on whether the meat is on or off the bone.

As soon as you get the meat home, unwrap it and transfer it to a clean dish (the dish should have a lip deep enough to catch any juices). Cover it with clingfilm and store in the refrigerator away from any cooked meats in order to prevent cross-contamination. Leave any prepackaged meat in its wrapping in the refrigerator and use by the 'best before' date. Unpackaged minced lamb, beef and pork is best used within 1–2 days of purchase. Fresh cuts of beef and pork will keep in the refrigerator for 2–3 days, and cooked beef and pork can be refrigerated for 4–5 days. Fresh lamb cuts will keep for up to 4 days in the refrigerator. Before cooking, bring out the meat (keep it covered) and allow it to come back to room temperature for about 30 minutes before cooking. You can freeze small cuts of beef or pork for up to 6 months, and lamb for up to 3 months. Make sure you thaw the meat thoroughly in a refrigerator or cool room before cooking: allow 6 hours per 450 g/1 lb.

Preparation techniques

There is a range of techniques you can use to prepare and/or improve your chosen cuts of meat before cooking. Some of them are done purely for presentation, while other techniques help to tenderize the meat or facilitate thorough cooking.

Lamb chops

Use a sharp knife to remove the excess fat around the edge.

Pork chops and rump steaks

Use a sharp knife to make incisions in the fat at intervals of 2.5 cm/1 inch around the edge. This helps prevent the meat curling up at the sides during cooking.

Braising steak

Use a sharp knife to remove any excess fat. Slice the meat across the grain, then cut across the slices to form smaller pieces or cubes of meat.

Choosing cuts of meat

There are many different cuts of meat available. Choosing the right cut will help to ensure the perfect result for your chosen recipe. When in doubt, ask your local butcher for advice.

Tenderize thin cuts of meat

Put the meat between sheets of greaseproof paper and pound with either a meat mallet or the base of a saucepan.

Stuff and tie a boneless joint

Put it skin-side down and arrange the stuffing evenly over the surface. Roll up the joint from the thick end, tie a piece of clean string lengthways around the joint, then knot it and trim off the ends. Now tie further pieces of string crossways around the joint at intervals of about 2.5 cm/1 inch. Knot each one in turn and trim the ends.

Butterfly a leg of lamb

Push a chef's knife into the cavity of the bone, then cut sideways to part the meat. Open it out and make a light incision down the centre of the meat so that it stays open and flat.

Prepare a rack of lamb

Remove the skin and excess fat, leaving a layer of fat about 1.5 cm/⅝ inch thick. Cut off the bone at the back, then remove the fat from the ends of the bones (to a length of about 5 cm/2 inches). Use a knife to scrape out the meat from between the bones.

Beef

For roasting, choose sirloin, topside fillet or rib. Fillet and steaks are excellent for grilling, pan-frying or barbecuing. For braising and stewing, use chuck or topside fillet or rib.

Pork

For roasting, choose the belly, leg, loin, shoulder, fillet, chops or steaks. For grilling, use the belly, escalopes, loin, shoulder, fillet, chops or steaks. The belly, loin, fillet, chops or steaks are excellent for barbecues. For frying, use the loin, fillet, chops and steaks, and also bacon. To stew or braise, use the leg, shoulder or loin.

Veal

The breast, loin and shoulder are best for roasting, while the loin, topside and cutlets are ideal for grilling and barbecuing. For pan-frying, choose the loin or topside, and for stewing or braising use the knuckle, shoulder or breast.

Lamb

The leg is the most popular choice for roasting, but you can also roast the shoulder, saddle, breast and best end of neck. For grilling, try chops, noisettes, leg and best end of neck. The leg or chops are ideal for barbecues, and for pan-frying use noisettes or the middle neck. Finally, for stewing, braising or casseroles, use the shoulder, shank or middle neck.

Cooking and carving techniques

Techniques for cooking and carving joints of meat are not difficult, but they do have to be performed properly in order to get the best out of the meat. Follow the instructions given here for perfect results every time.

Roasting and carving a boned joint

This technique is suitable for boned joints of lamb, pork and beef. Rub the surface with a little oil, followed by some salt and some crushed peppercorns (use a pestle and mortar for this). Place on a rack in a roasting tin, then roast in the oven, basting once or twice during cooking. Remove from the oven and cut off the strings. Wrap the meat in foil and leave to stand for 15–20 minutes. To carve, steady the meat with a fork, then carve slices downwards from one end.

Roasting and carving a leg of lamb

Using a sharp knife, score a criss-cross pattern in the fat, then rub all over the surface with a little oil, followed by some salt and freshly ground black pepper. Put the meat on a rack in a roasting tin and roast in the oven, basting once or twice during cooking.

To test if the meat is cooked all the way through, pierce a skewer or knife into the thickest part. The juices that run out will be clear if the meat is cooked. If not, return it to the oven and cook until it is done. Remove from the oven and wrap the meat in foil. Leave to stand for 15–20 minutes. To carve, turn the leg meat-side up, then steady the meat with a fork. Start carving from the knuckle end. When you have finished, turn over the leg and carve horizontal slices.

Using a meat thermometer

A meat thermometer is a useful device for testing whether a joint of meat is cooked thoroughly. Thorough cooking is particularly important in the case of pork, which can carry harmful bacteria and cause food poisoning if not cooked all the way through. Simply insert the thermometer into the thickest part of the meat at the start of cooking. Take care to ensure that the thermometer does not come into contact with any bone, because this could give a false reading. When the thermometer reaches the required temperature, the meat is cooked. The recommended temperatures for different meats are shown below.

COOKING TEMPERATURES

Lamb	Medium rare	75°C/167°F
	Well done	80°C/176°F
Pork	Well done	90°C/194°F
Beef	Rare	65°C/149°F
	Medium rare	70°C/158°F
	Well done	75°C/167°F

OVEN TEMPERATURES AND ROASTING TIMES

PLEASE NOTE THAT INDIVIDUAL OVEN TEMPERATURES AND COOKING TIMES VARY, SO THE FOLLOWING COOKING TIMES ARE APPROXIMATE ONLY. REMEMBER TO PREHEAT THE OVEN BEFORE COOKING IN ORDER TO ENSURE THE BEST RESULTS.

Meat	Joint	Weight	Temperature	Cooking time
Lamb	Whole leg	2.5 kg/5 lb 8 oz	180°C/350°F/Gas Mark 4	2¼ hours (medium rare) or 2½ hours (well done)
Lamb	Whole shoulder	2.5 kg /5 lb 8 oz	180°C/350°F/Gas Mark 4	2¼ hours (medium rare) or 2½ hours (well done)
Pork	Loin (boned)	2.5 kg/5 lb 8 oz	180°C/350°F/Gas Mark 4 220°C/425°F/Gas Mark 7	3 hours at lower temperature, then 20 minutes at higher temperature (well done)
Pork	Shoulder (boned)	2.5 kg/5 lb 8 oz	180°C/350°F/Gas Mark 4 220°C/425°F/Gas Mark 7	3 hours at lower temperature, then 20 minutes at higher temperature (well done)
Beef	Sirloin	2.5 kg/5 lb 8 oz	200°C/400°F/Gas Mark 6	1¾ hours (rare), 2¼ hours (medium rare) or 2½ hours (well done)
Beef	Topside	2 kg/4 lb 8 oz	180°C/350°F/Gas Mark 4	1½ hours (rare), 2 hours (medium rare) or 2½ hours (well done)

OVEN TEMPERATURES AND HEAT DESCRIPTIONS

YOU MAY COME ACROSS RECIPES THAT DO NOT GIVE A SPECIFIC TEMPERATURE: INSTEAD THEY WILL SIMPLY RECOMMEND COOKING IN A 'MODERATE' OR 'HOT' OVEN. HERE IS A LIST OF THESE HEAT DESCRIPTIONS AND THEIR CORRECT TEMPERATURES.

Oven heat description	Celsius	Fahrenheit	Gas mark
Very cool	110–120°	225–250°	¼–½
Cool	140–150°	275–300°	1–2
Moderate	160–180°	325–350°	3–4
Moderately hot	190–200°	375–400°	5–6
Hot	220°	425°	7
Very hot	230–240°	450–475°	8–9

Roast Beef

Serves 8

ingredients

- 2.7 kg/6 lb prime rib of beef
- 2 tsp dry English mustard
- 3 tbsp plain flour
- 300 ml/10 fl oz red wine
- 300 ml/10 fl oz beef stock
- 2 tsp Worcestershire sauce (optional)
- salt and pepper

for the Yorkshire pudding

- 100 g/3½ oz plain flour
- pinch of salt
- 1 egg, beaten
- 150 ml/5 fl oz milk
- 150 ml/5 fl oz water
- 2 tbsp roast beef dripping or olive oil

1 Preheat the oven to 230°C/450°F/ Gas Mark 8.

2 Season the meat with the salt and pepper and rub in the mustard and 1 tablespoon of the flour.

3 Place the meat in a roasting tin large enough to hold it comfortably and roast for 15 minutes. Reduce the heat to 190°C/375°F/Gas Mark 5 and cook for 15 minutes per 450 g/1 lb, plus 15 minutes (1 hour 45 minutes for this joint) for rare beef or 20 minutes per 450 g/1 lb, plus 20 minutes (2 hours 20 minutes) for medium beef. Baste the meat from time to time to keep it moist and if the tin becomes too dry, add a little stock or red wine.

4 Increase the oven temperature to 220°C/425°F Gas Mark 7. To make the Yorkshire pudding beat together the flour, salt, egg, milk and water, until a batter forms. Leave to stand for half an hour. Heat 2 tablespoons of roast beef dripping in a 20-cm/8-inch square roasting tin in the top of the oven. Remove the tin from the oven, pour in the batter and bake for 25–30 minutes until it is puffed up and golden brown.

5 Remove the meat from the oven and place on a hot serving plate, cover with foil and leave in a warm place for 10–15 minutes.

6 To make the gravy, pour off most of the fat from the tin, leaving behind the meat juices and the sediments. Place the tin on the top of the stove over a medium heat and scrape all the sediments from the base of the tin. Sprinkle in the remaining flour and quickly mix it into the juices with a small whisk. When you have a smooth paste, gradually add the wine and most of the stock, whisking all the time. Bring to the boil, then turn down the heat to a gentle simmer and cook for 2–3 minutes. Season with salt and pepper and add the remaining stock, if needed, and a little Worcestershire sauce, if liked.

7 When ready to serve, carve the meat into slices and serve on hot plates. Pour the gravy into a warm jug and take direct to the table. Serve with Yorkshire pudding.

Beef en Daube with Mustard Mash

Serves 2

ingredients

- 2 tsp vegetable oil
- 225 g/8 oz extra-lean braising steak, cut into 8 pieces
- 10 small shallots, peeled but left whole
- 1 clove garlic, peeled and crushed
- 1 medium tomato, chopped
- 100 g/3½ oz mushrooms, finely sliced
- 150 ml/¼ pint red wine
- 100 ml/3½ fl oz chicken stock
- 1 small bouquet garni
- 1 tsp cornflour
- salt and pepper

for the Mustard Mash

- 2 medium floury potatoes, peeled and sliced
- 1½–2 tbsp skimmed milk, heated
- 1 tsp Dijon mustard, to taste

1 Preheat the oven to 180°C/350°F/Gas Mark 4.

2 Heat the oil in a heavy-based flame-proof casserole. Add the meat and shallots and cook over a high heat, stirring, for 4–5 minutes to brown the meat on all sides. Add the garlic, tomato, mushrooms, wine and stock, and tuck the bouquet garni in well.

3 Bring to a simmer on the hob, cover and transfer to the oven to cook for 45–60 minutes, or until everything is tender.

4 About 30 minutes before the beef is ready, place the potatoes in boiling water and simmer for 20 minutes or until just tender. Remove from heat, drain well and put in a bowl. Add the milk and mash well. Stir in the mustard to taste, and keep warm.

5 Use a slotted spoon to transfer the meat and vegetables to a warmed serving dish. Cook the sauce on the hob over a high heat until reduced by half. Reduce the heat, remove the bouquet garni and check the seasoning.

6 Add the cornflour to the sauce, mixed with a little cold water to form a paste, stirring well, and bring back to a simmer. Pour the sauce over the meat and serve with the mustard mash.

Classic Beef Fajitas

Serves 4–6

ingredients
- 700 g/1 lb 9 oz beef skirt steak, cut into strips
- 6 garlic cloves, chopped
- juice of 1 lime
- large pinch of mild chilli powder
- large pinch of paprika
- large pinch of ground cumin
- 1–2 tbsp extra virgin olive oil
- 12 flour tortillas
- butter, for greasing
- vegetable oil, for frying
- 1–2 avocados, stoned, sliced and tossed with lime juice
- 125 ml/4 fl oz soured cream
- salt and pepper

for the salsa
- 8 ripe tomatoes, diced
- 3 spring onions, sliced
- 1–2 fresh green chillies, such as jalapeño or serrano, deseeded and chopped
- 3–4 tbsp chopped fresh coriander
- 5–8 radishes, diced
- ground cumin

1 Combine the beef with the garlic, lime juice, chilli powder, paprika, cumin and olive oil. Add salt and pepper, mix well and leave to marinate for at least 30 minutes at room temperature, or overnight in the refrigerator.

2 To make the salsa, place the tomatoes in a bowl with the spring onions, green chillies, coriander and radishes. Season to taste with cumin, and salt and pepper. Reserve.

3 Heat the tortillas one by one in a lightly greased non-stick frying pan, wrapping each in foil as you work, to keep it warm.

4 Heat a little oil in a large, heavy-based frying pan over a high heat. Add the meat and stir-fry until browned and just cooked through.

5 Serve the sizzling hot meat with the warm tortillas, the salsa, avocado and soured cream for each person to make their own fajitas.

Chilli con Carne

Serves 6

ingredients

- 4 tbsp sunflower oil
- 2 onions, chopped
- 1 garlic clove, chopped
- 1 tbsp plain flour
- 900 g/2 lb braising steak, diced
- 300 ml/10 fl oz beef stock
- 300 ml/10 fl oz red wine
- 2–3 fresh red chillies, deseeded and chopped
- 800 g/1 lb 12 oz canned red kidney beans, drained and rinsed
- 400 g/14 oz canned chopped tomatoes
- salt and pepper
- tortilla chips, to serve

1 Heat half of the oil in a heavy-based saucepan. Add half the chopped onion and the garlic and cook, stirring occasionally, for 5 minutes, until softened. Remove with a slotted spoon.

2 Place the flour on a plate and season well with salt and pepper, then toss the meat in the flour to coat. Cook the meat, in batches, until browned all over, then return the meat and the onion mixture to the saucepan. Pour in the stock and wine and bring to the boil, stirring. Reduce the heat and simmer for 1 hour.

3 Meanwhile, heat the remaining oil in a frying pan. Add the remaining onion and the chillies and cook, stirring occasionally, for 5 minutes. Add the beans and tomatoes with their juice and break up with a wooden spoon. Simmer for 25 minutes, until thickened.

4 Divide the meat between individual plates, top with the bean mixture and serve with tortilla chips.

Grilled Steak with Tomatoes & Garlic

Serves 4

ingredients

- 3 tbsp olive oil, plus extra for brushing
- 700 g/1 lb 9 oz tomatoes, peeled and chopped
- 1 red pepper, deseeded and chopped
- 1 onion, chopped
- 2 garlic cloves, finely chopped
- 1 tbsp chopped fresh flat-leaf parsley
- 1 tsp dried oregano
- 1 tsp sugar
- 4 175 g/6 oz entrecote (flesh from ribs) steaks or rump steaks
- salt and pepper
- green beans and new potatoes, to serve

1 Place the oil, tomatoes, red pepper, onion, garlic, parsley, oregano and sugar in a heavy-based saucepan and season to taste with salt and pepper. Bring to the boil, reduce the heat and simmer for 15 minutes.

2 Meanwhile, preheat the grill to high. Snip any fat around the outsides of the steaks. Season each generously with pepper (no salt) and brush with oil. Grill for 1 minute on each side, then reduce the heat to medium and cook according to taste: 1½–2 minutes each side for rare; 2½–3 minutes each side for medium; 3–4 minutes on each side for well done.

3 Transfer the steaks to warmed individual plates and spoon the sauce over them. Serve immediately with green beans and new potatoes.

Shepherd's Pie

Serves 4

ingredients

- 700 g/1 lb 9 oz fresh lean lamb mince
- 2 onions, chopped
- 225 g/8 oz carrots, diced
- 1–2 garlic cloves, crushed
- 1 tbsp plain flour
- 200 ml/7 fl oz lamb stock
- 200 g/7 oz canned chopped tomatoes
- 1 tsp Worcestershire sauce
- 1 tsp chopped fresh sage
- 1 kg/2 lb 4 oz potatoes
- 25 g/1 oz margarine
- 3–4 tbsp skimmed milk
- 125 g/4½ oz button mushrooms (optional)
- salt and pepper

1 Preheat the oven to 200°C/400°F/ Gas Mark 6. Place the lamb mince in a heavy-based saucepan with no extra fat and cook gently until the meat begins to brown.

2 Add the onions, carrots and garlic and continue to cook gently for 10 minutes. Stir in the plain flour and cook for about 1–2 minutes, then gradually stir in the stock and chopped tomatoes and bring to the boil.

3 Add the Worcestershire sauce, seasoning and sage, cover and simmer gently for 25 minutes, giving an occasional stir.

4 Meanwhile, cook the potatoes in boiling salted water until tender, then drain thoroughly and mash, beating in the margarine, seasoning and enough milk to give a piping consistency. Place in a piping bag fitted with a large star nozzle.

5 Slice the mushrooms (if using), stir into the meat, then taste and adjust the seasoning if necessary. Turn into a shallow ovenproof dish.

6 Pipe the potatoes evenly over the meat. Cook in the preheated oven for 30 minutes, or until piping hot and the potato is golden brown.

Moussaka

Serves 4

ingredients

- 2 aubergines, thinly sliced
- 450 g/1 lb fresh lean lamb mince
- 2 onions, thinly sliced
- 1 tsp finely chopped garlic
- 400 g/14 oz canned tomatoes
- 2 tbsp chopped fresh parsley
- 2 eggs
- 300 ml/10 fl oz low-fat natural yogurt
- 1 tbsp freshly grated Parmesan cheese
- salt and pepper

1 Preheat the oven to 180°C/350°F/Gas Mark 4. Dry-fry the aubergine slices, in batches, in a non-stick frying pan on both sides until browned. Remove from the pan.

2 Add the lamb mince to the frying pan and cook for 5 minutes, stirring, until browned. Stir in the onions and garlic and cook for 5 minutes, or until browned. Add the tomatoes, parsley and salt and pepper, then bring to the boil and simmer for 20 minutes, or until the meat is tender.

3 Arrange half the aubergine slices in a layer in an ovenproof dish. Add the meat mixture, then a final layer of the remaining aubergine slices.

4 Beat the eggs in a bowl, then beat in the yogurt and add salt and pepper to taste. Pour the mixture over the aubergines and sprinkle the grated cheese on top. Bake the moussaka in the oven for 45 minutes, or until golden brown. Serve straight from the dish.

Rack of Lamb

Serves 2

ingredients

- 1 trimmed rack of lamb (about 250–300 g/9–10½ oz)
- 1 garlic clove, crushed
- 150 ml/5 fl oz red wine
- 1 fresh rosemary sprig, crushed to release the flavour
- 1 tbsp olive oil
- 150 ml/5 fl oz lamb stock
- 2 tbsp redcurrant jelly
- salt and pepper

for the mint sauce

- small bunch of fresh mint leaves, chopped
- 2 tsp caster sugar
- 2 tbsp boiling water
- 2 tbsp white wine vinegar

1 Place the rack of lamb in a non-metallic bowl and rub all over with the garlic. Pour over the wine and place the rosemary sprig on top. Cover and leave to marinate in the refrigerator for 3 hours, or overnight if possible.

2 To make the mint sauce, combine the mint leaves with the sugar in a small bowl. Add the boiling water and stir to dissolve the sugar. Add the white wine vinegar and leave to stand for 30 minutes before serving with the lamb.

3 Preheat the oven to 220°C/425°F/ Gas Mark 7.

4 Remove the lamb from the marinade, reserving the marinade, dry the meat with kitchen paper and season well with salt and pepper. Place in a small roasting tin, drizzle with the oil and roast in the oven for 15–20 minutes, depending on whether you like your meat rare or medium. Remove the lamb from the oven and leave to rest, covered with foil, in a warm place for 5 minutes.

5 Meanwhile, place the marinade in a small pan, bring to the boil over a medium heat and bubble away for 2–3 minutes. Add the lamb stock and redcurrant jelly and simmer until a syrupy consistency is achieved.

6 Carve the lamb into cutlets and serve on warmed plates with the stock and redcurrant jelly sauce spooned over the top. Serve the mint sauce separately.

Irish Stew

Serves 4

ingredients

- 4 tbsp plain flour
- 1.3 kg/3 lb middle neck of lamb, trimmed of visible fat
- 3 large onions, chopped
- 3 carrots, sliced
- 450 g/1 lb potatoes, quartered
- ½ tsp dried thyme
- 850 ml/1½ pints hot beef stock
- salt and pepper
- 2 tbsp chopped fresh parsley, to garnish

1 Preheat the oven to 160°C/325°F/Gas Mark 3. Spread the flour on a plate and season with salt and pepper. Roll the pieces of lamb in the flour to coat, shaking off any excess, and arrange in the base of a casserole.

2 Layer the onions, carrots and potatoes on top of the lamb.

3 Sprinkle in the thyme and pour in the stock, then cover and cook in the preheated oven for 2½ hours. Garnish with the chopped fresh parsley and serve straight from the casserole.

Lamb Shanks with Roasted Onions

Serves 4

ingredients

- 4 350 g/12 oz lamb shanks
- 6 garlic cloves
- 2 tbsp extra virgin olive oil
- 1 tbsp fresh rosemary, very finely chopped
- 4 red onions
- 350 g/12 oz carrots, cut into thin batons
- 4 tbsp water
- salt and pepper

1 Preheat the oven to 180°C/350°F/Gas Mark 4. Trim off any excess fat from the lamb. Using a small, sharp knife, make 6 incisions in each shank. Cut the garlic cloves lengthways into 4 slices. Insert 6 garlic slices in the incisions in each lamb shank.

2 Place the lamb in a single layer in a roasting tin, drizzle with the olive oil, sprinkle with the rosemary and season with pepper. Roast in the preheated oven for 45 minutes.

3 Wrap each of the onions in a piece of foil. Remove the roasting tin from the oven and season the lamb with salt. Return to the oven and place the wrapped onions on the shelf next to it. Roast for a further 1–1¼ hours until the lamb is very tender.

4 Meanwhile, bring a large saucepan of water to the boil. Add the carrot batons and blanch for 1 minute. Drain and refresh in cold water.

5 Remove the roasting tin from the oven when the lamb is meltingly tender and transfer it to a warmed serving dish. Skim off any fat from the roasting tin and place it over a medium heat. Add the carrots and cook for 2 minutes, then add the water, bring to the boil and simmer, stirring constantly and scraping up the glazed bits from the base of the roasting tin.

6 Transfer the carrots and sauce to the serving dish. Remove the onions from the oven and unwrap. Cut off and discard about 1 cm/½ inch off the tops and add the onions to the dish. Serve immediately.

Pot-roast Pork

Serves 4

ingredients

- 1 tbsp sunflower oil
- 55 g/2 oz butter
- 1 kg/2 lb 4 oz boned and rolled pork loin joint
- 4 shallots, chopped
- 6 juniper berries
- 2 fresh thyme sprigs, plus extra to garnish
- 150 ml/5 fl oz dry cider
- 150 ml/5 fl oz chicken stock or water
- 8 celery sticks, chopped
- 2 tbsp plain flour
- 150 ml/5 fl oz double cream
- salt and pepper

1 Heat the oil with half the butter in a large, heavy-based saucepan or flameproof casserole. Add the pork and cook over a medium heat, turning frequently, for 5–10 minutes, or until browned. Transfer to a plate.

2 Add the shallots to the saucepan and cook, stirring frequently, for 5 minutes, or until softened. Add the juniper berries and thyme sprigs and return the pork to the saucepan, with any juices that have collected on the plate. Pour in the cider and stock, season to taste with salt and pepper, then cover and simmer for 30 minutes. Turn the pork over and add the celery. Re-cover the pan and cook for a further 40 minutes.

3 Meanwhile, make a beurre manié by mashing the remaining butter with the flour in a small bowl. Transfer the pork and celery to a platter with a slotted spoon and keep warm. Remove and discard the juniper berries and thyme. Whisk the beurre manié, a little at a time, into the simmering cooking liquid. Cook, stirring constantly, for 2 minutes, then stir in the cream and bring to the boil.

4 Slice the pork and spoon a little of the sauce over it. Garnish with the thyme sprigs and serve immediately. Hand around the remaining sauce separately.

Meatloaf

Serves 4

ingredients

- 1 thick slice white bread, crusts removed
- 700 g/1 lb 9 oz fresh beef, pork or lamb mince
- 1 small egg
- 1 tbsp finely chopped onion
- 1 beef stock cube, crumbled
- 1 tsp dried herbs
- salt and pepper
- sauce or gravy, mashed potatoes and freshly cooked runner beans, to serve

1 Preheat the oven to 180°C/350°F/ Gas Mark 4.

2 Put the bread into a small bowl and add enough water to soak. Leave to stand for 5 minutes, then drain and squeeze well to get rid of all the water.

3 Combine the bread and all the other ingredients in a bowl. Shape into a loaf, then place on a baking tray or in an ovenproof dish. Put the meatloaf in the oven and cook for 30–45 minutes until the juices run clear when it is pierced with a skewer.

4 Serve in slices with your favourite sauce or gravy, mashed potatoes and runner beans.

Sausage & Bean Casserole

Serves 4

ingredients

- 8 Italian sausages
- 3 tbsp olive oil
- 1 large onion, chopped
- 2 garlic cloves, chopped
- 1 green bell pepper, deseeded and sliced
- 225g/8 oz canned chopped tomatoes, skinned and chopped or 400 g/14 oz can tomatoes, chopped
- 2 tbsp sun-dried tomato purée
- 400 g/14 oz canned cannellini beans

1 Prick the sausages all over with a fork. Heat 2 tablespoons of the oil in a large, heavy-based frying pan. Add the sausages and cook over a low heat, turning frequently, for 10–15 minutes, until evenly browned and cooked through. Remove them from the frying pan and keep warm. Drain off the oil and wipe out the pan with kitchen paper.

2 Heat the remaining oil in the frying pan. Add the onion, garlic and pepper to the frying pan and cook for 5 minutes, stirring occasionally, or until softened.

3 Add the tomatoes to the frying pan and leave the mixture to simmer for about 5 minutes, stirring occasionally, or until slightly reduced and thickened.

4 Stir the sun-dried tomato purée, cannellini beans and Italian sausages into the mixture in the frying pan. Cook for 4–5 minutes or until the mixture is piping hot. Add 4–5 tablespoons of water if the mixture becomes too dry during cooking.

5 Transfer to serving plates and serve.

Macaroni with Sausage, Pepperoncini & Olives

Serves 6

ingredients

- 1 tbsp olive oil
- 1 large onion, finely chopped
- 2 garlic cloves, very finely chopped
- 450 g/1 lb pork sausage, peeled and roughly chopped
- 3 canned pepperoncini, or other hot red peppers, drained and sliced
- 400 g/14 oz canned chopped tomatoes
- 2 tsp dried oregano
- 125 ml/4 fl oz chicken stock or red wine
- 450 g/1 lb dried macaroni
- 12–15 stoned black olives, quartered
- 75 g/2¾ oz freshly grated cheese, such as Cheddar or Gruyère
- salt and pepper

1 Heat the oil in a large frying pan over a medium heat. Add the onion and cook for 5 minutes, until softened. Add the garlic and cook for a few seconds, until just beginning to colour. Add the sausage and cook until evenly browned.

2 Stir in the pepperoncini, tomatoes, oregano and stock. Season to taste with salt and pepper. Bring to the boil, then simmer over a medium heat for 10 minutes, stirring occasionally.

3 Meanwhile, bring a large saucepan of lightly salted water to the boil. Add the pasta, bring back to the boil and cook for 8–10 minutes, or until tender but still firm to the bite. Drain and transfer to a warmed serving dish.

4 Add the olives and half the cheese to the sauce, then stir until the cheese has melted.

5 Pour the sauce over the pasta. Toss well to mix. Sprinkle with the remaining cheese and serve immediately.

Chapter 4
Poultry & Game

Introduction

Poultry is rich in protein, and quick and easy to prepare and cook. Some birds, such as chicken and turkey, can be a low-fat choice as long as the fatty skin is removed, and they are very versatile. Duck is fattier, but makes a good dinner-party choice. Game birds and animals are becoming more widely available and make impressive dishes for entertaining.

Chicken

Guinea fowl

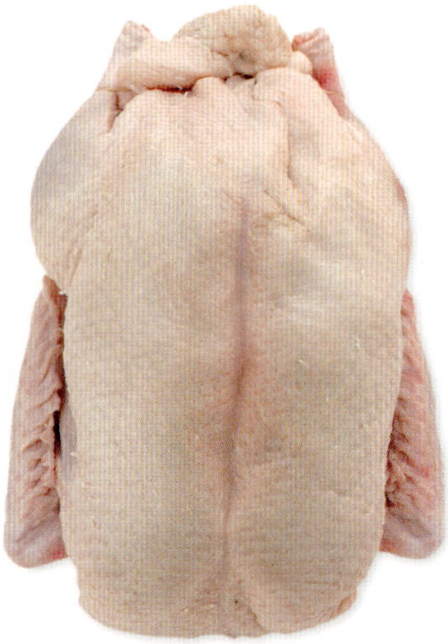

Duck

Quail

Buying and storing poultry and game

Always buy your poultry and game as fresh as possible and from a reputable supplier. Choose plump birds that have unblemished skin, and make sure that any wrapping or packaging is intact.

As soon as you get it home, remove the packaging (if it is a fresh bird) and transfer the giblets (if any) to a separate bowl. Place the bird on a rack in a dish, then cover it and any giblets loosely with clingfilm and store in the refrigerator. Keep it well away from cooked meats to prevent any cross-contamination. Whole birds will keep for 1–2 days in the refrigerator, and giblets no longer than 1 day.

Frozen birds can be stored in the freezer in their orignal packaging. Thaw in the refrigerator thoroughly before cooking: you will need to allow 5 hours per 450 g/1 lb for a chicken and 6 hours per 450 g/1 lb for a turkey.

Game birds are available fresh when in season and frozen all year round. If they are truly wild birds and not farmed, they will have a lower fat content and should therefore be wrapped in bacon or pork fat during roasting. Older birds are not recommended for roasting – they are more suited to soups, casseroles and stews. Game animals, such as venison and rabbit, tend to be less tender than farmed animals because they get more exercise in the wild. They should therefore be cooked slowly until tender, but not overcooked. Braising is a good method for keeping the meat moist, or it can be roasted if wrapped first in bacon or pork fat.

Types of bird

In addition to the flavour, the choice of bird may depend on the occasion, how many people you are catering for and how much preparation you wish to do.

Chicken
There are many different varieties of chicken available, including free range, organic and corn-fed. You can buy whole birds ready prepared for the oven or frozen. You can also buy a variety of joints – wing, breast, leg, thigh or drumstick – or you can joint a whole bird yourself. Chicken is delicious roasted, steamed, poached, grilled, casseroled, barbecued, chargrilled, stir-fried, pan-fried or deep-fried.

Poussin
A poussin is a very young, small chicken. Poussins weigh up to 450 g/1 lb and you should therefore allow one whole bird per person. They are suitable for roasting, barbecuing and grilling.

Guinea fowl
This bird is related to the chicken and the partridge, and has light and dark meat and a strong flavour. It is available fresh and frozen. Since guinea fowl has a low fat content, it is most suited to moist cooking methods such as casseroling. Alternatively, you can wrap it in bacon rashers or pork fat and roast it.

Turkey
These birds are much larger than chickens – some can grow to a massive 31.5 kg/70 lb – but the trend nowadays is for much smaller birds. This is because turkey suppliers would like to encourage their use all year round, rather than just during Christmas and other holiday periods. Turkeys have similar uses to chickens, and you can often interchange them with chickens in recipes. You can buy whole birds ready prepared for the oven or frozen. You can also buy separate joints, such as breast joints or drumsticks. Turkey is particularly suitable for roasting, casseroling, braising, stir-frying or pan-frying.

Duck
Ducks are available whole, fresh and frozen. Breast and leg joints are also available. Duck is fattier than chicken or turkey, and is therefore particularly suitable for roasting, grilling or pan-frying. Duck is often served with a tart fruit sauce, such as orange, in order to cut through any fatty aftertaste.

Partridge
This game bird has dark flesh and an earthy flavour. Its flesh can be tough so is best braised, stewed or casseroled. It can also be roasted.

Goose
Geese are larger than ducks, and can be bought fresh, although they are more often bought frozen. Although they are popular during holidays and at Christmas time, especially in Europe, they have become less popular year-round because of their very high fat content. Geese are best roasted, pot-roasted, braised or stewed. It is also a good idea to serve them with a tart fruit sauce in order to cut through any fatty aftertaste.

Grouse
These are small game birds, so allow one bird per person. If you are going to roast them, wrap them in bacon or pork fat during cooking. You can also pot-roast, braise, casserole or stew them.

Pheasant
These are medium-sized game birds. The male has more brilliant plumage than the female, but the female is juicier and more tender. Young pheasants can be roasted, but older birds should be wrapped in bacon or pork fat during roasting; they can also be braised, casseroled or stewed.

Quail
These small game birds are related to the partridge. The European variety has lean, medium-dark flesh, whereas the American variety has lean but lighter flesh. Both types have a sweet flavour. Quails are suitable for roasting, pot-roasting, braising, barbecuing, casseroling or grilling. Their small eggs have a speckled brown shell and a rich flavour.

Venison
Deer is a popular game animal and the meat is available wild or farmed. It is low in cholesterol, and usually available as leg or saddle joints, or as steaks. The best meat comes from a male deer under the age of two years. Venison meat is quite dry and is therefore more suited to casseroles.

Rabbit
This game animal has fine white meat and is available fresh or frozen; you can also buy it whole or boned and cut into pieces. Tender young rabbits are suitable for grilling, frying or roasting; older rabbits should be braised, casseroled or stewed.

Preparation and cooking techniques

It is essential to cook poultry all the way through in order to kill off any potentially harmful bacteria. If a bird is not cooked through when tested, return it to the oven to finish cooking, even if you have to exceed the recommended cooking time.

Making chicken stock

Chicken stock is easy to prepare and is ideal for adding to soups and sauces. It can be stored, covered with clingfilm, in the refrigerator for 2–3 days. You can also freeze it for up to 6 months. Put the chicken carcass into a large saucepan with 1 chopped onion, 1 sliced carrot, 1 chopped celery stick and 1 chopped leek. Add 1 bay leaf and 1 sprig of thyme, 3 stalks of parsley and some cracked black peppercorns. Cover with water and bring to the boil, then use a slotted spoon to skim off any scum from the surface. Reduce the heat, cover, and leave to simmer for 2–3 hours. Strain into a large bowl and discard the solids. Use the stock as required.

Spatchcocking a small bird

Spatchcocking helps to flatten the bird before grilling or barbecuing, ensuring quicker and more even cooking. Place the bird breast-side down (the legs are under the bird, the wings on top) on a clean chopping board. Cut along either side of the backbone and remove it (you can save it for making chicken stock or discard it). Open the bird out and turn it over. Using your palms, press down on the bird to flatten it against the chopping board.

Roasting a large chicken or a turkey

First wipe the bird inside and out with kitchen paper. If you are going to stuff it, pull back the skin around the neck cavity and insert the stuffing into the neck end only (do not overfill the bird or it will not cook through properly). If you are not stuffing the bird, simply season the cavity. Pull the skin over the top, then pull up the wings and tie with string. Pull the legs together and tie with string. Rub butter or oil over the skin of the bird, then season to taste with salt and pepper. Transfer to a wire rack in a roasting tin, and roast in a preheated oven, basting occasionally, until cooked through and tender. To test, insert a sharp knife or skewer into the thickest part of the bird: if the juices run clear, the bird is cooked. If not, return it to the oven and cook until done. Remove the bird from the oven and leave to rest, covered in foil, for 15–20 minutes before carving.

OVEN TEMPERATURES AND ROASTING TIMES

INDIVIDUAL OVEN TEMPERATURES AND COOKING TIMES VARY, SO COOKING TIMES ARE APPROXIMATE. PREHEAT THE OVEN BEFORE COOKING.

Bird	Weight	Temperature	Cooking Time
Chicken	3 kg/6 lb 8 oz	200°C/400°F/Gas Mark 6	2¼ hours
Turkey	5 kg/11 lb	180°C/350°F/Gas Mark 4	3½ hours
	8 kg/18 lb	180°C/350°F/Gas Mark 4	4¾–5 hours
Quail	450 g/1 lb	200°C/400°F/Gas Mark 6	30 minutes
Goose	5 kg/11 lb	220°C/425°F/Gas Mark 7 180°C/350°F/Gas Mark 4	30 minutes at higher temperature, then for 2–3 hours at lower temperature
Duck	2.5 kg/5 lb 8 oz	220°C/425°F/Gas Mark 7 180°C/350°F/Gas Mark 4	20 minutes at higher temperature, then for 2 hours at lower temperature

Roasting a goose

Wipe the goose inside and out with kitchen paper and pull out any excess fat from inside it. Season well with salt and pepper. If you are going to stuff the goose insert the stuffing as far as possible in the neck flap end, securing the flap with a skewer. Prick the goose all over with a fork, lay on a rack in a roasting tin and place in a preheated oven. To test that it is cooked all the way through, insert a skewer into the thickest part of the bird: if the juices run clear, the bird is cooked. Remove from the oven and leave to rest for 20 minutes before carving.

Carving a large bird

Place the cooked bird breast-side up on a clean chopping board. Use a carving knife to cut between one wing and the side of the breast. Remove the wing and cut thin, downward slices through the breast meat. Repeat with the other side, reserving the wings and the breast slices. Pull out one leg and cut through the joint. Repeat with the other side. Slice the meat from the thighs and drumsticks. Serve the wings and the meat slices.

Roasting and carving a duck

Wipe the duck inside and out with kitchen paper. Duck has a high fat content, so remove any surplus fat. Season inside the tail cavity and insert a bay leaf. Transfer the bird to a wire rack in a roasting tin. Use a fork to prick holes all over it, then season with salt and pepper. Roast in a preheated oven until cooked through and tender (turn and baste it halfway through the cooking time).

To test that the bird is cooked all the way through, insert a sharp knife or skewer into the thickest part of the bird: if the juices run clear, the bird is cooked. To serve the duck, joint it by cutting it in half lengthways. Alternatively, use a sharp knife to separate the legs from the body, then cut off the wings. Remove the breast meat and slice it. Serve the legs, wings and slices of breast meat.

JOINTING A WHOLE BIRD

1 TO CUT A LARGE RAW BIRD INTO JOINTS, REMOVE ANY STRING AND PLACE IT ON A CLEAN CHOPPING BOARD, BREAST-SIDE UP, WITH THE LEGS POINTING TOWARDS YOU.

2 USING A SHARP KNIFE, CUT THE SKIN BETWEEN ONE LEG AND THE SIDE OF THE BREAST, THEN USE YOUR HAND TO PRESS THE LEG DOWN FLAT TO THE BOARD. DO THE SAME WITH THE OTHER LEG. CUT THROUGH THE JOINT ATTACHING ONE OF THE LEGS AND REMOVE THE LEG FROM THE BODY. DO THE SAME FOR THE OTHER SIDE.

2

3 TURN THE BIRD TO FACE THE OTHER WAY AND LOCATE THE RIDGE ALONG THE MIDDLE OF THE BACK. USING A KNIFE, CUT AWAY ONE BREAST, TAKING A WING OFF WITH IT. DO THE SAME WITH THE OTHER BREAST.

4 TO DIVIDE THE LEGS INTO THIGHS AND DRUMSTICKS, PUT THEM SKIN-SIDE DOWN ON THE CHOPPING BOARD. CUT THROUGH THE LINE TO SEPARATE THE JOINT. RESERVE THE CARCASS FOR MAKING STOCK.

Traditional Roast Chicken

Serves 4

ingredients

- 25 g/1 oz butter, softened
- 1 garlic clove, finely chopped
- 3 tbsp finely chopped toasted walnuts
- 1 tbsp chopped fresh parsley
- 1 oven-ready chicken, weighing 1.8 kg/4 lb
- 1 lime, cut into quarters
- 2 tbsp vegetable oil
- 1 tbsp cornflour
- 2 tbsp water
- salt and pepper
- roast potatoes, to serve

1 Preheat the oven to 190°C/375°F/ Gas Mark 5. Mix 1 tablespoon of the butter with the garlic, walnuts and parsley together in a small bowl. Season well with salt and pepper. Loosen the skin from the breast of the chicken without breaking it. Spread the butter mixture evenly between the skin and breast meat. Place the lime quarters inside the body cavity.

2 Pour the oil into a roasting tin. Transfer the chicken to the tin and dot the skin with the remaining butter. Roast for 1¾ hours, basting occasionally, until the chicken is tender and the juices run clear when a skewer is inserted into the thickest part of the meat. Lift out the chicken and place on a serving platter to rest for 10 minutes.

3 Blend the cornflour with the water, then stir into the juices in the tin. Transfer to the hob. Stir over a low heat until thickened. Add more water if necessary. Spoon the thickened juices over the chicken and serve with roast potatoes.

Thai Green Chicken Curry

Serves 4

ingredients

- 2 tbsp groundnut or sunflower oil
- 2 tbsp ready-made Thai green curry paste
- 500 g/1 lb 2 oz skinless boneless chicken breasts, cut into cubes
- 2 kaffir lime leaves, roughly torn
- 1 lemon grass stalk, finely chopped
- 225 ml/8 fl oz canned coconut milk
- 16 baby aubergines, halved
- 2 tbsp Thai fish sauce
- fresh Thai basil sprigs and kaffir lime leaves, thinly sliced, to garnish

1 Heat 2 tablespoons of oil in a preheated wok or large, heavy-based frying pan. Add 2 tablespoons of the curry paste and stir-fry briefly until all the aromas are released.

2 Add the chicken, lime leaves and lemon grass and stir-fry for 3–4 minutes, until the meat is beginning to colour. Add the coconut milk and aubergines and simmer gently for 8–10 minutes, or until tender.

3 Stir in the fish sauce and serve immediately, garnished with Thai basil sprigs and lime leaves.

Chicken & Spinach Lasagne

Serves 4

ingredients

- 350 g/12 oz frozen chopped spinach, thawed and drained
- ½ tsp freshly grated nutmeg
- 450 g/1 lb lean, cooked chicken, skinned and diced
- 4 sheets dried no pre-cook lasagne verde
- 1½ tbsp cornflour
- 425 ml/15 fl oz milk
- 70 g/2½ oz freshly grated Parmesan cheese
- salt and pepper

for the tomato sauce

- 400 g/14 oz canned chopped tomatoes
- 1 onion, finely chopped
- 1 garlic clove, crushed
- 150 ml/5 fl oz white wine
- 3 tbsp tomato purée
- 1 tsp dried oregano
- salt and pepper

1 To make the tomato sauce, put the tomatoes into a pan and stir in the onion, garlic, wine, tomato purée and oregano. Bring to the boil and simmer for 20 minutes, until thick. Season well with salt and pepper.

2 Preheat the oven to 190°C/375°F/Gas Mark 5. Drain the spinach again and spread it out on kitchen paper to make sure that as much water as possible is removed. Layer the spinach in the base of a large ovenproof baking dish. Sprinkle with ground nutmeg and season to taste with salt and pepper.

3 Arrange the diced chicken over the spinach and spoon over the tomato sauce. Arrange the sheets of lasagne over the tomato sauce.

4 Blend the cornflour with a little of the milk to make a paste. Pour the remaining milk into a pan and stir in the paste. Heat, stirring, until the sauce thickens. Season well.

5 Spoon the sauce over the lasagne sheets and transfer the dish to a baking tray. Sprinkle the grated Parmesan cheese over the sauce and bake in the preheated oven for 25 minutes until golden, then serve.

Chicken Kiev

Serves 4

ingredients

- 115 g/4 oz butter, softened
- 3–4 garlic cloves, very finely chopped
- 1 tbsp chopped fresh parsley
- 1 tbsp snipped fresh chives
- finely grated rind and juice of ½ lemon
- 8 skinless, boneless chicken breasts, about 115 g/4 oz each
- 55 g/2 oz plain flour
- 2 eggs, lightly beaten
- 175 g/6 oz dry breadcrumbs
- groundnut or sunflower oil, for deep-frying
- salt and pepper

1 Beat the butter in a bowl with the garlic, herbs, lemon rind and juice. Season to taste with salt and pepper. Divide into 8 pieces, then shape into cylinders. Wrap in foil and chill for about 2 hours, until firm.

2 Place the chicken between 2 sheets of clingfilm. Pound gently with a rolling pin to flatten the chicken to an even thickness. Place a butter cylinder on each chicken piece and roll up. Secure with cocktail sticks.

3 Place the flour, eggs and breadcrumbs in separate shallow dishes. Dip the rolls into the flour, then the egg and, finally, the breadcrumbs. Place on a plate, cover and chill for 1 hour.

4 Heat the oil in a saucepan or deep-fat fryer to 180–190°C/350–375°F, or until a cube of bread browns in 30 seconds. Deep-fry the chicken in batches for 8–10 minutes, or until cooked through and golden brown. Drain on kitchen paper. Serve immediately.

Coq au Vin

Serves 4

ingredients

- 55 g/2 oz butter
- 2 tbsp olive oil
- 1.8 kg/4 lb chicken pieces
- 115 g/4 oz rindless smoked bacon, cut into strips
- 115 g/4 oz baby onions
- 115 g/4 oz chestnut mushrooms, halved
- 2 garlic cloves, finely chopped
- 2 tbsp brandy
- 225 ml/8 fl oz red wine
- 300 ml/10 fl oz chicken stock
- 1 bouquet garni
- 2 tbsp plain flour
- salt and pepper
- bay leaves, to garnish

1 Melt half the butter with the olive oil in a large, flameproof casserole. Add the chicken and cook over a medium heat, stirring, for 8–10 minutes, or until golden brown all over. Add the bacon, onions, mushrooms and garlic.

2 Pour in the brandy and set it alight with a match or taper. When the flames have died down, add the wine, stock and bouquet garni and season to taste with salt and pepper. Bring to the boil, reduce the heat and simmer gently for 1 hour, or until the chicken pieces are cooked through and tender. Meanwhile, make a beurre manié by mashing the remaining butter with the flour in a small bowl.

3 Remove and discard the bouquet garni. Transfer the chicken to a large plate and keep warm. Stir the beurre manié into the casserole, a little at a time. Bring to the boil, return the chicken to the casserole and serve immediately, garnished with bay leaves.

Peking Duck

Serves 4

ingredients
- 1.8 kg/4 lb duck
- 1.8 litres/3¼ pints boiling water
- 4 tbsp clear honey
- 2 tsp dark soy sauce
- carrot strips, to garnish

for the sauce
- 2 tbsp sesame oil
- 125 ml/4 fl oz hoisin sauce
- 125 g/4½ oz caster sugar
- 125 ml/4 fl oz water

to serve
- Chinese pancakes
- cucumber matchsticks
- shredded spring onions

1 Place the duck on a rack set over a roasting tin and pour 1.2 litres/2 pints of the boiling water over it. Remove the duck and rack and discard the water. Pat dry with clean kitchen paper, replace the duck and rack, cover and reserve for several hours.

2 Mix the honey, 600 ml/1 pint of boiling water and soy sauce together. Brush the mixture as a glaze over the skin and inside the duck. Reserve the remaining glaze. Set aside for 1 hour, until the glaze has dried.

3 Coat the duck with another layer of glaze. Leave to dry and repeat until all of the glaze is used.

4 Preheat the oven to 190°C/375°F/ Gas Mark 5. For the sauce, heat the oil in a saucepan. Add the hoisin sauce, sugar and water. Simmer for 2–3 minutes, until thickened. Cool and chill until required.

5 Cook the duck in the preheated oven for 30 minutes. Turn the duck over and cook for 20 minutes. Turn the duck again and cook for 20–30 minutes, or until the meat is cooked through and the skin is crisp.

6 Remove the duck from the oven and leave to stand for 10 minutes. Meanwhile, heat the Chinese pancakes in a bamboo steamer for 5–7 minutes. Cut the duck skin and meat into strips and divide between individual serving plates. Garnish with carrot strips and serve with the pancakes, cucumber matchsticks, shredded spring onions and sauce.

Duck Breasts with Chilli & Lime

Serves 4

ingredients
- 4 boneless duck breasts
- 1 tsp vegetable oil
- 125 ml/4 fl oz chicken stock
- 2 tbsp plum jam
- salt and pepper

for the marinade
- 2 garlic cloves, crushed
- 4 tsp light soft brown sugar
- 3 tbsp lime juice
- 1 tbsp soy sauce
- 1 tsp chilli sauce

to serve
- lime wedges
- freshly cooked rice

1 To make the marinade, mix the garlic, sugar, lime juice, and the soy and chilli sauces together.

2 Using a small sharp knife, cut deep slashes in the skin of the duck breasts to make a diamond pattern. Place the duck breasts in a wide, non-metallic dish.

3 Spoon the marinade over the duck breasts, turning to coat them evenly in the mixture. Cover the dish with clingfilm and leave to marinate in the refrigerator for at least 3 hours, or overnight if possible.

4 Drain the duck, reserving the marinade. Heat a large, heavy-based pan until very hot and brush with the oil. Add the duck breasts, skin-side down, and cook for 4–5 minutes until the skin is browned and crisp. Pour off the excess fat.

5 Turn the duck breasts and cook on the other side for 2–3 minutes to brown. Add the reserved marinade, and the stock and jam and simmer for 2 minutes. Adjust the seasoning to taste and spoon the juices over the meat. Serve with lime wedges and freshly cooked rice.

Roast Duck with Apple

Serves 4

ingredients

- 4 duck portions, about 350 g/12 oz each
- 4 tbsp dark soy sauce
- 2 tbsp light muscovado sugar
- 2 red-skinned apples
- 2 green-skinned apples
- juice of 1 lemon
- 2 tbsp clear honey
- a few bay leaves
- salt and pepper
- assorted freshly cooked vegetables, to serve

for the apricot sauce

- 400 g/14 oz canned apricots in fruit juice
- 4 tbsp sweet sherry

1 Preheat the oven to 190°C/375°F/Gas Mark 5. Wash the duck and trim away any excess fat. Place on a wire rack over a roasting tin and prick all over with a fork or a clean, sharp needle.

2 Brush the duck with the soy sauce. Sprinkle over the sugar and season with pepper. Cook in the preheated oven, basting occasionally, for 50–60 minutes, or until the meat is cooked through and the juices run clear when a skewer is inserted into the thickest part of the meat.

3 Meanwhile, core the apples and cut each into 6 wedges, then place in a small bowl and mix with the lemon juice and honey. Transfer to a small roasting tin, add a few bay leaves and season to taste with salt and pepper. Cook alongside the duck, basting occasionally, for 20–25 minutes until tender. Discard the bay leaves.

4 To make the sauce, place the apricots in a blender or food processor with the can juices and the sherry. Process until smooth. Alternatively, mash the apricots with a fork until smooth and mix with the juice and sherry.

5 Just before serving, heat the apricot sauce in a small saucepan. Remove the skin from the duck and pat the flesh with kitchen paper to absorb any fat. Serve the duck with the apple wedges, apricot sauce and freshly cooked vegetables.

Roast Turkey with Bread Sauce

Serves 8

ingredients

- 4 tbsp stuffing
- one 5-kg/11-lb turkey
- 40 g/1½ oz butter

for the Bread Sauce

- 1 onion, peeled
- 4 cloves
- 600 ml/1 pint milk
- 115 g/4 oz fresh white breadcrumbs
- 55 g/2 oz butter
- salt and pepper

1 Preheat the oven to 220°C/425°F/Gas Mark 7. If you are planning on stuffing the turkey, spoon the stuffing into the neck cavity and close the flap of skin with a skewer. If you prefer to cook the stuffing separately, cook according to the recipe's instructions.

2 Place the bird in a large roasting tin and rub it all over with the butter. Roast in the preheated oven for 1 hour, then lower the oven temperature to 180°C/350°F/Gas Mark 4 and roast for a further 2½ hours. You may need to pour off the fat from the roasting tin occasionally.

3 Meanwhile, make the bread sauce. Stud the onion with the cloves, then place in a saucepan with the milk, breadcrumbs and butter. Bring just to boiling point over a low heat, then remove from the heat and leave to stand in a warm place to infuse. Just before serving, remove the onion and cloves and reheat the sauce gently, beating well with a wooden spoon. Season to taste with salt and pepper.

4 Check that the turkey is cooked by inserting a skewer or the point of a sharp knife into the thigh – if the juices run clear, it is ready. Transfer the bird to a carving board, cover loosely with foil and leave to rest.

5 Carve the turkey and serve with the warm bread sauce and stuffing.

Lemon & Mint Turkey Burgers

Serves 6

ingredients

- 500 g/1 lb 2 oz fresh turkey mince
- ½ small onion, grated
- finely grated rind and juice of 1 small lemon
- 1 garlic clove, finely chopped
- 2 tbsp finely chopped fresh mint
- ½ tsp pepper
- 1 tsp sea salt
- 1 egg, beaten
- 1 tbsp olive oil, plus extra for frying
- lemon wedges, to serve

1 Place all the ingredients in a bowl and mix well with a fork. Shape the mixture into 12 balls rolling them with the palm of your hand. Flatten into rounds about 2 cm/¾ inch thick. Cover and leave in the refrigerator for at least 1 hour, or overnight.

2 Heat about 5 tablespoons of oil in a large heavy-based frying pan. When the oil starts to look hazy add the burgers, cooking in batches if necessary. Cook over a medium–high heat for 4–5 minutes on each side, until golden brown and cooked through.

3 Drain the burgers on kitchen paper and transfer to a warmed serving dish. Serve with lemon wedges.

Roast Goose with Cinnamon-spiced Red Cabbage

Serves 6

ingredients

- 1 oven-ready goose, weighing about 4.5 kg/10 lb
- 2 onions, quartered
- 1 bunch fresh thyme
- 2 bay leaves
- salt and pepper

for the Red Cabbage

- 3 tbsp olive oil
- 1 large onion, sliced
- 1 red cabbage, shredded
- 1 large cooking apple, peeled, cored and chopped
- 3 tbsp raisins
- 300 ml/10 fl oz red wine
- 50 ml/2 fl oz red wine vinegar
- 2 tsp caster sugar, or to taste
- 1 cinnamon stick

1 Preheat the oven to 200°C/400°F/Gas Mark 6.

2 Cut away any excess fat from the tail area of the goose. Season the goose cavity to taste with salt and pepper and push in the onion quarters, bay leaves and thyme, reserving a few sprigs for the garnish. Put the goose on a rack set over a roasting tin and prick the skin all over with a skewer. Season the outside of the goose to taste with salt and pepper. Roast in the preheated oven for 15 minutes per 450 g/1 lb, plus an extra 15 minutes. Remove from the oven, cover loosely with foil and leave to rest for 15 minutes before carving.

3 While the goose is roasting, prepare the red cabbage. Heat the oil in a large frying pan over a medium heat, add the onion and cook, stirring frequently, for 3–4 minutes until softened but not coloured. Add all the remaining ingredients, cover and cook for 30–40 minutes until the cabbage is tender and the liquid has reduced. Remove the cinnamon stick before serving.

4 Carve the goose and serve in slices, alongside the red cabbage and garnished with the reserved thyme.

Roast Pheasant with Red Wine & Herbs

Serves 4

ingredients

- 100 g/3½ oz butter, slightly softened
- 1 tbsp chopped fresh thyme
- 1 tbsp chopped fresh parsley
- 2 oven-ready young pheasants
- 4 tbsp vegetable oil
- 125 ml/4 fl oz red wine
- salt and pepper

to serve

- roast parsnips
- sautéed potatoes

1 Preheat the oven to 190°C/ 375°F/ Gas Mark 5. Place the butter in a small bowl and mix in the chopped herbs. Lift the skins off the pheasants, taking care not to tear them, and push the herb butter under the skins. Season to taste with salt and pepper.

2 Pour the oil into a roasting tin, add the pheasants and cook in the preheated oven for 45 minutes, basting occasionally. Remove from the oven, pour over the red wine, then return to the oven and cook for a further 15 minutes, or until cooked through. Check that each bird is cooked by inserting a knife between the legs and body. If the juices run clear, they are cooked.

3 Remove the pheasants from the oven, cover with foil and leave to stand for 15 minutes. Divide between individual serving plates, and serve with roast parsnips and sautéed potatoes.

Quails with Grapes

Serves 4

ingredients

- 4 tbsp olive oil
- 8 quails, gutted
- 280 g/10 oz green seedless grapes
- 225 ml/8 fl oz grape juice
- 2 cloves
- about 150 ml/5 fl oz water
- 2 tbsp Spanish brandy
- salt and pepper

for the potato pancake

- 600 g/1 lb 5 oz unpeeled potatoesa
- 35 g/1¼ oz unsalted butter or pork fat
- 1½ tbsp olive oil

1 Preheat the oven to 230°C/450°F/ Gas Mark 8. For the pancake, parboil the potatoes for 10 minutes. Drain and leave to cool completely, then peel, coarsely grate and season with salt and pepper to taste. Reserve until required.

2 Take a heavy-based frying pan or flameproof casserole large enough to hold the quails in a single layer and heat the oil over a medium heat. Add the quails and fry on all sides until they are golden brown.

3 Add the grapes, grape juice, cloves, enough water to come halfway up the side of the quails, and salt and pepper to taste. Cover and simmer for 20 minutes. Transfer the quails and all the juices to a roasting tin, or casserole, and sprinkle with brandy. Roast, uncovered, in the preheated oven for 10 minutes.

4 Meanwhile, to make the potato pancake, melt the butter or pork fat with the oil in a 30-cm/12-inch non-stick frying pan over a high heat. When the fat is hot, add the grated potato and spread into an even layer. Reduce the heat and simmer for 10 minutes. Place a plate over the frying pan and, wearing oven gloves, invert them so the potato pancake drops on to the plate. Slide the potato back into the frying pan and continue cooking on the other side for 10 minutes, or until cooked through and crisp. Slide out of the frying pan and cut into 4 wedges. Keep the pancake warm until the quail is ready.

5 Place a pancake wedge and 2 quails on each individual serving plate. Taste the grape sauce and adjust the seasoning if necessary. Spoon the sauce over the quails and serve immediately.

Game Pie

Serves 4–6

ingredients

- oil, for greasing
- 700 g/1 lb 9 oz mixed game, cut into 3-cm/1¼-inch pieces
- 2 tbsp plain flour, plus extra for dusting
- 3 tbsp vegetable oil
- 1 onion, roughly chopped
- 1 garlic clove, finely chopped
- 350 g/12 oz large field mushrooms, sliced
- 1 tsp crushed juniper berries
- 125 ml/4 fl oz port or Marsala
- 450 ml/16 fl oz chicken or game stock
- 1 bay leaf
- 400 g/14 oz ready-made puff pastry
- 1 egg, beaten
- salt and pepper

1 Preheat the oven to 160°C/325°F/Gas Mark 3. Grease a 1.2-litre/2-pint pie dish. Put the meat into a large plastic bag with the flour and salt and pepper and shake to coat the meat.

2 Heat the oil in a large flameproof casserole dish over a high heat and brown the meat in batches. Remove with a slotted spoon and keep warm. Fry the onion and garlic for 2–3 minutes until softened, then add the mushrooms and cook for about 2 minutes, stirring constantly, until they start to wilt. Add the juniper berries, then the port and scrape the bits from the base of the casserole. Add the stock, stirring constantly, and bring to the boil. Bubble for 2–3 minutes. Add the bay leaf and return the meat to the casserole. Cover and cook in the oven for 1½–2 hours until the meat is tender. Check for seasoning and add more salt and pepper if necessary. Remove from the oven and cool. Chill overnight in the refrigerator to develop the flavours. Remove the bay leaf.

3 Preheat the oven to 200°C/400°F/Gas Mark 6.

4 Roll out the pastry on a lightly floured work surface to about 7 cm/2¾ inches larger than the pie dish. Cut off a 3-cm/1¼-inch strip around the edge. Moisten the rim of the dish and press the pastry strip onto it. Place a pie funnel in the centre of the dish and spoon in the meat filling. Don't overfill; keep any extra gravy to serve separately.

5 Moisten the pastry collar with a little water and put on the pastry lid. Crimp the edges of the pastry firmly and glaze with the egg.

6 Bake the pie on a tray near the top of the oven for about 30 minutes. If necessary, cover it with foil and reduce the oven temperature a little. The pie should be golden brown and the filling bubbling hot.

Chapter 5
Vegetables & Salads

Introduction

Vegetables are very nutritious: they are rich in vitamins and minerals and low in fat. They are also very quick and easy to prepare and cook. You can also use surplus or leftover vegetables in other dishes, such as stock or stews.

Buying and storing vegetables

Choose vegetables when they are in season because this is when they are at their best. Try to buy them in small quantities on a frequent basis to ensure a constant fresh supply – the fresher the vegetables, the better they will taste and the more nutrients they will have. Here are some of the main varieties.

Root vegetables

Root vegetables are delicious and vary greatly in terms of flavour. They provide a colourful contrast to leafy green vegetables and are particularly good roasted or in casseroles or stews.

Carrots

These are available all year round. Carrots should be peeled first, then you can grate them raw into salads, or slice and boil them. After boiling, you can mash them if desired. You can also steam, stir-fry or roast them.

Beetroots

These are available all year round and are excellent washed and grated raw into salads. Alternatively, you can boil or roast them whole. You can also buy beetroots ready-cooked.

Radishes

These are available in many sizes, shapes and colours all year round, the most common variety being the small red radish, which is either round or oval. Washed, trimmed and served raw, radishes give a distinctive peppery taste to salads and make excellent garnishes, whole or sliced.

Celeriac

This knobbly vegetable is usually available in the autumn, winter and spring. It is very good peeled and boiled, then mashed. You can also parboil and roast celariac.

Parsnips

Fresh parsnips are best during autumn and winter, although they are available all year round. They should always be cooked. You can boil and mash, or parboil and roast them. You can also steam or sauté parsnips, and they are very good in soups.

Potatoes

Available all year round and usually classified as either floury or waxy, this versatile and popular vegetable comes in many shapes, sizes and colours including long white, round white and rounded. Potatoes range in size from small new potatoes, which are ideal for boiling and for salads, to large baking potatoes, which are excellent for baking in their skins or for making chips. Sweet potatoes are not botanically related to the potato, but they have a delicious sweet flavour and can be substituted for potatoes in many recipes. When cooking potatoes, you can either peel them first, or simply scrub them and leave them unpeeled. Potato skins are very nutritious, and delicious when cooked, so it is often a good idea to leave the skins on, unless you are making mashed potatoes, when it is better to remove them. Potatoes are excellent boiled, mashed, fried, baked and roasted. You can serve them hot or cold. After buying your potatoes, store them in a cool, dark place.

Swede

This root vegetable is available all year round and should always be peeled and cooked. You can boil and mash it or parboil and roast it. It is delicious mashed with carrots.

Turnips

Although available all year round, the peak season for turnips is in winter. Like swedes, these root vegetables are best peeled and boiled, then mashed. You can also parboil and roast them.

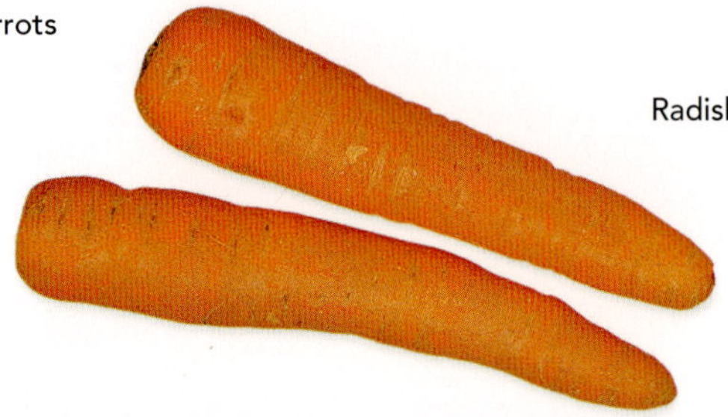

Carrots

Radishes

Parsnips

Baby new potatoes

Leafy vegetables and salad leaves

Leafy vegetables and salad leaves are very good for us, which is why nutritionists recommend eating plenty of them. They also make attractive accompaniments to many dishes.

White Sante potato

Spinach

Salad leaves

Our appetite for salad leaves has grown in recent years. Different varieties of lettuce include round, Webbs, cos, frisée and little gem, as well as the red lollo rosso and radicchio. Lettuce is rich in iron, calcium and vitamins A and C, yet is very low in calories and fat. It is a popular favourite in salads, makes a good garnish and is delicious lightly sautéed. Other popular salad leaves include rocket, a member of the brassica family, and watercress, a rich source of vitamin C.

Spinach

Although a good source of iron and vitamins A and C, the oxalic acid content of spinach actually prevents the body's absorption of iron and calcium, so it is probably best eaten in moderation. Baby spinach leaves can be washed and used raw in salads, or you can boil, stir-fry, steam or sauté the leaves. When spinach is cooked, it reduces in weight considerably, so you'll need to allow substantially more raw spinach to ensure that you have enough when it is cooked. It is best lightly steamed. You can also buy spinach frozen or tinned.

Maris Bard potatoes

Red salad potatoes

Lettuce

Brassicas

These vegetables are excellent boiled, steamed or stir-fried. Take care not to overcook them, however – brassicas are best when they are tender but still slightly crisp to the bite.

Chinese leaves

Broccoli

Savoy cabbage

Brussels sprouts

Cauliflower

Brussels sprouts

These look like tiny cabbages and are, in fact, related to the cabbage family. They are available fresh during autumn and winter, or frozen all year round. They are very good boiled or steamed, or shredded and added to stir-fries. However, due to their sulphur content, they have a strong flavour that some people dislike.

Cauliflower

Like cabbage, cauliflower comes in different colours: white, green and red, although the white variety is the most popular. You can eat it raw, or cook it by boiling, steaming, stir-frying, sautéeing or baking.

Pak choi

This is available all year round. It looks a little like celery and has crunchy white stalks and dark green leaves. It is related to Chinese leaves botanically, and is often confused with them but is not the same. However, it does have similar uses and can be used raw in salads, or stir-fried, sautéed, steamed, braised or baked.

Cabbages

These come in many shapes and colours, ranging from white and green to red and the purplish-black cavolo nero. Look for cabbage that is crisp and fresh. You can wash and eat it raw in salads and coleslaw, or cook it in a variety of ways such as boiling, steaming or stir-frying.

Broccoli

This popular vegetable is available all year round and is very nutritious. It can be boiled, steamed, stir-fried, sautéed or baked.

Chinese leaves

These crinkly, cream-coloured leaves with green tips are available all year round. They can be used raw in salads, or sautéed, steamed, braised or baked. They are also popular in stir-fries.

The onion family

These members of the onion family contain sulphuric compounds that give them their unmistakable aroma and flavour. Their taste varies from mild to pungent.

Shallots

These are small onions that resemble large garlic cloves when they are peeled. Use shallots when you need a milder onion flavour. They are particularly good in stir-fries and bakes, and in kebabs.

Spring onions

These very small onions are available all year round but their peak season is during the spring and summer. They can be used raw in salads or sliced to make an attractive garnish, or they can be boiled, steamed, sautéed or baked. Spring onions are also excellent in stir-fries and soups.

Garlic

This versatile bulb was popular with the ancient Egyptians for its medicinal qualities and has many uses in modern cooking. It has an unmistakable taste, due to its sulphur content, and adds a delicious flavour to many different recipes. It can be boiled, steamed, sautéed, stir-fried, baked and roasted. When garlic is cooked with wine, it gives off a wonderful flavour and the combination is excellent in soups and sauces. It can also be used to liven up dressings and marinades.

Leeks

These have a very mild onion flavour and range in size from small baby leeks to large. They can be boiled, steamed, sautéed, stir-fried or baked, and can be substituted for onions in most recipes.

Onions

These are available all year round in a variety of colours, from yellow and white to red. They also range in size from tiny button onions, to medium-sized French onions, to the large Spanish onions, and vary in flavour from mildly pungent to very strong. Once peeled and trimmed, they can be eaten raw in salads or as a garnish, or cooked in a wide variety of dishes, from stir-fries to bakes. You can also pickle onions.

Vegetable fruits

The tastes of the vegetables in this category vary from the mild, creamy flavour of avocados, to the sweet freshness of tomatoes and the fiery heat of chillies. They are popular in a wide range of international dishes.

Aubergines

These come in different sizes and colours, from the large, deep-purple variety, to the tiny greeen pea aubergine. Aubergines must always be cooked, and unless you are using them in a moist recipe with lots of liquid, you should degorge them to remove bitter juices first. Simply cut the aubergine into slices about 1 cm/½ inch thick, spread them out in a large, shallow dish and sprinkle over plenty of salt. Leave the slices for 30 minutes, then transfer to a colander and rinse off the salt with plenty of cold running water. Pat dry with kitchen paper, then use.

Avocados

These green or purplish-black vegetable fruits are shaped like pears but have a soft, buttery interior. Look for avocados that are just beginning to yield to the touch when pressed, and have no bruises. You can use them halved as a starter, sliced in salads or mashed in dips. Avocados discolour quickly when cut, so use them straight away after cutting, or brush them with lemon juice to prevent discolouration.

Chillies

These fiery vegetable fruits usually come in red or green, and in many different sizes and shapes, from 5 mm/¼ inch to 30 cm/12 inches in length. Generally, the smaller the chilli, the hotter the flavour; the small ones can be so fiery that they can burn the skin. Always wear protective gloves when handling chillies, and keep them away from your eyes. Chillies add a spicy kick to many recipes and are particularly good in sauces and stir-fries, and in dishes such as chilli con carne. Deseed chillies before use in order to reduce their fiery heat.

Peppers

When sweet peppers are young they are green and quite bitter, then as they ripen and get sweeter they turn red. You can also get yellow, orange, purple and brown peppers, or peppers in different shapes, such as the long pointed red Mediterranean peppers. Once sliced and deseeded, they can be used raw in salads or as crudités, or cooked in a variety of dishes. Roasting or grilling brings out their sweet flavour. They can also be sautéed, stir-fried, steamed, braised and baked.

Tomatoes

These are available all year round and come in many different sizes and shapes, from tiny cherry tomatoes to large beef tomatoes. Make sure your tomatoes are firm when you buy them. Tomatoes left on the vine are particularly flavourful: in order to preserve their flavour, store them on the vine until you intend to use them. You can eat tomatoes raw in salads and snacks, or cook them. You can also stuff them. They make excellent sauces, soups and pizza toppings, and are delicious sautéed, stir-fried, grilled and baked.

Pod vegetables

Pod vegetables have a delicious flavour, and some varieties, such as sugar snap peas, are tender enough to have an edible pod, so you can eat them whole. They are very good stir-fried.

Pods

These are young vegetables that have edible pods, such as sugar snap peas, mangetout, green beans and runner beans. They have a delicious sweet flavour and can be steamed, boiled, sautéed or stir-fried.

Shelled peas and beans

These are seeds that are allowed to grow in the pod, then are served shelled. They include garden peas, petit pois (smaller peas) and broad beans, which are green and slightly kidney-shaped. All of them can be boiled or steamed.

Peas

Green beans

Mangetout

Other vegetables

Mushrooms and sweetcorn are delicious in salads, risottos and stir-fries, but try experimenting with more exotic varieties of vegetables too, such as Asian vegetables and seaweeds.

Squashes

Squashes have become increasingly popular, and are suitable for use in a variety of dishes. Smaller varieties tend to be more flavourful.

Butternut squash

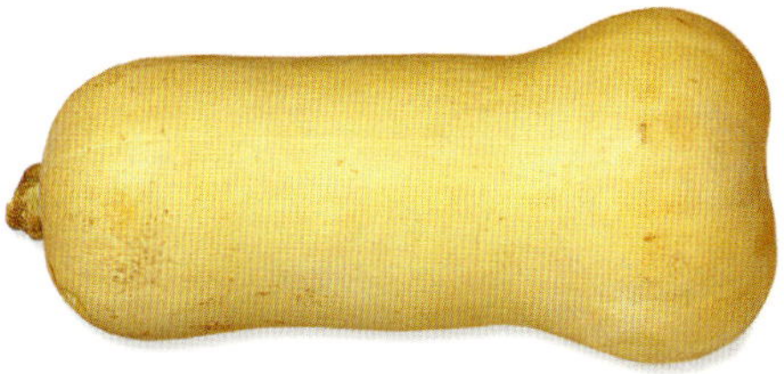

Sweetcorn

White mushrooms

Exotic vegetables

There is a great variety of exotic vegetables available nowadays, and they come from all over the world. Some of the most popular include kombu, which is a dried form of kelp that is used in Japanese cooking; mooli, a long white root that is used in Asian cooking; and wakame, an edible seaweed popular in Asia.

Sweetcorn

The most popular type of sweetcorn these days is the yellow corn. The husks and silks need to be removed before cooking, then you can simply cook the corn whole on the cob, or remove the kernels and cook them on their own. Sweetcorn comes into season in the summer months, but you can also buy it frozen or canned all year round. It is delicious boiled on the cob, or the kernels can be cooked and used in soups, salads and bakes. You can also buy baby corn, which can be boiled, steamed or stir-fried.

Mushrooms

Both cultivated or wild mushrooms are available all year round. The former include the common white or chestnut, button, and large, flat field mushrooms. Wild mushrooms vary enormously in size, shape and colour, and include shiitake, porcini and pieds de moutons. They are available fresh or dried. Mushrooms can absorb a lot of water, so it is better to wipe them with a clean, damp cloth rather than wash them. They can be sautéed, stir-fried, deep-fried in batter, grilled or baked.

Courgettes

This member of the squash family is shaped like a cucumber and comes in various shades of green, sometimes with yellow stripes. It also comes in a variety of sizes, from 10 cm/4 inches to 60 cm/2 feet long (the largest are known as marrows). The smaller varieties tend to have the most flavour. You can also get small round courgettes, ideal for stuffing. Courgettes are available all year round, and are very versatile. They can be steamed, grilled, stir-fried, chargrilled, sautéed, deep-fried, baked and roasted, or you can eat them raw in salads. Courgette flowers, if you can get them, are wonderful stuffed and cooked, or battered and fried.

Cucumbers

Although best known as a salad vegetable, the cucumber is, in fact, a member of the squash family. It can be cut into crudités, with or without its skin, served raw with dips, or lightly sautéed or stir-fried.

Pumpkins

This large squash is available in autumn and winter. The large variety is popular at Hallowe'en, when it is carved out and made into a mask or lantern. The smaller, orange variety has a sweeter flavour and is more suitable for cooking. Pumpkin pie is a particular favourite. You can also use pumpkin in soups and casseroles.

Other squashes

Butternut, acorn and spaghetti squashes are classed as winter squashes. They are large and have thick skins and firm flesh. Once deseeded, they can be roasted, baked or steamed. Summer squashes, such as patty pans, are smaller and can be sautéed, steamed or baked.

Chunky Vegetable Soup

Serves 6

ingredients

- 2 carrots, sliced
- 1 onion, diced
- 1 garlic clove, crushed
- 350 g/12 oz new potatoes, diced
- 2 celery sticks, sliced
- 115 g/4 oz closed-cup mushrooms, quartered
- 400 g/14 oz canned chopped tomatoes
- 600 ml/1 pint vegetable stock
- 1 bay leaf
- 1 tsp dried mixed herbs or 1 tbsp chopped fresh mixed herbs
- 85 g/3 oz sweetcorn kernels, frozen or canned, drained
- 55 g/2 oz green cabbage, shredded
- freshly ground black pepper
- sprigs of fresh basil, to garnish (optional)

1 Put the carrots, onion, garlic, potatoes, celery, mushrooms, tomatoes and stock into a large saucepan. Stir in the bay leaf and herbs. Bring to the boil, then reduce the heat, cover and simmer for 25 minutes.

2 Add the sweetcorn and cabbage and return to the boil. Reduce the heat, cover and simmer for 5 minutes, or until the vegetables are tender. Remove and discard the bay leaf. Season to taste with pepper.

3 Ladle into warmed soup bowls, garnish with basil, if using, and serve immediately.

Leek & Potato Soup

Serves 4

ingredients

- 2 tbsp butter
- 2 garlic cloves, chopped
- 3 large leeks
- 450 g/1 lb potatoes
- 2 tbsp chopped fresh parsley
- 1 tbsp chopped fresh oregano
- 1 bay leaf
- 850 ml/1½ pints vegetable stock
- 200 ml/7 fl oz single cream
- 100 g/3½ oz smoked firm cheese, grated
- salt and pepper
- snipped chives, to garnish

1 Melt the butter in a large saucepan over a medium heat. Add the garlic and cook, stirring, for 1 minute. Trim and slice the leeks. Peel the potatoes and cut into bite-sized chunks. Add the leeks and cook, stirring, for 2 minutes. Add the potatoes, half the parsley, all the oregano and the bay leaf and stock, then season to taste with salt and pepper. Bring to the boil, then reduce the heat, cover the saucepan and leave to simmer for 25 minutes. Remove from the heat, leave to cool for 10 minutes, then remove and discard the bay leaf.

2 Transfer half of the soup to a food processor and process until smooth (you may need to do this in batches). Return to the saucepan with the rest of the soup, stir in the cream and reheat gently. Adjust the seasoning, if necessary.

3 Remove from the heat and stir in the cheese. Ladle into warmed soup bowls, garnish with the snipped chives and remaining parsley, and serve.

Niçoise Pasta Salad

Serves 4

ingredients

- 350 g/12 oz dried conchiglie
- 115 g/4 oz green beans
- 50 g/1¾ oz canned anchovy fillets, drained
- 2 tbsp milk
- 2 small crisp lettuces
- 3 large beef tomatoes
- 4 hard-boiled eggs
- 225 g/8 oz canned tuna, drained
- 115 g/4 oz stoned black olives
- salt

for the vinaigrette dressing

- 3 tbsp extra virgin olive oil
- 2 tbsp white wine vinegar
- 1 tsp wholegrain mustard
- salt and pepper

1 Bring a large pan of lightly salted water to the boil over a medium heat. Add the pasta and cook for 8–10 minutes, until tender but still firm to the bite. Drain and refresh in cold water.

2 Bring a small pan of lightly salted water to the boil over a medium heat. Add the green beans and cook for 10–12 minutes, or until tender but still firm to the bite. Drain, refresh in cold water, drain again and reserve.

3 Put the anchovies in a shallow bowl, pour over the milk and leave to stand for 10 minutes. Meanwhile, tear the lettuces into large pieces. Blanch the tomatoes in boiling water for 1–2 minutes, then drain, skin and roughly chop the flesh. Shell the eggs and cut into quarters. Flake the tuna into large chunks.

4 Drain the anchovies and the pasta. Put all the salad ingredients into a large bowl and gently mix together.

5 To make the vinaigrette dressing, beat together the oil, vinegar and mustard and season to taste with salt and pepper. Chill in the refrigerator until required. Just before serving, pour the vinaigrette dressing over the salad.

Caesar Salad

Serves 4

ingredients

- 1 large egg
- 2 cos lettuces or 3 Little Gem lettuces
- 6 tbsp olive oil
- 2 tbsp lemon juice
- 8 canned anchovy fillets, drained and roughly chopped
- 85 g/3 oz fresh Parmesan cheese shavings
- salt and pepper

for the garlic croûtons

- 4 tbsp olive oil
- 2 garlic cloves
- 5 slices white bread, crusts removed, cut into 1-cm/½-inch cubes

1 Bring a small, heavy-based saucepan of water to the boil.

2 Meanwhile, make the garlic croûtons. Heat the olive oil in a heavy-based frying pan. Add the garlic and diced bread and cook, stirring and tossing frequently, for 4–5 minutes, or until the bread is crispy and golden all over. Remove from the frying pan with a slotted spoon and drain on kitchen paper.

3 While the bread is frying, add the egg to the boiling water and cook for 1 minute, then remove from the saucepan and reserve.

4 Arrange the lettuce leaves in a salad bowl. Mix the olive oil and lemon juice together, then season to taste with salt and pepper. Crack the egg into the dressing and whisk to blend. Pour the dressing over the lettuce leaves, toss well, then add the croûtons and chopped anchovies and toss the salad again. Sprinkle with Parmesan cheese shavings and serve.

Greek Feta Salad

Serves 4

ingredients

- a few vine leaves
- 4 tomatoes, sliced
- ½ cucumber, peeled and sliced
- 1 small red onion, sliced thinly
- 115 g/4 oz feta cheese, cubed
- 8 black olives

for the dressing

- 3 tbsp extra virgin olive oil
- 1 tbsp lemon juice
- ½ tsp dried oregano
- salt and pepper

1 To make the dressing, put the oil, lemon juice, oregano, and salt and pepper in a screw-top jar and shake together until blended.

2 Arrange the vine leaves on a serving dish and then the tomatoes, cucumber and onion. Scatter the cheese and olives on top. Pour the dressing over the salad and serve.

Roast Summer Vegetables

Serves 4

ingredients

- 2 tbsp olive oil
- 1 fennel bulb
- 2 red onions
- 2 beef tomatoes
- 1 aubergine
- 2 courgettes
- 1 yellow pepper
- 1 red pepper
- 1 orange pepper
- 4 garlic cloves
- 4 fresh rosemary sprigs
- pepper
- crusty bread, to serve (optional)

1 Preheat the oven to 200ºC/400ºF/ Gas Mark 6. Brush a large ovenproof dish with a little of the oil. Prepare the vegetables. Cut the fennel, red onions and tomatoes into wedges. Slice the aubergine and courgettes thickly, then deseed all the peppers and cut into chunks. Arrange the vegetables in the dish and tuck the garlic cloves and rosemary sprigs among them. Drizzle with the remaining oil and season to taste with pepper.

2 Roast the vegetables in the preheated oven for 10 minutes. Remove the dish from the oven and turn the vegetables over with a slotted spoon. Return to the oven and roast for a further 10–15 minutes until tender and beginning to turn golden brown.

3 Serve the vegetables straight from the dish, or transfer to a warmed serving plate. Serve with crusty bread, if desired.

Crisp Noodle & Vegetable Stir-fry

Serves 4

ingredients

- groundnut oil, for deep-frying
- 115 g/4 oz rice vermicelli, broken into 7.5-cm/3-inch lengths
- 115 g/4 oz green beans, cut into short lengths
- 2 carrots, cut into thin batons
- 2 courgettes, cut into thin batons
- 115 g/4 oz shiitake mushrooms, sliced
- 2.5-cm/1-inch piece fresh ginger, shredded
- ½ small head Chinese leaves, shredded
- 4 spring onions, shredded
- 85 g/3 oz beansprouts
- 2 tbsp dark soy sauce
- 2 tbsp Chinese rice wine
- large pinch of sugar
- 2 tbsp roughly chopped fresh coriander

1 Half-fill a wok or deep, heavy-based frying pan with oil. Heat to 180–190°C/350–375°F, or until a cube of bread browns in 30 seconds.

2 Add the noodles, in batches, and cook for 1½–2 minutes, or until crisp and puffed up. Remove and drain on kitchen paper. Pour off all but 2 tablespoons of oil from the wok.

3 Heat the remaining oil over a high heat. Add the green beans and stir-fry for 2 minutes.

4 Add the carrot and courgette batons, sliced mushrooms and ginger and stir-fry for a further 2 minutes.

5 Add the shredded Chinese leaves and spring onions with the beansprouts and stir-fry for a further 1 minute.

6 Add the soy sauce, rice wine and sugar and cook, stirring constantly, for 1 minute.

7 Add the noodles and chopped coriander and toss well. Serve immediately.

Ratatouille

Serves 4

ingredients

- 1 aubergine, about 250 g/9 oz
- 4 tbsp olive oil
- 2 garlic cloves, chopped
- 1 large onion, chopped
- 2 red peppers, deseeded and cut into bite-sized chunks
- 800 g/1 lb 12 oz canned chopped tomatoes
- 2 courgettes, sliced
- 1 celery stick, sliced
- 1 tsp sugar
- 2 tbsp chopped fresh thyme
- salt and pepper

1 Trim the aubergine and cut it into bite-sized chunks, then place it in a colander. Sprinkle with salt and leave to stand for 30 minutes.

2 Heat the oil in a large saucepan over a medium heat. Add the garlic and onion and cook, stirring, for 3 minutes until softened slightly. Rinse the aubergine and drain well, then add it to the saucepan with the red peppers. Reduce the heat and cook gently, stirring frequently, for a further 10 minutes.

3 Stir in the tomatoes, courgettes, celery, sugar and thyme, and season to taste with salt and pepper. Bring to the boil, then reduce the heat, cover the saucepan, and leave to simmer gently for 30 minutes.

4 Remove the saucepan from the heat, transfer to bowls and serve.

Vegetable Cannelloni

Serves 4

ingredients

- 12 dried cannelloni tubes
- 1 aubergine
- 125 ml/4 fl oz olive oil, plus extra for brushing
- 225 g/8 oz spinach
- 2 garlic cloves, crushed
- 1 tsp ground cumin
- 85 g/3 oz mushrooms, chopped
- 55 g/2 oz mozzarella cheese, sliced
- salt and pepper
- lamb's lettuce, to garnish

for the tomato sauce

- 1 tbsp olive oil
- 1 onion, chopped
- 2 garlic cloves, crushed
- 800 g/1 lb 12 oz canned chopped tomatoes
- 1 tsp caster sugar
- 2 tbsp chopped fresh basil

1 Preheat the oven to 190°C/375°F/Gas Mark 5. Bring a large heavy-bottom saucepan of lightly salted water to the boil. Add the cannelloni tubes, return to the boil and cook for 8–10 minutes, or until tender but still firm to the bite. Transfer the pasta to a plate and pat dry with kitchen paper. Brush a large ovenproof dish with oil.

2 Cut the aubergine into small dice. Heat the oil in a frying pan over a medium heat. Add the aubergine and cook, stirring frequently, for about 2–3 minutes.

3 Add the spinach, garlic, cumin and mushrooms and reduce the heat. Season to taste with salt and pepper and cook, stirring, for about 2–3 minutes. Spoon the mixture into the cannelloni tubes and put into the dish in a single layer.

4 To make the sauce, heat the oil in a pan over a medium heat. Add the onion and garlic and cook for 1 minute. Add the tomatoes, sugar and basil and bring to the boil. Reduce the heat and simmer for about 5 minutes. Spoon the sauce over the cannelloni tubes.

5 Arrange the mozzarella cheese on top of the sauce and bake in the preheated oven for about 30 minutes, or until the cheese is golden brown and bubbling. Serve garnished with lamb's lettuce.

Griddled Courgette Bruschetta

Serves 4

ingredients

- 1 tbsp olive oil, plus extra for drizzling
- ½ tsp ground cumin
- 2 courgettes (about 300 g/10½ oz total weight), cut in half crossways, then thinly sliced lengthways
- 1 red onion, thinly sliced
- 2 large plum or vine-ripened tomatoes, thickly sliced (each cut into 4 slices)
- 8 slices (each about 2 cm/¾ inch thick) plain ciabatta bread (or 8 slices cut from a large French baguette or white flute)
- 1 clove garlic, halved
- salt and pepper

1 In a large bowl, whisk together the olive oil, cumin and seasoning. Add the courgette and onion slices and toss gently to coat all over. Heat a non-stick ridged griddle pan over a medium heat. Place a layer of courgette and onion slices on the pan and cook for about 6–8 minutes or until lightly browned and tender, turning occasionally. When the first batch is cooked, remove and keep warm, then add the remaining courgette and onion slices to the griddle pan and cook as before. Remove and keep warm.

2 Add the tomato slices to the griddle pan and cook briefly on both sides (about 1 minute on each side), then remove and keep warm. Carefully wipe out any stray tomato pips from the pan using kitchen paper, if necessary. Add the bread slices to the griddle pan and toast each side, turning once. Remove from the pan to warmed serving plates.

3 Rub the toasts on one side with the cut garlic halves, then drizzle with a little olive oil. Arrange the griddled vegetables on top of the garlicky toasts and serve immediately.

Stuffed Red Peppers with Basil

Serves 4

ingredients

- 140 g/5 oz long-grain white or brown rice
- 4 large red peppers
- 2 tbsp olive oil
- 1 garlic clove, chopped
- 4 shallots, chopped
- 1 celery stick, chopped
- 3 tbsp chopped toasted walnuts
- 2 tomatoes, peeled and chopped
- 1 tbsp lemon juice
- 50 g/1¾ oz raisins
- 4 tbsp freshly grated Cheddar cheese
- 2 tbsp chopped fresh basil
- salt and pepper

1 Preheat the oven to 180°C/ 350°F/ Gas Mark 4. Cook the rice in a saucepan of lightly salted boiling water for 20 minutes if using white rice, or 35 minutes if using brown. Drain, rinse under cold running water, then drain again.

2 Meanwhile, using a sharp knife, cut the tops off the peppers and reserve. Remove the seeds and white cores, then blanch the peppers and reserved tops in boiling water for 2 minutes. Remove from the heat and drain well. Heat half the oil in a large frying pan. Add the garlic and shallots and cook, stirring, for 3 minutes. Add the celery, walnuts, tomatoes, lemon juice and raisins and cook for a further 5 minutes. Remove from the heat and stir in the rice, cheese, chopped basil and seasoning.

3 Stuff the peppers with the rice mixture and arrange them in a baking dish. Place the tops on the peppers, drizzle over the remaining oil, loosely cover with foil and bake in the preheated oven for 45 minutes. Remove from the oven and serve.

Classic Roast Potatoes

Serves 4

ingredients

- 900 g/2 lb medium–large floury potatoes, peeled
- ½ tsp salt
- paprika
- 100 ml/3½ fl oz vegetable oil
- pepper

1 Preheat the oven to 200°C/400°F/ Gas Mark 6. Using a sharp knife, cut the potatoes in half, or into quarters if very large, then arrange in a roasting tin. Sprinkle over the salt, then season to taste with pepper and paprika.

2 Pour the oil over the potatoes, then turn them in the oil until well coated. Transfer to the preheated oven and roast, basting occasionally, for 1½ hours, or until golden brown and tender. Remove from the oven and serve immediately.

Braised Red Cabbage

Serves 6

ingredients

- 2 tbsp sunflower oil
- 2 onions, thinly sliced
- 2 eating apples, peeled, cored and thinly sliced
- 900 g/2 lb red cabbage, cored and shredded
- 4 tbsp red wine vinegar
- 2 tbsp sugar
- ¼ tsp ground cloves
- 55 g/2 oz raisins
- 125 ml/4 fl oz red wine
- 2 tbsp redcurrant jelly
- salt and pepper

1 Heat the oil in a large saucepan. Add the onions and cook, stirring occasionally, for 10 minutes, or until softened and golden. Stir in the apple slices and cook for 3 minutes.

2 Add the cabbage, vinegar, sugar, cloves, raisins and red wine and season to taste with salt and pepper. Bring to the boil, stirring occasionally. Reduce the heat, cover and cook, stirring occasionally, for 40 minutes, or until the cabbage is tender and most of the liquid has been absorbed.

3 Stir in the redcurrant jelly, transfer to a warmed dish and serve.

Risotto with Artichoke Hearts

Serves 4

ingredients

- 225 g/8 oz canned artichoke hearts
- 1 tbsp olive oil
- 40 g/1½ oz butter
- 1 small onion, finely chopped
- 280 g/10 oz risotto rice
- 1.2 litres/2 pints hot vegetable stock
- 85 g/3 oz freshly grated Parmesan cheese or Grana Padano cheese
- salt and pepper
- fresh flat-leaf parsley sprigs, to garnish

1 Drain the artichoke hearts, reserving the liquid, and cut them into quarters.

2 Heat the oil with 25 g/1 oz of the butter in a deep saucepan over a medium heat until the butter has melted. Stir in the onion and cook gently, stirring occasionally, for 5 minutes, or until soft and starting to turn golden. Do not brown.

3 Add the rice and mix to coat in oil and butter. Cook, stirring constantly, for 2–3 minutes, or until the grains are translucent.

4 Gradually add the artichoke liquid and the hot stock, a ladle at a time. Stir constantly and add more liquid as the rice absorbs each addition. Increase the heat to medium so that the liquid bubbles. Cook for 15 minutes, then add the artichoke hearts. Cook for a further 5 minutes, or until all the liquid is absorbed and the rice is creamy. Season to taste with salt and pepper.

5 Remove the risotto from the heat and add the remaining butter. Mix well, then stir in the cheese until it melts. Season, if necessary. Spoon the risotto into warmed bowls, garnish with parsley sprigs and serve immediately.

Chapter 6
Herbs & Spices

Introduction

There is a wide range of fresh herbs available all year round in your local supermarket, as well as a tempting array of fragrant and exotic spices. You can also buy frozen herbs, which are a good substitute when fresh herbs are unavailable. It is a good idea to keep some pots of fresh herbs on a windowsill and a selection of dried herbs and spices in your storecupboard. Note that if you are substituting a dried herb for fresh, you will need only half the quantity, since the flavour is more concentrated.

Buying and storing herbs and spices

If you buy fresh herbs as pot plants, place them on a windowsill where they can get plenty of light, and water them regularly. Basil, in particular, needs lots of water, so make sure you do not allow it to dry out. Packaged fresh herbs should be stored in their wrapping in the refrigerator. If you grow herbs in your garden, after picking keep them in a jug of clean water until you are ready to use them. Store dried herbs and ground spices in a cool, dark place – an airy storecupboard is ideal. Use all fresh herbs by their 'best before' date, and go through your storecupboard regularly and throw out any dried herbs and spices that are past their best.

Basil

There are many species of this herb. It thrives in a warm, Mediterranean climate, and therefore in cold climates it will do better indoors on a windowsill with plenty of sunshine and water. It has a sweet, aromatic flavour, and is particularly good with tomatoes and mozzarella cheese. It is also delicious with poultry, fish and seafood, salads and sauces. This herb is fragile and should therefore be added to recipes towards the end of the cooking time.

Tarragon

The dark green pointed leaves of tarragon have an aromatic, aniseed-like flavour. It adds a distinctive flavour to poultry, fish, eggs, sauces, salads and dressings. It is best to use this herb on its own, since its strong flavour can overpower other herbs if mixed with them.

Coriander

Chives

Rosemary

Bay

Dill

Thyme
This herb comes in different varieties, and several of them are commonly used in cooking. The leaves add a pungent, aromatic flavour to meat, poultry, egg and potato dishes, and are good in soups, sauces, roasts, casseroles and stews.

Oregano
This green herb is related to marjoram. It has a pungent flavour and should be used sparingly. It is popular in Italian cookery, particularly on pizzas, and adds an aromatic flavour to meat and poultry, eggs and cheese.

Coriander
This pungent herb has bright green leaves and is very popular in Mediterranean and Asian cooking. It adds a distinctive flavour to salads, cooked vegetables and stir-fries.

Fennel
There are two types of fennel. One has a bulbous base, which can be cooked and used like a vegetable; the other variety has no bulb. Fennel has a strong aniseed flavour. The leaves of both types can be snipped into soups and sauces, and are excellent with fish and egg dishes.

Marjoram
This ancient herb has pale green leaves and a delicate, sweet flavour. It is ideal with meat, poultry, cheese, tomatoes, eggs and dressings.

Rosemary
The silvery, needle-shaped leaves of rosemary have a strong aromatic flavour. It is used in soups, salads, roasts, stuffings, dressings and marinades, as well as on pizzas. The herb also makes delicious skewers for kebabs. It pairs particularly well with potatoes and bread, as well as meat, poultry, fish and eggs.

Bay
The leaves of this aromatic herb come from the Mediterranean laurel tree. The fresh leaves, if you can get them, have more flavour than the dried, but either type will add a good, pungent flavour to soups, sauces, stocks and casseroles. They are usually discarded once the food has absorbed their flavour.

Sage
This herb has greyish oval leaves and a pungent, slightly bitter taste. It is very common in stuffings, especially those containing onion, and is excellent with pork, poultry, beans, cheese, rice and pasta. It is also used to flavour drinks.

Chervil
The dark green, curly leaves of chervil have an aromatic flavour with a hint of aniseed. It is especially good in chicken, fish and egg dishes.

Mint
There are many species of mint, the two best-known being peppermint and spearmint. Peppermint has a more peppery flavour, while spearmint has a fresher mint taste. Mint is a hardy plant and can take over a herb garden if not carefully controlled. Use it to flavour cooked potatoes, peas, sauces, soups, meat dishes, desserts and drinks.

Dill
This herb has feathery green leaves and a mild flavour. Dill is excellent with fish, as well as in salads, cheese dishes and sauces.

Chives
These relatives of the onion family have long, hollow stems and edible purple flowers. The fresh stems are snipped into small pieces and added to salads, soups, cream cheese and egg dishes. You can also buy them frozen and dried.

Parsley
This versatile herb is rich in vitamins A and C and comes in many varieties. The two most popular types have green leaves that are either curly or flat. Curly parsley is common all year round, while flat-leaf parsley may be found only in some supermarkets and specialist delicatessens. Parsley is used in a wide range of dishes, including soups, salads, sauces, stir-fries and bakes, as well as stuffings, dressings and marinades. It adds a spicy, lingering flavour to meat, poultry, fish, eggs and vegetables, and helps to offset the sulphur aftertaste of garlic. It also makes an attractive garnish, particularly the flat-leaf variety.

Oregano

Thyme

Basil

Types and uses of spices

Spices used to be costly when international travel was comparatively slow and difficult – now they are less expensive and more widely available.

Cardamom pods

Chilli powder

Ground cinnamon

Cinnamon sticks

Paprika

This spice is made from ground red pepper pods and its flavour can vary from mild, sweet and pungent to fiery hot. It is excellent in salads and as a garnish. It also goes well with meat, poultry, eggs, vegetables, cream cheese, pasta, rice and beans.

Cardamom

This aromatic spice is related to ginger and has a pungent lemon flavour. You can grind and use the whole pod, or use just the seeds inside. Cardamom is widely used in Asian and Middle Eastern dishes, and adds a distinctive flavour to soups, stews, curries, pastry, bread and cakes.

Allspice

This small berry comes from the West Indies and South America and has a sweet flavour of nutmeg, cinnamon and cloves. You can buy it whole or ground. It is used with meat, onions and fruit desserts, as well as in cakes and bread.

Mustard

This hot, acrid spice is available as whole seeds, ground, or processed into a paste that ranges in intensity from mild to strong. It goes well with meat, poultry, seafood, eggs, beans, potatoes, cheese, cream and butter sauces, bread, marinades, chutneys and relishes.

Chilli powder

This powdered mixture of spices includes dried chillies, cumin, coriander and cloves. It has a fiery heat but you can also buy mild chilli powder. Use it to flavour soups and stews. It goes well with seafood, meat, poultry, vegetables, beans and eggs.

Fennel seeds

You can buy fennel seeds whole or ground. They have a sweet, mildly aniseed flavour and can be used in savoury and sweet dishes, including marinades, pizzas, stuffings, bread, cakes, biscuits and a variety of desserts and drinks. Fennel goes particularly well with meat, poultry, fish, beetroot, onions, potatoes, tomatoes, cucumber, beans, pasta, rice, cheese, eggs and fruit.

Star anise

This star-shaped brown pod comes from an Asian tree. It has a warm, aromatic, slightly bitter aniseed flavour and is available whole or ground. It is popular in Chinese cooking, and is used in marinades, stir-fries, bakes, cakes, fruit and some drinks. It goes particularly well with pork, poultry and fish.

Caraway

These seeds have a nutty, aniseed flavour and can be bought whole or ground. They are popular in German and Austrian cookery, and are used to flavour soups, stews, meat, cheese, vegetables, sauerkraut, bread, cakes and the liqueur kümmel.

Juniper

These berries are available dried and are usually crushed to release their pungent pine flavour. Use them to flavour various meats as well as pâtés, stuffings and sauces.

Mace

This sweet, fragrant spice is most often sold ground and is used to flavour a wide range of savoury and sweet dishes, including beef, chicken, fish, vegetables, pasta, beans, cheese, chocolate, fruit, cakes, marinades, biscuits, chutneys and mulled wine.

Cayenne pepper

This type of pepper is made from tropical chillies and it has a hot, spicy flavour. Use it to add a kick to South American and Caribbean dishes. It is especially good with seafood and chutneys.

Peppercorns

The dried berries from the pepper plant come in black, white and green. Black peppercorns are the most widely used, and are available whole, cracked or ground. They deteriorate quickly when ground, so it is best to buy them whole and grind them yourself. They have an aromatic flavour and can be used in almost every savoury recipe and some sweet fruit dishes, such as balsamic strawberries.

Cinnamon

This spice comes from the bark of a tropical tree. The bark is dried and curled into quills or sticks; it can also be bought ground. Cinnamon has a sweet, aromatic smell and flavour, and is popular in Middle Eastern dishes. It is used to flavour a wide range of savoury and sweet dishes, such as stews, curries, pies, bread and cakes, and a whole host of desserts and drinks.

Whole nutmeg

Coriander seeds

Garam masala

Ground ginger

Nutmeg
Nutmeg has a sweet, fragrant flavour and is available whole or ground. It is used in a wide variety of savoury and sweet dishes, from meat, poultry, vegetables, beans, rice, cheese and eggs to chocolate, fruit, cream sauces and drinks.

Coriander
The dried seeds of the coriander plant are fragrant and lemony and can be used whole or ground. They are popular in marinades, chutneys, curries and bakes, and go particularly well with meat, poultry, fish, cheese, vegetables, beans, chocolate and jam.

Saffron
This spice has a pungent, slightly bitter flavour. It comes from the purple crocus and is available in threads or powdered. It is used to tint and flavour marinades, soups, stews, rice dishes, breads and bakes. This is the spice that gives the rice in Spanish paella its characteristic yellow colour. Saffron is expensive, so the less expensive turmeric is often used in its place.

Cloves
These come from the buds of the tropical clove tree. The dried brown buds are sold whole or powdered, and have a sweet, pungent flavour. Push whole cloves into ham, pork, onions and oranges to flavour them, or use them ground in soups, stews, bread, cakes, desserts and chutneys. You can also use them whole in drinks such as mulled wine (but you should always remove whole cloves before serving).

Mixed spice
This blend of spices usually consists of allspice, cinnamon, cloves, ginger, coriander and nutmeg. It has a warm, sweet flavour and is delicious in fruit desserts, bread, cakes, biscuits and drinks.

Cumin
These dried seeds have a pungent, nutty flavour and are also available ground. Cumin is popular in Asian and Mexican cooking, and goes well with beef, pork, salmon, shellfish, beans, pasta, eggs, cheese and rice.

Five spice
Chinese five-spice powder is, as its name implies, a blend of five spices, usually cloves, cinnamon, fennel seeds, Szechuan peppercorns and star anise. It has a sweet, pungent flavour and is popular in Chinese and Vietnamese cooking. It is especially good in stir-fries. There is also a Tunisian version, which consists of cloves, cinnamon, nutmeg, pepper, and grains of paradise (which are also known as melegueta pepper).

Curry powder
This powder contains a mixture of spices including cardamom, chillies, cloves, coriander, fenugreek and turmeric. It is available mild or hot, and is used in curries, cream sauces and chutneys. It also goes well with beef, chicken, turkey, seafood, root vegetables, rice, eggs and cheese.

Turmeric
This spice comes from the root of a tropical plant and has a pungent, somewhat bitter flavour. The powdered variety has a bright orange-yellow colour, so is used to tint foods as well as to flavour them. Turmeric is often used as a cheaper alternative to saffron to colour food. Use this spice to colour or flavour seafood, poultry, pasta, cheese, eggs, curries, risottos, chutneys, marinades, bread and beans.

Garam masala
The blend of spices in garam masala varies, but it often includes cumin, cinnamon, cloves, cardamom, chillies, fennel, fenugreek, garlic, ginger and black pepper. It is popular in Indian cooking, especially in curries, and also goes well with vegetables, eggs, cheese and rice.

Ginger
Ginger is available fresh or dried. The fresh root has a warm, lemon flavour and can be used chopped or grated. It is especially useful in marinades, salads, soups, stews and stir-fries; it can also be preserved in syrup. Powdered ginger has a more pungent, spicy flavour, and is particularly good with chocolate, cream, fruit, gingerbread, cakes, biscuits, jams, chutneys and drinks.

Minty Pea & Bean Soup

Serves 4–6

ingredients

- 1½ tbsp olive oil
- 1 bunch spring onions, trimmed and chopped
- 1 large celery stick, chopped
- 1 garlic clove, crushed
- 1 floury potato, about 150 g/5½ oz, peeled and diced
- 1.2 litres/2 pints vegetable stock
- 1 bay leaf
- 150 g/5½ oz peas
- 400 g/14 oz canned flageolet beans, drained and rinsed
- salt and pepper
- finely shredded fresh mint, to garnish
- mixed-grain bread rolls, to serve

1 Heat the oil in a large saucepan over a medium–high heat. Add the spring onions, celery and garlic and cook, stirring, for about 3 minutes until soft. Add the potato and stir for a further minute.

2 Add the stock, bay leaf and salt and pepper to taste and bring to the boil, stirring. Reduce the heat to low, cover the pan and simmer for 20 minutes, or until the potatoes are tender.

3 Add the peas and beans and return the soup to the boil. Reduce the heat, re-cover the pan and continue to simmer until the peas are tender.

4 Remove the bay leaf, then tip the soup into a food processor or blender and blend until smooth. Place a metal sieve over the rinsed-out pan and use a wooden spoon to push the soup through the sieve.

5 Add salt and pepper to taste and reheat. Ladle the soup into warmed bowls, sprinkle with mint and serve with the bread rolls.

Basil & Pine Kernel Pesto

Serves 4

ingredients

- about 40 fresh basil leaves
- 3 garlic cloves, crushed
- 25 g/1 oz pine kernels
- 50 g/1¾ oz Parmesan cheese, finely grated, plus extra to garnish
- 2–3 tbsp extra virgin olive oil
- 675 g/1 lb 8 oz fresh pasta or 350 g/12 oz dried pasta
- salt and pepper

1 Rinse the basil leaves and pat them dry with kitchen paper.

2 Place the basil leaves, garlic, pine kernels and grated Parmesan cheese in a food processor and process for 30 seconds, or until smooth. Alternatively, pound all of the ingredients by hand, using a pestle and mortar.

3 If you are using a food processor, keep the motor running and slowly add the olive oil. Alternatively, add the oil drop by drop while stirring briskly. Season to taste with salt and pepper.

4 Bring a large, heavy-based saucepan of water to the boil. Add the pasta, return to the boil and cook for 3–4 minutes for fresh pasta or 8–10 minutes for dried, until tender but still firm to the bite. Drain the pasta thoroughly and stir in the pesto.

5 Transfer to warmed serving bowls, garnish with the Parmesan cheese and serve hot.

Tarragon Chicken

Serves 4

ingredients

- 4 skinless, boneless chicken breasts, about 175 g/6 oz each
- 125 ml/4 fl oz dry white wine
- 225–300 ml/8–10 fl oz chicken stock
- 1 garlic clove, finely chopped
- 1 tbsp dried tarragon
- 175 ml/6 fl oz double cream
- 1 tbsp chopped fresh tarragon
- salt and pepper
- green vegetables, to serve

1 Season the chicken with salt and pepper and place in a single layer in a large, heavy-based frying pan. Pour in the wine and enough chicken stock just to cover and add the garlic and dried tarragon. Bring to the boil, reduce the heat and cook gently for 10 minutes, or until the chicken is tender and cooked right through.

2 Remove the chicken with a slotted spoon or tongs, cover and keep warm. Strain the poaching liquid through a sieve into a clean frying pan and skim off any fat from the surface. Bring to the boil and cook for 12–15 minutes, or until reduced by about two-thirds.

3 Stir in the cream, return to the boil and cook until reduced by about half. Stir in the fresh tarragon.

4 Transfer the chicken breasts to warmed plates. Spoon over the sauce and serve with green vegetables.

Herbed Mixed Bean Salad with Fried Halloumi Cheese

Serves 4–6

ingredients

- 5 tbsp extra virgin olive oil
- 2 tbsp tarragon vinegar
- ½ tsp mixed grain mustard
- pinch of sugar
- 115 g/4 oz French beans, topped and tailed and cut into bite-sized pieces
- 115 g/4 oz shelled broad beans, grey outer skins removed if not young
- 115 g/4 oz fresh or frozen shelled peas
- 400 g/14 oz canned cannellini beans, drained and rinsed
- 1 small red onion, thinly sliced
- 2 tbsp chopped fresh parsley
- 1 tbsp snipped fresh chives
- 85 g/3 oz rocket or watercress leaves
- salt and pepper

fried halloumi cheese

- ½ tbsp olive oil
- 350 g/12 oz halloumi cheese, drained, cut into 12 slices
- plain flour, for dusting

1 Put the olive oil, vinegar, mustard, sugar and salt and pepper to taste in a small screw-top jar and shake until blended and emulsified. Set aside.

2 Prepare a bowl of iced water. Bring a saucepan of lightly salted water to the boil. Add the French beans and the broad beans and blanch for 3 minutes, or until just tender. Use a slotted spoon to remove the beans from the water and immediately transfer them to the iced water.

3 Return the water to the boil and blanch the peas for 3 minutes, or until tender. Remove from the water and add to the iced water to cool. Drain the beans and peas and pat dry with kitchen paper. Transfer to a large bowl, add the dressing, cannellini beans, onion and herbs and toss. Cover and chill.

4 To make the fried halloumi cheese, heat the oil in a pan over a medium–high heat. Dust the cheese with flour, shaking off the excess and add to the pan. Fry for 3–6 minutes, or until golden. Flip the cheese over and cook the other side, then remove and keep warm while you fry the remaining pieces.

5 Divide the salad ingredients and the rocket leaves between individual plates and arrange the hot cheese alongside. Drizzle the cheese with olive oil and serve.

Fusilli with Smoked Salmon & Dill

Serves 4

ingredients

- 450 g/1 lb dried fusilli
- 55 g/2 oz unsalted butter
- 1 small onion, finely chopped
- 6 tbsp dry white wine
- 425 ml/15 fl oz double cream
- 225 g/8 oz smoked salmon
- 2 tbsp snipped fresh dill, plus extra sprigs to garnish
- 1–2 tbsp lemon juice
- salt and pepper

1 Bring a large heavy-based saucepan of lightly salted water to the boil. Add the pasta, return to the boil and cook for 8–10 minutes, or until tender but still firm to the bite.

2 Meanwhile, melt the butter in a heavy-based saucepan. Add the onion and cook over a low heat, stirring occasionally, for 5 minutes, or until softened. Add the wine, bring to the boil and continue boiling until reduced by two thirds. Pour in the cream and season to taste with salt and pepper. Bring to the boil, reduce the heat and simmer for 2 minutes, or until slightly thickened. Cut the smoked salmon into squares and stir into the saucepan with the snipped dill and lemon juice to taste.

3 Drain the pasta and transfer to a warmed serving dish. Add the smoked salmon mixture, toss well, garnish with dill sprigs and serve immediately.

Marinated Sardine Fillets with Oregano & Fennel

Serves 6

ingredients

- 8 large sardines, gutted and descaled
- 6 tbsp extra virgin olive oil
- 1 tbsp white wine vinegar
- 1 tbsp dried oregano
- 2 garlic cloves, crushed
- 1 tsp black peppercorns, crushed
- ½ tsp sea salt
- ¼ tsp dried chilli flakes
- ½ red onion, sliced thinly
- 1 fennel bulb, trimmed, quartered lengthways and sliced thinly
- 4 tomatoes, deseeded and sliced into thin segments
- 2 tbsp shredded fresh basil

1 Preheat the oven to 180°C/350°F/ Gas Mark 4. Place the sardines in an ovenproof baking dish. Combine the oil, vinegar, oregano and garlic, and season with the crushed pepper, sea salt and chilli flakes. Pour the mixture over the sardines. Bake for 20–25 minutes until the flesh is no longer translucent around the backbone.

2 Remove the sardines from the oven and leave to cool in the baking dish. Sprinkle with the red onion slices, cover with clingfilm and leave to marinate in the fridge for up to 3 days. Remove from the fridge an hour or two before serving.

3 Arrange the fennel and tomato segments on top of the sardines, spooning over some of the oily juices from the dish. Sprinkle with the basil just before serving.

Tuna & Herbed Fusilli Salad

Serves 4

ingredients

- 200 g/7 oz dried fusilli
- 1 red pepper, deseeded and quartered
- 1 red onion, sliced
- 4 tomatoes, sliced
- 200 g/7 oz canned tuna in brine, drained and flaked

for the dressing

- 6 tbsp basil-flavoured oil or extra virgin olive oil
- 3 tbsp white wine vinegar
- 1 tbsp lime juice
- 1 tsp mustard
- 1 tsp honey
- 4 tbsp chopped fresh basil, plus extra sprigs to garnish

1 Bring a large saucepan of lightly salted water to the boil. Add the pasta, return to the boil and cook for 8–10 minutes until tender but still firm to the bite.

2 Meanwhile, put the pepper quarters under a preheated hot grill and cook for 10–12 minutes until the skins begin to blacken. Transfer to a polythene bag, seal and set aside.

3 Remove the pasta from the heat, drain and set aside to cool. Remove the pepper quarters from the bag and peel off the skins. Slice the pepper into strips.

4 To make the dressing, put all the dressing ingredients in a large bowl and stir together well. Add the pasta, pepper strips, onion, tomatoes and tuna. Toss together gently, then divide between serving bowls. Garnish with basil sprigs and serve.

Spicy Potato Chips

Serves 4

ingredients

- 4 large waxy potatoes
- 2 sweet potatoes
- 4 tbsp butter, melted
- ½ tsp chilli powder
- 1 tsp garam masala
- salt

1 Cut both the potatoes and sweet potatoes into slices about 1 cm/½ inch thick, then cut them into finger-shaped chips. Place the potatoes in a large bowl of cold salted water. Leave to soak for 20 minutes.

2 Remove the potato slices with a slotted spoon and drain thoroughly. Pat with kitchen paper until they are completely dry.

3 Pour the melted butter on to a baking tray. Transfer the potato slices to the baking tray. Sprinkle with the chilli powder and garam masala, turning the potato slices to coat them with the spice mixture.

4 Cook the chips in a preheated oven, 200°C/400°F/Gas Mark 6, turning frequently, for 40 minutes, until browned and cooked through.

5 Drain the chips well on kitchen paper to remove the excess oil and serve immediately.

Vegetarian Samosas

Makes 8

ingredients

- 1 carrot, diced
- 200 g/7 oz sweet potato, diced
- 85 g/3 oz frozen peas
- 2 tbsp ghee or vegetable oil
- 1 onion, chopped
- 1 garlic clove, chopped
- 2.5-cm/1-inch piece fresh ginger, grated
- 1 tsp ground turmeric
- 1 tsp ground cumin
- ½ tsp chilli powder
- ½ tsp garam masala
- 1 tsp lime juice
- salt and pepper
- lime wedges, to serve
- sweet chilli dipping sauce, to serve

for the pastry

- 150 g/5½ oz plain flour, plus extra for dusting
- 40 g/1½ oz butter, diced
- 4 tbsp warm milk
- vegetable oil, for frying

1 Bring a saucepan of water to the boil, add the carrot and cook for 4 minutes. Add the sweet potato and continue to cook for 4 minutes, then add the peas and cook for a further 3 minutes. Drain.

2 Heat the ghee in a saucepan over a medium heat, add the onion, garlic, ginger, spices and lime juice and cook, stirring, for 3 minutes. Add the drained vegetables and season to taste with salt and pepper. Cook, stirring, for 2 minutes. Remove from the heat and leave to cool for 15 minutes.

3 To make the pastry, put the flour into a bowl and rub in the butter. Add the milk and mix to form a dough. Knead briefly and divide into 4 pieces. On a lightly floured work surface, form each piece into a ball and roll out into a circle measuring 17 cm/6½ inches in diameter. Halve each circle, divide the filling between them and brush the edges with water, then fold over into triangles and seal the edges.

4 Heat 2.5 cm/1 inch of oil in a frying pan to 180–190°C/350–375°F, or until a cube of bread browns in 30 seconds. Cook the samosas in batches for 3–4 minutes, or until golden. Remove the samosas with a slotted spoon and drain on kitchen paper.

5 Transfer to serving bowls and serve hot with the lime wedges and sweet chilli dipping sauce.

Spicy Fragrant Black Bean Chilli

Serves 4

ingredients

- 400 g/14 oz dried black beans
- 2 tbsp olive oil
- 1 onion, chopped
- 5 garlic cloves, roughly chopped
- ½–1 tsp ground cumin
- ½–1 tsp mild chilli powder
- 1 red pepper, deseeded and diced
- 1 carrot, diced
- 400 g/14 oz fresh tomatoes, diced
- 1 bunch fresh coriander, roughly chopped, plus extra to garnish
- salt and pepper

1 Soak the beans overnight, then drain. Place in a saucepan, cover with water and bring to the boil. Boil for 10 minutes, then reduce the heat and simmer for 1½ hours, or until tender. Drain well, reserving 250 ml/8 fl oz of the cooking liquid.

2 Heat the oil in a frying pan. Add the onion and garlic and cook for 2 minutes, stirring, until softened.

3 Stir in the cumin and chilli powder and continue to cook for 20–30 seconds. Add the red pepper, carrot and tomatoes. Cook over a medium heat for 5 minutes.

4 Add half the coriander and the beans and their reserved liquid. Season to taste with salt and pepper. Simmer for 30–45 minutes, or until very flavourful and thickened.

5 Season to taste with salt and pepper. Transfer to warmed serving bowls, garnish with the remaining coriander and serve.

Spiced Mackerel with Tomato Salad

Serves 4

ingredients

- 4 garlic cloves, well crushed
- finely grated zest and juice of 1 lemon
- 1 heaped tsp ground cumin
- 1 heaped tsp smoked paprika
- 2–3 tbsp olive oil
- 4 large mackerel fillets, about 200 g/7 oz each, or 8 small, about 100 g/3½ oz each

for the Tomato Salad

- 300 g/10½ oz juicy ripe tomatoes
- 1 small red onion, thinly sliced
- 1 heaped tbsp chopped fresh herbs, such as thyme, mint or parsley
- 2 tbsp olive oil
- 1 tbsp white wine vinegar
- pinch of caster sugar
- salt and pepper

1 Mix the garlic, lemon zest and juice, cumin, paprika and oil together in a small bowl. Put the mackerel fillets in a shallow, non-metallic dish and thoroughly rub both sides with the spice mixture. Cover and leave to marinate in a cool place for 30 minutes, if possible.

2 Preheat the grill to high. Lay the mackerel fillets in the grill pan and cook under the preheated grill for 3 minutes on one side, then turn over, drizzle with any remaining marinade and cook for a further 2–3 minutes, or until the mackerel is cooked through.

3 Meanwhile, prepare the salad. Slice the tomatoes and arrange with the onion on a serving platter. Put the herbs, oil, vinegar, sugar and a little salt and pepper to taste in a screw-top jar and shake well to combine.

4 Drizzle the dressing over the salad and serve with the hot mackerel fillets.

Chicken Casserole with a Herb Crust

Serves 4

ingredients

- 4 whole chicken legs, dusted in flour
- 1 tbsp olive oil
- 1 tbsp butter
- 1 onion, chopped
- 3 cloves garlic, sliced
- 4 parsnips, peeled and cut into large chunks
- 150 ml/5 fl oz dry white wine
- 900 ml/1½ pint chicken stock
- 3 leeks, white parts only, sliced
- 75 g/3 oz prunes, halved (optional)
- 1 tbsp English mustard
- bouquet garni sachet (shop-bought)
- 100 g/4 oz fresh breadcrumbs
- 75 g/3 oz Caerphilly cheese, crumbled
- salt and pepper
- 50 g/2 oz mixed chopped tarragon and flat-leaf parsley

1 Preheat oven to 180°C/350°F/ Gas Mark 4.

2 Fry the chicken in a casserole with the olive oil and butter, until golden brown. Remove with a slotted spoon and keep warm. Add the onion, garlic and parsnips to the casserole and cook for 20 minutes or until the mixture is golden brown. Add the wine, stock, leeks, prunes (if using), English mustard and bouquet garni and season with salt and pepper.

3 Add the chicken to the casserole, place on the lid and cook in the oven for 1 hour. Meanwhile mix together the breadcrumbs, cheese and herbs.

4 Remove the casserole from the oven and increase the heat to 200°C/400°F/ Gas Mark 6.

5 Remove the lid of the casserole and sprinkle over the crust mixture. Return to the oven for 10 minutes, uncovered, until the crust starts to brown slightly.

6 Remove from the oven and serve.

Spicy Red Lentil Soup

Serves 4–6

ingredients

- 300 g/10½ oz red lentils, picked over and rinsed
- 2 litres/3½ pints vegetable stock or water
- 2 fresh green chillies, halved lengthways
- 1 tsp ground turmeric
- 2 tbsp sunflower oil
- 1½ onions, thinly sliced
- 2 large garlic cloves, crushed
- 2 tsp curry paste, mild, medium or hot, to taste
- salt and pepper
- Greek-style yogurt and chopped fresh coriander leaves, to garnish
- warmed naan breads, to serve

1 Put the lentils and stock into a large saucepan with a tight-fitting lid. Place over a high heat and slowly bring to the boil, skimming the surface as necessary. Add the chillies and turmeric, reduce the heat to very low, cover the pan and leave the lentils to simmer for 25–30 minutes, until they are very soft and mushy.

2 Meanwhile, heat the oil in a separate large saucepan over a medium heat. Add the onions and garlic and fry for 5–7 minutes, until the onions are tender but not brown. Add the curry paste and cook, stirring, for about a minute.

3 Tip the lentils and any remaining water into the pan with the onion mixture and stir together.

4 Put the mixture into a blender or food processor and whizz until blended. Return the mixture to the rinsed-out pan and add enough water to make a thin soup. Slowly bring to the boil. Reduce the heat, season to taste with salt and pepper and simmer for 2 minutes.

5 Ladle into warmed soup bowls, swirl in a spoonful of yogurt and sprinkle with coriander. Serve with the warmed naan breads.

Meatballs with Tomato Sauce

Serves 4

ingredients

- 3 tbsp olive oil
- 3 onions, finely chopped
- 3 garlic cloves, crushed
- 2 heaped tsp dried mixed herbs or oregano
- 450 g/1 lb fresh beef mince
- 1 large egg, beaten
- salt and pepper
- 2–3 tbsp freshly grated Parmesan or mozzarella cheese, to serve

for the Tomato Sauce

- 400 g/14 oz canned chopped tomatoes
- 1 tbsp tomato purée
- pinch of soft light brown sugar

1 Heat 2 tablespoons of the oil in a saucepan over a medium heat, add the onions and cook, stirring occasionally, for 5 minutes, or until transparent. Add the garlic and cook, stirring, for a further minute, then stir in the herbs. Transfer half the contents of the saucepan to a bowl and leave to cool slightly.

2 To make the tomato sauce, add all the sauce ingredients, with a very little salt and pepper to taste, to the saucepan, stir well and bring to a simmer. Simmer for 20–30 minutes, stirring once or twice, until you have a rich sauce. Meanwhile, stir the mince, egg and a very little salt and pepper to taste into the onion mixture in the bowl. Combine thoroughly and then form into 16 small balls.

3 When the tomato sauce is nearly ready, heat the remaining oil in a non-stick frying pan over a medium–high heat, add the meatballs and cook, turning a few times, for 5–6 minutes, or until golden on all sides and cooked through. Serve with the tomato sauce, with the cheese sprinkled over.

Chapter 7

Rice, Pasta, Pulses & Grains

Introduction

Carbohydrates such as rice, pasta, noodles and grains provide a good, inexpensive source of energy, especially the wholewheat/wholegrain varieties, and are a valuable source of dietary fibre. Combine them with protein-rich pulses, and you have a delicious meal that is nutritious, satisfying and healthy.

Buying and storing pasta

You can buy fresh and dried pasta in a wide variety of colours, shapes and sizes. It is usually made with durum wheat or wholewheat flour. Fresh pasta usually keeps for up to 2 days in the refrigerator, and dried pasta for up to 2 years in the storecupboard. Always use them by their 'best before' date.

Buying and storing noodles

In addition to Italian pasta, there are also different types of Asian noodles. Asian noodles should be stored in a cool, dry place, and used by their 'best before' date.

How to cook pasta

Cooking pasta is quick and easy. Simply bring a large saucepan of lightly salted water to the boil, add the pasta and bring back to the boil, stirring at intervals to prevent it sticking together. Reduce the heat slightly and cook until it is tender but still firm to the bite; this is known as 'al dente'. Remove from the heat, drain and serve tossed with olive oil or accompanied by your chosen sauce or recipe.

Cellophane noodles

These thread-like noodles are also known as Chinese vermicelli and are made from the starch of mung beans. Dried cellophane noodles should be soaked briefly before use, although this is not necessary in dishes that contain a lot of liquid, such as soups.

Egg noodles

These are very popular in Asian cooking, especially in Chinese stir-fries. Check the cooking instructions on the packet: some need to be soaked in hot water for about 4–5 minutes, while others can be put straight into the wok.

Ramen noodles

These noodles are deep-fried and sold packaged, often accompanied by ready-to-use broth mix.

Rice noodles

These delicate, fine, white noodles are simply soaked in hot water for 4–5 minutes. They are very good added to soups and stir-fries, and when deep-fried they become deliciously crunchy. They make a good gluten-free alternative to wheat-based pasta.

Soba noodles

These thin noodles are made from wheat flour and buck-wheat. They are popular in Japanese cooking.

Udon noodles

These thick Japanese noodles are like spaghetti, except that they can be square as well as round. They are made from cornflour or wheat flour, and are available both fresh and dried.

Thick egg noodle

Fine egg noodle

Medium egg noodle

Conchigliette
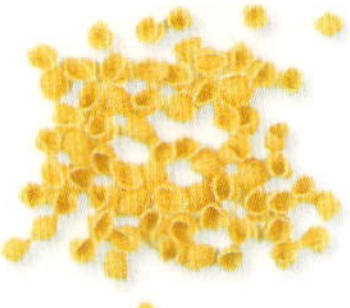

Cannelloni

Lumaconi

Penne

Fusilli

Rigatoni

Making your own fresh pasta

You can buy good-quality fresh pasta nowadays, but if you prefer to make your own, the process is simple. You might also like to invest in a pasta machine in order to create perfect pasta shapes of your choice.

Home-made pasta

Serves 6

280 g/10 oz plain flour, plus extra for dusting
1 tsp salt
2 eggs, lightly beaten
3 tbsp tomato purée (optional – use if you want a red, tomato-flavoured pasta)

Lightly dust a clean work surface with flour. Sift the flour and salt into a mound on the work surface.

Make a well in the centre of the flour, add the beaten eggs, and tomato purée if using, and mix to a stiff dough. If necessary, stir in a few tablespoons of water.

Knead the dough vigorously for about 8 minutes, then wrap it in clingfilm and leave it to rest for 30 minutes, or for up to 2 days if not required straight away. Roll out the dough to the desired thickness, then use a sharp knife to cut it into pieces of the required shape and size.

Alternatively, use a pasta machine to cut the dough. The pasta is now ready to be cooked.

PASTA NAMES

Anelli Very small rings
Cannelloni Large, hollow tubes
Conchiglie Ridged shells
Farfalle Bows
Fettucine Long, narrow ribbons
Fusilli Spirals
Lasagne Large, flat rectangular sheets
Linguine Long, narrow ribbons with flattened edges
Lumaconi Snail shapes
Macaroni Long or short narrow tubes, often curved
Penne Hollow quills
Ravioli Square cushions
Spaghetti Long, narrow strings
Tagliatelle Long ribbons, a little wider than fettucine
Vermicelli Long, very fine, hair-like strings

Buying and storing pulses

Beans, lentils and peas all fall into the category of pulses. You can buy these protein-rich foods dried, or ready to use in cans if you are short of time. When buying dried pulses, store them in airtight containers in a cool, dry place and use by the 'best before' date, or, if there is no date on the package, within 1 year for best results. Do not mix old and new beans because they will take different lengths of time to cook. Once cooked, refrigerate leftover beans and use within 3 days, or freeze them in an airtight container and use within 6 months.

Preparing and cooking pulses

Most pulses need soaking for at least 8 hours, then boiling rapidly for 10 minutes, followed by further cooking for at least 45 minutes or until they are tender. The main exceptions are soya beans, which need 12 hours to soak and 4 hours to cook, and chickpeas, which need 8 hours to soak and 2 hours to cook. Haricot beans need to soak overnight and need up to 1½ hours to cook. Lentils and split peas usually need no soaking and can be cooked in around 25–30 minutes.

Chickpeas

These round and cream-coloured peas have a nutty flavour, and are excellent in soups, salads, dips and stews, as well as pasta or grain dishes. Chickpeas can also be roasted for snacks, and are used in falafel, a Middle Eastern dish in which the mashed beans are formed into balls and deep-fried. Soak chickpeas for at least 8 hours before use. After soaking, drain and rinse them, then cover with fresh water and bring to the boil. Lower the heat and simmer for 2 hours until they are thoroughly cooked.

Soya beans

The most common colour of soya beans is pale yellow. These beans are good in soups and other savoury dishes, such as curries. Remember that they need to be soaked for at least 12 hours. After soaking, drain and rinse them, then cover with fresh water and bring to the boil. Boil them for the first hour of cooking, then simmer for another 3 hours until they are thoroughly cooked.

Aduki beans

These small red beans are good in soups and salads.

Long-grain rice

Pudding rice

Cannellini beans

Add these long creamy-white beans to soups and salads.

Split peas

These disc-shaped yellow or green peas are split along a natural seam. They can be cooked and puréed, and used in soups, bakes and other savoury dishes.

Lentils

These are small, disc-shaped pulses. Use red or orange lentils puréed and in soups and sauces; green or brown lentils are best in salads, sauces, stews and other savoury dishes.

Red kidney beans

These red, kidney-shaped beans can be added to soups, salads and stews. They must be boiled rapidly for a full 10 minutes, otherwise they can cause food poisoning. They should be precooked before being added to slow cookers, which do not reach a sufficiently high cooking temperature to eliminate the toxins.

Haricot beans

These white beans can be used in a wide variety of savoury dishes, including soups, salads, stews and casseroles. They are also the beans commonly used as baked beans with tomato sauce.

Butter beans

These white, kidney-shaped beans are excellent in soups and salads.

Flageolet beans

These small green beans are excellent in salads and as an accompaniment to meat dishes.

Borlotti beans

These oval beans vary in colour from pale pink to maroon-streaked skin. Use them in soups, dips and other savoury dishes.

Black-eyed beans

These small beige beans have a circular black 'eye'. Use them in sauces, stir-fries and soups.

Chickpeas

Soya beans

Split peas

Black-eyed beans

Buying and storing rice

There are many different varieties of rice available. Store rice in airtight containers for up to 3 years in a cool, dry place, or use by the 'best before' date if sooner.

Short-grain rice

This rice has short, fat grains that are more starchy and moist than medium- and long-grain rice. Varieties of short-grain rice include arborio and carnaroli rice, which are used in risottos.

Medium-grain rice

These grains are a little shorter than long-grain rice. They are more moist and therefore tend to clump together when cooked. Medium-grain rice is used in savoury dishes.

Long-grain rice

Both white and brown long-grain rice are excellent for savoury dishes because the grains stay separate when cooked.

Basmati rice

This Himalayan long-grain rice has a nutty flavour and is excellent in savoury dishes. It is available in white or brown and the grains stay dry and separate when cooked.

Jasmine rice

This tender rice has a delicate, fragrant, aromatic flavour. It is popular in both Vietnamese and Thai cooking.

Arborio rice

This starchy, short-grain creamy rice is ideal in risottos.

Carnaroli rice

This short-grain rice has often been called 'the king of Italian rice'. It has a high starch content and makes a lovely creamy risotto.

Pudding rice

This rice has a high starch content and becomes very sticky and creamy when cooked. It is popular in desserts, especially rice pudding.

Easy-cook rice

These rice grains are polished and partly boiled so that they are quick to cook. They stay fluffy and separate when cooked, but have less flavour than white or brown rice.

Red rice

This rice is grown in the Camargue region of France and in China. It has a pale red colour and a nutty flavour that is similar to brown rice.

Wild rice

This grain is in fact a marsh grass, not a rice. The grains are long and black, with a nutty flavour. It is often mixed with brown long-grain rice for reasons of economy.

How to cook long-grain and basmati rice

To cook rice for four people, put 300 g/10½ oz rice into a sieve and rinse under cold running water. Transfer to a large saucepan and pour in 600 ml/1 pint cold water. Add a large pinch of salt, then bring to the boil. Reduce the heat, stir briefly, then cover the pan and simmer gently until the rice is tender and all the liquid has been absorbed (but do not let the rice burn). As a rough guide, white rice will need 15 minutes, and brown rice will need 25–30 minutes. Remove from the heat and leave to stand for 5 minutes with the lid on. Fluff the grains with a fork and serve.

Other grains

It is always worthwhile experimenting with other types of grain. Try using them in salads, soups and stews, or piling them on to a platter and topping them with tasty cooked vegetables and sauces.

Barley

The polished variety of barley, known as pearl barley, is the kind most widely available. You can also buy pot barley, which is unpolished, from specialist shops and health-food shops. Barley is delicious and excellent in soups, casseroles and stews.

Millet

This protein-rich grain is a staple in Africa and Asia, and is boiled in a similar way to rice.

Couscous

This is not a true grain, but pieces of semolina. Steam it in accordance with the instructions on the packet. It makes an excellent bed of grains on which to pile meats and vegetables.

Polenta

This yellow grain is made from cornmeal and features widely in Italian cooking. Follow the cooking instructions on the packet because methods and cooking times vary. To serve cold, once the mixture pulls away from the pan, pour it into a baking tray, leave it to cool, then cut it into squares and serve. To serve hot, at the same stage stir in a generous knob of butter, then remove it from the heat and stir vigorously until the polenta stays firm.

Bulgar wheat

This comprises wheat kernels that have been precooked. It is a golden-brown grain with a nutty flavour. Since it has already been cooked, you simply need to soak it in plenty of cold water for 20–30 minutes, then strain it in a sieve, pressing out as much water as possible. This grain is excellent in salads, especially in the Middle Eastern dish known as 'tabbouleh'. It is also good in pilaus.

Quinoa Salad with Sun-dried Tomatoes, Olives & Feta

Serves 4

ingredients

for the salad

- 235 g/8½ oz quinoa
- 500 ml/18 fl oz water
- 10 sun-dried tomatoes (in oil, drained)
- 50 g/1¾ oz feta cheese, crumbled
- 2 spring onions, white parts, chopped
- 20 g/¾ oz mixed fresh herbs (basil, parsley, coriander), chopped
- 50 g/1¾ oz stoned black olives, chopped

for the dressing

- 5 tbsp roasted tomato oil
- 3 tbsp fresh lemon juice
- 1 garlic clove, crushed
- salt and freshly ground black pepper

1 Spread the quinoa on a dish and pick out any pieces of grit. Rinse the grains thoroughly in a fine-mesh sieve and drain.

2 In a medium saucepan, bring the water to the boil over a high heat, stir in the quinoa and return to the boil. Lower the heat, cover, and simmer for about 15 minutes or until all the liquid has been absorbed. Remove from the heat, fluff up the quinoa with a fork and transfer to a bowl. Leave to cool a little.

3 Add the remaining ingredients to the bowl and mix with the quinoa.

4 Whisk the dressing ingredients together, pour over the quinoa, toss and serve.

Chicken & Butternut Casserole

Serves 4–6

ingredients

- 2 tbsp olive oil
- 4 skinless, boneless chicken thighs, about 100 g/3½ oz each, cut into bite-sized pieces
- 1 large onion, sliced
- 2 leeks, chopped
- 2 garlic cloves, chopped
- 1 butternut squash, peeled, deseeded and cut into cubes
- 2 carrots, diced
- 400 g/14 oz canned chopped tomatoes and herbs
- 400 g/14 oz canned mixed beans, drained and rinsed
- 100 ml/3½ fl oz vegetable or chicken stock, plus extra if needed
- salt and pepper

1 Preheat the oven to 160°C/325°F/ Gas Mark 3.

2 Heat half the oil in a large, flameproof casserole over a high heat, add the chicken and cook, turning frequently, for 2–3 minutes until browned all over. Reduce the heat to medium, remove the chicken with a slotted spoon and set aside.

3 Add the remaining oil to the casserole, add the onion and leeks and cook, stirring occasionally, for 10 minutes, or until soft. Add the garlic, squash and carrots and cook, stirring, for 2 minutes. Add the tomatoes and their juice, beans, the chicken pieces and stock, stir well and bring to a simmer.

4 Cover, transfer to the preheated oven and cook for 1–1¼ hours, stirring once or twice – if the casserole looks too dry, add a little extra stock. Season with a very little salt and pepper to taste before serving.

Spiced Lentils with Spinach

Serves 4–6

ingredients

- 2 tbsp olive oil
- 1 large onion, finely chopped
- 1 large garlic clove, crushed
- ½ tbsp ground cumin
- ½ tsp ground ginger
- 250 g/9 oz Puy lentils
- about 600 ml/1 pint vegetable stock
- 100 g/3½ oz baby spinach leaves
- 2 tbsp fresh mint leaves
- 1 tbsp fresh coriander leaves
- 1 tbsp fresh flat-leaf parsley
- lemon juice
- salt and pepper
- strips of lemon rind, to garnish

1 Heat the oil in a large frying pan over a medium heat. Add the onion and cook, stirring occasionally, for about 6 minutes. Stir in the garlic, cumin and ginger and cook, stirring occasionally, until the onion starts to brown.

2 Stir in the lentils. Pour in enough stock to cover the lentils by 2.5 cm/1 inch and bring to the boil. Lower the heat and simmer for 20–30 minutes until the lentils are tender.

3 Meanwhile, rinse the spinach leaves in several changes of cold water and shake dry. Finely chop the mint, coriander leaves and parsley.

4 If there isn't any stock left in the pan, add a little extra. Add the spinach and stir through until it just wilts. Stir in the mint, coriander and parsley. Adjust the seasoning, adding lemon juice and salt and pepper. Transfer to a serving bowl and serve, garnished with lemon rind.

Vegetable Stew with Green Lentils

Serves 6

ingredients

- 1 tbsp olive oil
- 1 onion, finely chopped
- 1 garlic clove, finely chopped
- 1 carrot, halved and thinly sliced
- 450 g/1 lb young green cabbage, cored, quartered and thinly sliced
- 400 g/14 oz canned chopped tomatoes
- ½ tsp dried thyme
- 2 bay leaves
- 1.5 litres/2¾ pints chicken or vegetable stock
- 200 g/7 oz Puy lentils
- 450 ml/16 fl oz water
- salt and pepper
- chopped fresh flat-leaf parsley, to garnish

1 Heat the oil in a large saucepan over a medium heat, add the onion, garlic and carrot and cook for 3–4 minutes, stirring frequently, until the onion starts to soften. Add the cabbage and cook for a further 2 minutes.

2 Add the tomatoes, thyme and 1 bay leaf, then pour in the stock. Bring to the boil, reduce the heat to low and cook gently, partially covered, for about 45 minutes until the vegetables are tender.

3 Meanwhile, put the lentils in another saucepan with the remaining bay leaf and the water. Bring just to the boil, reduce the heat and simmer for about 25 minutes until tender. Drain off any remaining water, and set aside.

4 Allow the stew to cool, then transfer to a food processor or blender and process until smooth, working in batches, if necessary. (If using a food processor, strain off the cooking liquid and reserve. Purée the solids with enough cooking liquid to moisten them, then combine with the remaining liquid.)

5 Return the stew to the saucepan and add the cooked lentils. Taste and adjust the seasoning, and cook for about 10 minutes to heat through. Ladle into warmed bowls and garnish with parsley.

Chinese Fried Rice

Serves 4

ingredients

- 700 ml/1¼ pints water
- ½ tsp salt
- 300 g/10½ oz long-grain rice
- 2 eggs
- 4 tsp cold water
- 3 tbsp sunflower oil
- 4 spring onions, sliced diagonally
- 1 red, green or yellow pepper, cored, deseeded and thinly sliced
- 3–4 lean bacon rashers, rinded and cut into strips
- 200 g/7 oz fresh beansprouts
- 125 g/4½ oz frozen peas, thawed
- 2 tbsp soy sauce (optional)
- salt and pepper

1 Pour the water into the wok with the salt and bring to the boil. Rinse the rice in a sieve under cold running water until the water runs clear, drain thoroughly and add to the boiling water. Stir well, then cover the wok tightly with the lid and simmer gently for 12–13 minutes. (Do not remove the lid during cooking or the steam will escape and the rice will not be cooked.)

2 Remove the lid, give the rice a good stir and spread out on a large plate or baking tray to cool and dry.

3 Meanwhile, beat each egg separately with salt and pepper and 2 teaspoons of cold water. Heat 1 tablespoon of oil in a preheated wok, pour in the first egg, swirl it around and leave to cook undisturbed until set. Transfer to a chopping board and cook the second egg. Cut the omelettes into thin slices.

4 Add the remaining oil to the wok and, when really hot, add the spring onions and sliced pepper and stir-fry for 1–2 minutes. Add the bacon and continue to stir-fry for a further 2 minutes. Add the beansprouts and peas and toss together thoroughly. Stir in the soy sauce, if using.

5 Add the rice, and salt and pepper to taste, and stir-fry for 1 minute, then add the strips of omelette and continue to stir-fry for 2 minutes, or until the rice is piping hot. Serve immediately.

Parmesan Risotto with Mushrooms

Serves 6

ingredients

- 2 tbsp olive oil or vegetable oil
- 225 g/8 oz risotto rice
- 2 garlic cloves, crushed
- 1 onion, chopped
- 2 celery sticks, chopped
- 1 red or green pepper, deseeded and chopped
- 225 g/8 oz mushrooms, thinly sliced
- 1 tbsp chopped fresh oregano or 1 tsp dried oregano
- 1 litre/1¾ pints vegetable stock
- 55 g /2 oz sun-dried tomatoes in olive oil, drained and chopped (optional)
- 55 g/2 oz finely grated Parmesan cheese
- salt and pepper
- fresh flat-leaf parsley sprigs or bay leaves, to garnish

1 Heat the oil in a deep saucepan. Add the rice and cook over a low heat, stirring constantly, for 2–3 minutes, until the grains are thoroughly coated in oil and translucent.

2 Add the garlic, onion, celery and pepper and cook, stirring frequently, for 5 minutes. Add the mushrooms and cook for 3–4 minutes. Stir in the oregano.

3 Gradually add the hot stock, a ladle at a time. Stir constantly and add more liquid as the rice absorbs each addition. Increase the heat to medium so that the liquid bubbles. Cook for 20 minutes, or until all the liquid is absorbed and the rice is creamy. Add the sun-dried tomatoes, if using, 5 minutes before the end of the cooking time and season to taste with salt and pepper.

4 Remove the risotto from the heat and stir in half the Parmesan until it melts. Transfer the risotto to warmed bowls. Top with the remaining cheese, garnish with flat-leaf parsley and serve immediately.

Wok-fried Soba Noodles

Serves 4

ingredients

- 300 g/10½ oz dry thin soba (buckwheat) noodles
- 3 tbsp sunflower or groundnut oil
- 1 tsp ground ginger
- 1 tbsp Chinese rice wine vinegar
- 1½ tsp sesame oil
- 1 tsp light soy sauce
- 100 g/3½ oz beansprouts
- 85 g/3 oz mangetout, thinly sliced
- 4 spring onions, chopped
- 2 garlic cloves, crushed
- 1 red pepper, halved, deseeded and very thinly sliced
- ½ head cabbage, cored and thinly shredded
- small handful fresh coriander leaves
- pepper
- toasted sesame seeds, to garnish

1 Bring a saucepan of water to the boil, add the noodles and boil for 3 minutes, or according to the packet instructions. Drain well, then add to a bowl of cold water and use your hand to swish around to remove all the starch. Drain again, then put into another bowl of cold water and set aside.

2 Put 2 tablespoons of the sunflower oil into a large bowl and stir in the ginger. Beat in the vinegar, sesame oil and soy sauce. Add pepper to taste.

3 Drain the noodles very well, shaking off any excess water, then add to the bowl with the oil. Add the beansprouts, mangetout, spring onions, garlic, red pepper and cabbage and use your hands to mix together. Season to taste. If you're not cooking immediately, cover the bowl with clingfilm and chill until 10 minutes before you want to cook.

4 When you are ready to cook, heat a wok over a high heat until a splash of water 'dances' on the surface. Add the remaining oil to the wok and heat until it shimmers.

5 Tip in the noodles and vegetables and stir-fry for 3–5 minutes until all the vegetables are hot and just tender. Add the coriander leaves and stir them through. Taste and adjust the seasoning.

6 Transfer the noodles and vegetables to serving bowls and sprinkle with the sesame seeds.

Vegetable Couscous

Serves 4

ingredients

- 2 tbsp vegetable oil
- 1 large onion
- 1 carrot, chopped
- 1 turnip, chopped
- 600 ml/1 pint vegetable stock
- 175 g/6 oz couscous
- 2 tomatoes
- 1 red pepper
- 2 courgettes
- 125 g/4½ oz French beans
- grated rind of 1 lemon
- pinch of turmeric (optional)
- 1 tbsp finely chopped fresh coriander
- salt and pepper

1 Heat the oil in a large saucepan. Chop the onion, then add to the pan with the carrot and turnip and fry for 3–4 minutes. Add the stock, bring to the boil, cover and leave to simmer for 20 minutes.

2 Meanwhile, place the couscous in a bowl and moisten with a little boiling water, stirring, until the grains have swollen and separated.

3 Peel and quarter the tomatoes, deseed and chop the red pepper then chop the courgettes and French beans.

4 Add the tomatoes, red pepper, courgettes and French beans to the pan and stir. Stir the lemon rind into the couscous, add the turmeric if using, and mix thoroughly. Place the couscous in a steamer and position it over the saucepan of vegetables. Simmer the vegetables so that the couscous steams for 8–10 minutes.

5 Pile the couscous on to warmed serving plates. Ladle the vegetables and some of the liquid over the top. Scatter over the finely chopped coriander and serve immediately.

Tabbouleh

Serves 4

ingredients

- 175 g/6 oz bulgar wheat
- 3 tbsp extra virgin olive oil
- 4 tbsp lemon juice
- 4 spring onions
- 1 green pepper, deseeded and sliced
- 4 tomatoes, chopped
- 2 tbsp chopped fresh parsley
- 2 tbsp chopped fresh mint
- 8 black olives, stoned
- salt and pepper

1 Place the bulgar wheat in a large bowl and add enough cold water to cover. Leave to stand for 30 minutes, or until the wheat has doubled in size. Drain well and press out as much liquid as possible. Spread out the wheat on kitchen paper to dry.

2 Place the wheat in a serving bowl. Mix the olive oil and lemon juice together in a jug and season to taste with salt and pepper. Pour the lemon mixture over the wheat and leave to marinate for 1 hour.

3 Using a sharp knife, finely chop the spring onions, then add to the bowl with the green pepper, tomatoes, parsley and mint and toss lightly to mix. Top the salad with the olives and serve.

Spaghetti Bolognese

Serves 4

ingredients

- 3 tbsp olive oil
- 2 garlic cloves, crushed
- 1 large onion, finely chopped
- 1 carrot, diced
- 225 g/8 oz fresh lean beef or chicken mince
- 85 g/3 oz chicken livers, finely chopped
- 100 g/3½ oz lean Parma ham, diced
- 150 ml/5 fl oz Marsala wine
- 280 g/10 oz canned chopped plum tomatoes
- 1 tbsp chopped fresh basil leaves
- 2 tbsp tomato purée
- 450 g/1 lb dried spaghetti
- salt and pepper
- shavings of fresh Parmesan cheese, to garnish

1 Heat 2 tablespoons of the oil in a large saucepan. Add the garlic, onion and carrot and fry for 6 minutes.

2 Add the mince, chicken livers and Parma ham to the saucepan and cook over a medium heat for 12 minutes, or until well browned.

3 Stir in the Marsala, tomatoes, basil and tomato purée and cook for 4 minutes. Season to taste with salt and pepper. Cover and leave to simmer for 30 minutes.

4 Remove the lid from the saucepan, stir and leave to simmer for a further 15 minutes.

5 Meanwhile, bring a large saucepan of lightly salted water to the boil. Add the spaghetti and the remaining oil, return to the boil and cook for 12 minutes, or until tender, but still firm to the bite. Drain and transfer to a serving dish. Pour the sauce over the pasta, scatter over some fresh Parmesan shavings and serve hot.

Golden Polenta

Serves 4

ingredients

- 1.5 litres/2¾ pints water
- 1½ tsp salt
- 300 g/10½ oz polenta or cornmeal flour
- vegetable oil, for frying and oiling
- 2 beaten eggs (optional)
- 125 g/4½ oz fresh fine white breadcrumbs (optional)

for the tomato sauce

- 2 tbsp olive oil
- 1 small onion, chopped
- 1 garlic clove, chopped
- 400 g/14 oz canned chopped tomatoes
- 2 tbsp chopped fresh parsley
- 1 tsp dried oregano
- 2 bay leaves
- 2 tbsp tomato purée
- 1 tsp sugar
- salt and pepper

1 Bring the water and salt to the boil in a large saucepan and gradually sprinkle in the polenta, stirring constantly to prevent lumps forming. Simmer gently, stirring frequently, for 30 minutes, or until the polenta becomes very thick and begins to draw away from the sides of the pan.

2 Thoroughly oil a 28 x 18-cm/11 x 7-inch shallow tin, then spoon in the polenta. Spread out evenly, using a wet wooden spoon or spatula. Allow to cool, then leave to stand for 2 hours at room temperature, if possible.

3 Cut the polenta into 30–36 squares. Heat the oil in a frying pan. Add the pieces and fry until golden brown all over, turning several times, for about 5 minutes. Alternatively, dip each piece of polenta in beaten egg and coat in breadcrumbs before frying in the hot oil. Keep warm.

4 For the tomato sauce, heat the oil in a pan over a medium heat. Add the onion and fry for 2 minutes until translucent. Add the garlic and fry for 1 minute. Stir in the chopped tomatoes, herbs, tomato purée and sugar, and salt and pepper to taste. Bring to the boil, then simmer, uncovered, for 20 minutes, or until the sauce has reduced by half. Discard the bay leaves.

5 Serve the polenta pieces with the hot tomato sauce.

Penne with Mixed Beans

Serves 4

ingredients

- 1 tbsp olive oil
- 1 onion, chopped
- 1 garlic clove, finely chopped
- 1 carrot, finely chopped
- 1 celery stick, finely chopped
- 425 g/15 oz canned mixed beans, drained and rinsed
- 225 ml/8 fl oz passata
- 1 tbsp chopped fresh chervil, plus extra leaves to garnish
- 350 g/12 oz dried penne
- salt and pepper

1 Heat the oil in a large heavy-based frying pan. Add the onion, garlic, carrot and celery and cook over a low heat, stirring occasionally, for 5 minutes, or until the onion has softened.

2 Add the mixed beans, passata and chopped chervil to the frying pan and season the mixture to taste with salt and pepper. Cover and simmer gently for 15 minutes.

3 Meanwhile, bring a large heavy-based saucepan of lightly salted water to the boil. Add the pasta, return to the boil and cook for 8–10 minutes, or until tender but still firm to the bite. Drain the pasta and transfer to a warmed serving dish. Add the mixed bean sauce, toss well and serve immediately, garnished with extra chervil.

Vegetable Lasagne

Serves 4

ingredients

- 1 aubergine, sliced
- 3 tbsp olive oil
- 2 garlic cloves, crushed
- 1 red onion, halved and sliced
- 3 mixed peppers, deseeded and diced
- 225 g/8 oz mixed mushrooms, sliced
- 2 celery sticks, sliced
- 1 courgette, diced
- ½ tsp chilli powder
- ½ tsp ground cumin
- 2 tomatoes, chopped
- 300 ml/10 fl oz passata
- 2 tbsp chopped fresh basil
- 8 no pre-cook lasagne verde sheets
- salt and pepper

for the cheese sauce

- 2 tbsp butter or margarine
- 1 tbsp flour
- 150 ml/5 fl oz vegetable stock
- 300 ml/10 fl oz milk
- 75 g/2¾ oz Cheddar cheese, grated
- 1 tsp Dijon mustard
- 1 tbsp chopped fresh basil
- 1 egg, beaten

1 Place the aubergine slices in a colander, sprinkle with salt and leave for 20 minutes. Rinse under cold water, drain and reserve.

2 Preheat the oven to 180°C/ 350°F/ Gas Mark 4. Heat the oil in a saucepan. Add the garlic and onion and sauté for 1–2 minutes. Add the peppers, mushrooms, celery and courgette and cook, stirring constantly, for 3–4 minutes.

3 Stir in the chilli powder and cumin and cook for 1 minute. Mix in the tomatoes, passata and basil and season to taste with salt and pepper.

4 For the sauce, melt the butter in a saucepan. Stir in the flour and cook for 1 minute. Remove from the heat, gradually stir in the stock and milk, return to the heat, then add half the cheese and all the mustard. Boil, stirring, until thickened. Stir in the basil. Remove from the heat and stir in the egg.

5 Place half the lasagne in an ovenproof dish. Top with half the vegetables, half the tomato sauce, then half the aubergines. Repeat and then spoon the cheese sauce on top. Sprinkle with the remaining cheese and bake for 40 minutes, or until golden and bubbling.

Rice Pudding

Serves 4–6

ingredients

- 1 tbsp melted butter
- 115 g/4 oz pudding rice
- 55 g/2 oz caster sugar
- 850 ml/1½ pints full-cream milk
- ½ tsp vanilla extract
- 40 g/1½ oz unsalted butter
- whole nutmeg, for grating
- cream, jam, fruit purée, stewed fruit or ice cream, to serve (optional)

1 Preheat the oven to 300ºC/150ºF/Gas Mark 2. Grease a 1.2-litre/2-pint baking dish (a gratin dish is good) with the melted butter. Place the rice in the dish and sprinkle with the sugar.

2 Heat the milk in a saucepan until almost boiling, then pour over the rice. Add the vanilla extract and stir well to dissolve the sugar.

3 Cut the butter into small pieces and scatter over the surface of the pudding.

4 Grate the whole nutmeg over the top, using as much as you like to give a good covering.

5 Place the dish on a baking tray and bake in the centre of the oven for 1½–2 hours until the pudding is well browned on the top. You can stir it after the first half hour to disperse the rice.

6 Serve hot and, if desired, with some cream, jam, fresh fruit purée, stewed fruit or ice cream. It is also good cold with fresh fruit or honey.

Chapter 8
Fruit

Introduction

Fruit is a healthy choice because it is full of vitamins and very low in fat. It is also very versatile – delicious in savoury dishes and chutneys, and delightful in a wide range of desserts and cakes.

Orchard fruits

Orchard fruits, such as apples, pears and peaches, are delicious and very versatile. They can be eaten raw on their own and in fruit salads, or in cooked dishes such as fruit tarts and pies.

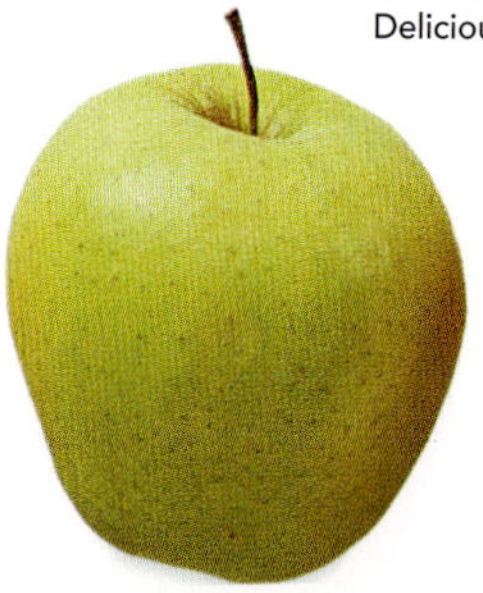
Golden Delicious apple

Pear

Nectarine

Apricot

Plum

Buying and storing fruit

Some fruits, such as apples and pears, are available fresh all year round, whereas others, such as cherries, have a limited season. Always buy your fruit as fresh as possible from a reputable supplier. Avoid any fruits that are bruised or damaged, or that are showing signs of mould. Choose fruits that are plump and free from blemishes: they should feel firm to the touch and not too soft. Many fruits, such as apples, pears and oranges, can be stored for around a week at room temperature, or even longer in the refrigerator. Other fruits, such as blueberries, have a short shelf life and should be kept in the refrigerator and eaten by the 'best before' date, but usually within a couple of days. You can also freeze a wide range of fruits, such as bananas and mangoes (peel and slice them first) – even grapes are excellent frozen whole and used instead of ice cubes in drinks.

Apples

There are countless different varieties of apple in existence, in a range of colours from pale yellow to deep red. Some have a sweet flavour, while others are more acidic. Some apples, such as Golden Delicious and Braeburn, are excellent eaten raw as a snack or in salads. They also pair very well with cheese. Other varieties of apple are excellent for cooking, such as Bramley's Seedling, Cox's Orange Pippin and Granny Smith. They make excellent desserts, and are delicious stuffed and baked, or made into pie fillings. They can also be used in some savoury dishes, such as curries, and make very good sauces and purées.

Pears

Like apples, there are thousands of different types of pear, although we see only a selection of these in our shops. Pears bruise easily, so buy them while they are still hard and let them ripen at home. Many varieties, such as Comice or Conference pears, are delicious eaten as a snack, and they are excellent in salads and with cheese. Some types, such as Williams, are also very good for cooking. They can be stuffed and baked like apples, and are excellent peeled and poached in red wine.

Peaches

These fruits are similar to nectarines except that they have downy skin instead of smooth skin. Store and use them in the same way as nectarines.

Nectarines

These fruits are usually available in summer and autumn. Their smooth skins should be yellow with patches of red, with no green areas and no bruises. They will keep in the refrigerator for 5–6 days. You can eat nectarines raw as a snack or sliced in desserts. You can also poach or bake them. If they need further ripening, leave them out at room temperature for 1–2 days. If they do not soften during this time, they will not be suitable for eating raw, so cook them instead.

Orange

Lime

Lemon

Cherries

There are two main varieties of cherry: the larger sweet cherries, which are delicious eaten raw, and the smaller sour cherries, which are too tart to eat raw but can be cooked and made into excellent desserts and jams. Cherries are usually available during late spring and in the early summer, and should be stored in the refrigerator before use.

Apricots

These fruits are usually yellow or orange and have a large central stone. Some varieties are sweet enough to eat raw as a snack, while others need to be cooked. Cooked apricots make excellent desserts and jams, and can also be used in some savoury dishes. Dried apricots are also very popular. The deep orange varieties have been treated with sulphur dioxide in order to preserve their colour. Untreated dried apricots are dark brown, so some people may find them less attractive, but they have just as much, if not more, flavour and goodness.

Plums

Hundreds of varieties of plum exist, and all tend to have a large, central stone. Their colour varies from yellow or green to red or purple, and they can grow to up to 7.5 cm/3 inches in diameter. They are in season through the summer months until early autumn, and will keep at room temperature for several days, or a little longer if stored in the refrigerator. Ripe plums are deliciously sweet and juicy and can be eaten raw as a snack or in a salad. They can also be cooked. Plum crumble is a popular baked dessert, and consists of a dish of plums covered with a crunchy topping. Plums also make excellent jam.

Citrus fruits

The fragrance and juicy tang of a ripe citrus fruit is irresistible, and wonderful in a whole host of chilled and cooked desserts. These fruits are also rich sources of vitamin C.

Oranges

These citrus fruits are available all through the year and come in many different varieties, such as the sweet oranges that can be eaten as a snack and sliced in salads and desserts. A variation of these is the blood orange, which is just as sweet and juicy, but which has redder flesh. Some oranges are seedless, while others have many seeds. You can also buy bitter oranges, such as Seville oranges: they are too sour to eat but they make excellent marmalade. Oranges will keep at room temperature for up to a week, but are better stored in the refrigerator to preserve their vitamin C content. They will keep in the refrigerator for up to 2 weeks. Oranges make excellent garnishes or decorations, and are popular in a wide range of savoury and sweet dishes.

Grapefruits

Grapefruits can be seeded or seedless, and vary in colour from yellow to pink to red. They are available all year round, and are usually eaten raw. However, they can also be sprinkled with brown sugar and lightly grilled.

Lemons

These oval, yellow fruits have a tart flavour but a wide range of uses. They are available all year round and will keep at room temperature for around a week, and in the refrigerator for up to 3 weeks (but less time if cut). Lemons make an excellent flavouring and a good garnish or decoration for savoury and sweet dishes. You can use the juice, grated zest or the flesh.

Limes

These green citrus fruits are smaller than lemons and have a milder flavour, but can replace lemons in many savoury and sweet dishes. They will keep whole in the refrigerator for up to 10 days.

Mandarin orange family

These small, round, orange fruits include mandarins, clementines, satsumas and tangerines. They are generally available in the winter months. Mandarins and tangerines have thick skins that are easy to peel. Clementines have thinner skins, and no seeds. Satsumas are also easy to peel, and are seedless. They are delicious eaten raw as a snack and in salads, and they all pair well with cream cheese.

Soft fruits

Juicy berries are delicious in desserts such as sorbets, ice creams, fools, puddings, fruit crumbles and pies, but they can also be used in a variety of savoury dishes, such as chicken with blackberries.

Strawberries

These juicy red berries are available all year round, but peak season for strawberries is spring and early summer. Fresh strawberries will keep for up to 3 days in the refrigerator, and are delicious eaten raw, perhaps with whipped cream or marinated in balsamic vinegar. They also make excellent jams and syrups, and are very popular in a range of desserts. Dried strawberries have a deliciously tangy flavour and are wonderful in muesli.

Gooseberries

These large berries are usually green, but can also come in white and yellow. They are available in the summer months and are usually cooked before eating. Gooseberries make excellent jams and fillings for sweet pies. They will keep in the refrigerator for up to 4 days.

Blackberries

Blackberries are also known as 'brambles', and they grow wild on bushes. They are also cultivated. Blackberries come into season in the summer months. Use them straight away, or refrigerate them for up to 2 days. You can eat blackberries raw or cooked in sweet pies and desserts. They are often paired with apples. Blackberries also make good jam.

Raspberries

The most common colour of the raspberry is red. These fruits are very popular with dieters, since they are very low in calories and fat, and yet have a delicious flavour. They will keep in the refrigerator for up to 3 days, and are delicious raw in a wide range of desserts. They can also be cooked, and make good coulis and fillings for puddings, as well as excellent jam.

Blueberries

These small, round, dark-blue berries are sweet and can be eaten raw or cooked in sweet pies and other desserts. Like most berries, they make excellent jam. They are available during the summer and early autumn, and will keep in the refrigerator for 4–5 days.

Cranberries

These small, shiny, red berries are available in late autumn and will keep in the refrigerator for 6–8 weeks and in the freezer for around 9 months. They have a tart flavour and therefore are usually mixed with sweeter fruits, such as apple – cranberry and apple juice is a very popular combination. Cranberries can also be cooked and make an excellent sauce. They can be used in sweet pies and other cooked desserts.

Currants

Fresh currants are tiny berries that can be white, red or black. White- and redcurrants can be eaten raw and make excellent decorations for sweet dishes. Blackcurrants are quite tart and are better cooked and made into syrup or jam. Fresh currants are available in summer and will keep in the refrigerator for 3–4 days. They should not be confused with dried currants, which are like dark raisins.

Strawberries

Raspberries

Grapes

Lychees

Star fruit

Fig

Pineapple

Other fruits

Other well-known fruits, such as bananas, grapes and melons, are widely available. They are very popular as snacks in their own right, and are also used in a wide range of desserts and cakes.

Grapes

These small oval fruits range in colour from yellowish-green to purplish-black, and can be seeded or seedless. The eating varieties are sweet and juicy, and are delicious eaten raw as a snack or added to salads. They also make excellent decorations and are wonderful paired with cheese. Other varieties of grapes are made into grape juice, wine, jam or raisins.

Bananas

These long fruits start off green, but turn yellow when they have ripened. Contrary to popular opinion, very fresh bananas can be stored in the refrigerator: the skins will turn brown but the flesh will be unaffected. If you prefer your bananas to stay yellow, store them at room temperature for a day or two. Bananas are delicious peeled and eaten as they are or added to desserts and cakes. They can also be lightly grilled or baked.

Rhubarb

Rhubarb has edible red stalks, and comes into season in spring. The stalks will keep in the refrigerator for up to 3 days. Rhubarb has a tart flavour but, once cooked and sweetened, will make a good jam, sweet pie filling or other dessert. It also pairs well with ginger.

Melons

These fruits come in many sizes and colours. The popular edible types include galia, charentais, watermelon and cantaloupe. They are delicious eaten fresh on their own, or as a starter, perhaps combined with figs and ham, or alternatively with port wine. They are also good in fruit salads.

Pineapples

These golden oval fruits have a tough, prickly exterior and spearlike leaves. Large pineapples are the most common, but baby pineapples are also available. The flesh is juicy with a tangy flavour, and is delicious sliced and eaten on its own or added to fruit salads or other desserts. It is also good when cooked. It can be lightly grilled, or baked in a cake. Fresh pineapple will keep in the refrigerator for up to 3 days. You can also buy canned pineapple chunks or rings.

Exotic fruits

There is a wonderful range of exotic fruits available nowadays, from physalis to dragon fruit. Here is just a small selection of some of the popular ones you may find in your local supermarket – there are many more.

Mangoes

These large oval fruits vary in colour from yellow to red. Eat them raw, perhaps in a fruit salad, or frozen in a sorbet.

Star fruit

These star-shaped yellow fruits make beautiful decorations when cut across in slices.

Dates

These oval fruits are available fresh or dried. Chopped dried dates are delicious in muesli and desserts.

Kiwi fruit

These oval fruits have brown 'hairy' skin and soft green flesh. Eat the flesh with a teaspoon. Alternatively, peel and slice them and add them to fruit salads and other desserts.

Lychees

These small fruits are available fresh or canned. They have a rough, pink, inedible skin, but the flesh inside is juicy and fragrant. You can eat them raw or lightly poached.

Figs

These soft, pear-shaped fruits are delicious eaten raw or poached. Dried figs are also good.

Passion fruit

Cut these brown-skinned, wrinkly fruits in half and eat the pulp by scooping it out with a teaspoon.

Pawpaws

These large, pear-shaped fruits are cooked when green and unripe, or eaten raw when they are ripe and golden-yellow. Pawpaws are good in salads.

Couscous with Nuts & Dried Fruit

Serves 6

ingredients

- 250 g/9 oz couscous
- 600 ml/1 pint water
- 70 g/2½ oz ready-to-eat dried apricots
- 40 g/1½ oz blanched almonds
- 600 ml/1 pint vegetable stock, chicken stock or water
- 1 tsp extra virgin olive oil
- 2 tbsp chopped fresh coriander
- salt and pepper

1 Put the couscous into a bowl and pour in the water. Leave to soak, stirring frequently with a fork to separate the grains, for 30 minutes, until almost all the liquid has been absorbed.

2 Meanwhile, using a sharp knife, cut the apricots into thin strips and set aside. Heat a heavy-based frying pan, add the almonds and cook over a low heat, shaking the pan frequently, for 1–2 minutes, until lightly toasted. Remove the pan from the heat.

3 Pour the stock into a saucepan and bring to the boil. Line a steamer with muslin. Stir the apricots into the soaked couscous, season with salt and pepper and spoon into the steamer. Cover with a tight-fitting lid, set the steamer over the pan and steam for 20 minutes.

4 Transfer the couscous mixture to a warmed serving dish and stir in the olive oil, coriander and almonds. Serve immediately.

Smoked Chicken & Cranberry Salad

Serves 4

ingredients

- 1 smoked chicken, weighing 1.3 kg/3 lb
- 115 g/4 oz dried cranberries
- 2 tbsp apple juice or water
- 200 g/7 oz sugar snap peas
- 2 ripe avocados
- juice of ½ lemon
- 4 lettuce hearts
- 1 bunch of watercress, trimmed
- 55 g/2 oz rocket
- 55 g/2 oz walnuts, chopped, to garnish (optional)

for the dressing

- 2 tbsp olive oil
- 1 tbsp walnut oil
- 2 tbsp lemon juice
- 1 tbsp chopped fresh mixed herbs, such as parsley and lemon thyme
- salt and pepper

1 Carve the chicken carefully, slicing the white meat. Divide the legs into thighs and drumsticks and trim the wings. Cover with clingfilm and refrigerate.

2 Put the cranberries in a bowl. Stir in the apple juice, cover with clingfilm and leave to soak for 30 minutes.

3 Meanwhile, blanch the sugar snap peas, refresh under cold running water and drain.

4 Peel, stone and slice the avocados, then toss in the lemon juice to prevent browning.

5 Separate the lettuce hearts and arrange on a large serving platter with the avocados, sugar snap peas, watercress, rocket and chicken.

6 Put all the dressing ingredients, with salt and pepper to taste, in a screw-top jar, screw on the lid and shake until well blended.

7 Drain the cranberries and mix them with the dressing, then pour over the salad.

8 Serve immediately, scattered with walnuts if you are using them.

Pear & Roquefort Open Sandwiches

Serves 4–6

ingredients

- 4 slices walnut bread or pain Poilâne, about 1 cm/½ inch thick
- 2 ripe pears, such as Conference, peeled, halved, cored and thinly sliced lengthways
- 100 g/3½ oz Roquefort cheese, very thinly sliced

1 Preheat the grill to a medium–high setting. Toast the bread slices on the rack in the grill pan until crisp, but not brown, on both sides. Do not turn off the grill.

2 Divide the pear slices equally between the breads. Lay the cheese slices on top.

3 Return the breads to the grill until the cheese melts and bubbles. Serve.

Warm Salmon & Mango Salad

Serves 4

ingredients

- 115 g/4 oz sungold or red cherry tomatoes
- 85 g/3 oz salmon fillets, skinned and cut into small cubes
- 1 large ripe mango (about 150 g/5½ oz peeled fruit), peeled and cut into small chunks
- 2 tbsp orange juice
- 1 tbsp soy sauce
- 115 g/4 oz assorted salad leaves
- ½ cucumber, trimmed and sliced into batons
- 6 spring onions, trimmed and chopped

for the dressing

- 4 tbsp low fat natural yogurt
- 1 tsp soy sauce
- 1 tbsp finely grated orange rind

1 Soak 4 wooden skewers in a bowl of cold water for 30 minutes to prevent them burning during cooking. Cut half the tomatoes in half and set aside.

2 Thread the salmon with the whole tomatoes and half the mango chunks onto 4 kebab sticks. Mix the orange juice and soy sauce together in a small bowl and brush over the kebabs. Leave to marinate for 15 minutes, brushing with the remaining orange juice mixture at least once more.

3 Arrange the salad leaves on a serving platter with the reserved halved tomatoes, mango chunks, the cucumber batons and the spring onions.

4 Preheat the grill to high and line the grill rack with foil. To make the dressing, mix the yogurt, soy sauce and grated orange rind together in a small bowl and reserve.

5 Place the salmon kebabs on the grill rack, brush again with the marinade and grill for 5–7 minutes, or until the salmon is cooked. Turn the kebabs over halfway through cooking and brush with any remaining marinade.

6 Divide the prepared salad between 4 plates, top each with a kebab, and then drizzle with the dressing.

Cherry with Brandy Jam

Makes about 2.25 kg/5 lb

ingredients

- 1.8 kg/4 lb dark cherries, such as Morello, rinsed and stoned
- 125 ml/4 fl oz freshly squeezed lemon juice or 1½ tsp citric or tartaric acid
- 150 ml/5 fl oz water (optional)
- 1.25 kg/2 lb 12 oz granulated sugar
- 1 tsp butter
- 4 tbsp brandy
- 225 ml/8 fl oz liquid pectin

1 Roughly chop the cherries and place in a large preserving pan with the lemon juice. If using citric or tartaric acid, add to the pan with the water. Place the pan over a gentle heat, cover and simmer gently for 20 minutes, or until the cherries have collapsed and are very soft.

2 Add the sugar and heat, stirring frequently, until the sugar has completely dissolved. Add the butter and brandy, bring to the boil and boil rapidly for 3 minutes. Remove from the heat and stir in the pectin.

3 Leave to cool for 10 minutes then pot into warmed sterilized jars and cover the tops with waxed discs. When completely cold, cover with cellophane or lids, label and store in a cool place.

Fruity Apple Chutney

Makes about 3.5 kg/7 lb 10 oz

ingredients

- 900 g/2 lb Bramley apples, peeled, cored and chopped
- 450 g/1 lb onions, chopped
- 450 g/1 lb ripe plums, rinsed, stoned and chopped
- rind and juice of 2 lemons (preferably unwaxed and organic), scrubbed
- 225 g/8 oz fresh cranberries (if fresh are unavailable, use dried)
- 450 g/1 lb soft brown sugar
- 4 kiwi fruit, peeled and sliced
- 450 ml/16 fl oz malt vinegar
- 2 tbsp balsamic vinegar

1 Place the apples, onions and plums in a preserving pan with the lemon rind, juice and cranberries. Cook over a gentle heat, stirring frequently, for 12 minutes, or until the cranberries are beginning to 'pop'.

2 Stir in all the remaining ingredients and heat gently, stirring occasionally, until the sugar has completely dissolved. Bring to the boil, then reduce the heat and simmer for 35–40 minutes, or until a thick consistency is reached.

3 Remove from the heat, leave to cool slightly then pot into warmed sterilized jars. Cover with non-metallic lids, label and store in a cool place.

Spiced Tea-soaked Dried Fruit Salad

Serves 8

ingredients

- 175 g/6 oz dried apricots
- 100 g/3½ oz dried apple rings, chopped
- 100 g/3½ oz dried pears
- 100 g/3½ oz sultanas
- 100 g/3½ oz dried cherries
- 5 lemon-ginger tea bags
- several strips freshly pared lemon peel
- 2 cinnamon sticks
- 2 star anise

to serve

- Greek-style yogurt
- sliced banana (optional)
- honey (optional)

1 Put the dried fruit and the tea bags in a heatproof bowl and pour over enough boiling water to cover the fruit by 2.5 cm/1 inch. Set aside and leave the fruit to stew in the water for at least 2 hours, but ideally overnight, stirring occasionally.

2 Tip the fruit and any remaining soaking liquid, the lemon peel, cinnamon stick and star anise into a saucepan over a medium heat. If necessary add extra water so the fruit is just covered and simmer for 10–20 minutes until the fruit is plump and soft.

3 Remove the pan from the heat and leave the fruit and liquid to cool. Transfer to an airtight container, seal and store in the fridge for up to two weeks.

4 To serve, spoon the fruit into a bowl and top with yogurt. Add some sliced banana and honey, if using.

Summer Fruit Slush

Serves 2

ingredients

- 4 tbsp orange juice
- 1 tbsp lime juice
- 100 ml/3½ fl oz sparkling water
- 350 g/12 oz frozen summer fruits (such as blueberries, raspberries, blackberries and strawberries)
- 4 ice cubes

1 Pour the orange juice, lime juice and sparkling water into a blender and blend gently until combined.

2 Add the summer fruits and ice cubes and blend until a slushy consistency has been reached.

3 Pour the mixture into glasses and serve.

Fruit Crudités with Chocolate Sauce

Serves 4

ingredients

- 200 g/7 oz good-quality plain chocolate, at least 60% cocoa solids
- 12 fresh strawberries
- 2 fresh pineapple rings
- 1 orange
- 1 large banana
- 4 tbsp semi-skimmed milk, at room temperature

1 Break the chocolate into a heatproof bowl that will fit snugly over a small saucepan on the hob so that when you put 2 cm/¾ inch water in the saucepan, the base of the bowl doesn't touch the water. Set the bowl over the saucepan and heat the water to a slow simmer. Leave the chocolate, undisturbed, to melt very slowly - this will take about 10 minutes.

2 Meanwhile, prepare the fruit. Hull the strawberries and, if large, halve. Remove the central core from the pineapple rings and cut the flesh into chunks. Peel the orange, and remove all the pith. Cut the flesh into segments. Peel the banana and cut into 4-cm/1½-inch chunks. Arrange the fruit on a platter.

3 When the chocolate has melted, remove the bowl from the saucepan and stir in the milk. Pour the sauce into a serving bowl and serve with the fruit for dipping.

Tarte au Citron

Serves 6–8

ingredients

- grated rind of 2–3 large lemons
- 150 ml/5 fl oz lemon juice
- 100 g/3½ oz caster sugar
- 125 ml/4 fl oz double cream or crème fraîche, plus extra to serve
- 3 large eggs
- 3 large egg yolks
- icing sugar, for dusting
- fresh whole raspberries, to serve

for the pastry

- 175 g/6 oz plain flour, plus extra for dusting
- ½ tsp salt
- 115 g/4 oz cold unsalted butter, diced
- 1 egg yolk beaten with 2 tbsp ice-cold water

1 To make the pastry, sift the flour and salt into a large bowl. Add the butter and rub it in with your fingertips until the mixture resembles fine breadcrumbs. Add the egg yolk and water and stir to mix to a dough.

2 Gather the dough into a ball, wrap in clingfilm and leave to chill for at least 1 hour.

3 Preheat the oven to 200°C/ 400°F/ Gas Mark 6. Roll the dough out on a lightly floured work surface and use to line a fluted tart tin measuring 23–25 cm/ 9–10 inches in diameter with a removable base. Prick the base of the pastry all over with a fork and line with baking paper and baking beans.

4 Bake for 15 minutes until the pastry looks set. Remove the paper and beans. Reduce the oven temperature to 190°C/375°F/Gas Mark 5.

5 Beat the lemon rind, lemon juice and sugar together until blended. Slowly beat in the cream, then beat in the eggs and yolks, one by one.

6 Set the pastry case on a baking sheet and pour in the filling. Transfer to the preheated oven and bake for 20 minutes until the filling is set.

7 Leave to cool completely on a wire rack. Dust with icing sugar and serve with whole raspberries.

Berry Yogurt Ice Cream

Serves 4

ingredients

- 125 g/4½ oz raspberries
- 125 g/4½ oz blackberries
- 125 g/4½ oz strawberries
- 1 large egg
- 175 ml/6 fl oz Greek yogurt
- 125 ml/4 fl oz red wine
- 2¼ tsp powdered gelatine
- fresh berries, to decorate

1 Place the raspberries, blackberries and strawberries in a blender or food processor and process until a smooth purée forms. Rub the purée through a sieve into a bowl to remove the seeds.

2 Break the egg and separate the yolk and white into separate bowls. Stir the egg yolk and yogurt into the berry purée and set the egg white aside.

3 Pour the wine into a heatproof bowl set over a saucepan of water. Sprinkle the gelatine on the surface of the wine and leave to stand for 5 minutes to soften. Heat the pan of water and simmer until the gelatine has dissolved. Pour the mixture into the berry purée in a steady stream, whisking constantly. Transfer the mixture to a freezerproof container and freeze for 2 hours, or until slushy.

4 Whisk the egg white in a spotlessly clean, grease-free bowl until very stiff. Remove the berry mixture from the freezer and fold in the egg white. Return to the freezer and freeze for 2 hours, or until firm. To serve, scoop the berry yogurt ice into glass dishes and decorate with fresh berries of your choice.

Orange Sorbet

Serves 4

ingredients

- 500 ml/18 fl oz water
- 200 g/7 oz caster sugar
- 4 large oranges
- 2 tbsp orange liqueur, such as Cointreau

1 Heat the water and sugar in a saucepan over a low heat, stirring, until dissolved. Boil without stirring for 2 minutes. Pour into a heatproof bowl. Cool to room temperature.

2 Grate the rind from 2 oranges and extract the juice. Extract the juice from 2 more oranges. Mix the juice and rind in a bowl, cover with clingfilm and reserve. Discard all the squeezed oranges. Stir the orange juice, grated rind and orange liqueur into the cooled syrup. Cover with clingfilm and leave to chill for 1 hour. Transfer to an ice cream machine and churn for 15 minutes.

3 If you do not have an ice cream machine, place the mixture in a freezerproof container. Freeze for 1 hour, then transfer to a bowl. Beat to break up the crystals, then return it to the freezerproof container and freeze for 30 minutes. Repeat twice more, freezing for 30 minutes and whisking each time.

4 Divide the frozen sorbet between 4 bowls and serve immediately.

Fruit & Nut Squares

Makes 9

ingredients

- 115 g/4 oz unsalted butter, plus extra for greasing
- 2 tbsp honey
- 1 egg, beaten
- 85 g/3 oz ground almonds
- 115 g/4 oz no-soak dried apricots, finely chopped
- 55 g/2 oz dried cherries
- 55 g/2 oz toasted chopped hazelnuts
- 25 g/1 oz sesame seeds
- 85 g/3 oz rolled oats

1 Lightly grease an 18-cm/7-inch shallow, square baking tin with butter. Beat the remaining butter with the honey in a bowl until creamy, then beat in the egg with the almonds.

2 Add the remaining ingredients and mix together. Press into the prepared tin, ensuring that the mixture is firmly packed. Smooth over the top.

3 Bake in a preheated oven, 180°C/350°F, for 20–25 minutes or until firm to the touch and golden brown.

4 Remove from the oven and allow to cool for 10 minutes before marking into squares. Cool completely before removing from the tin. Store in an airtight container.

Rhubarb & Orange Crumble

Serves 6

ingredients

- 500 g/1 lb 2 oz rhubarb
- 500 g/1 lb 2 oz cooking apples
- grated rind and juice of 1 orange
- ½–1 tsp ground cinnamon
- 85 g/3 oz light soft brown sugar

for the topping

- 225 g/8 oz plain flour
- 125 g/4½ oz unsalted butter or margarine
- 125 g/4½ oz light brown sugar
- 40–55 g/1½–2 oz toasted chopped hazelnuts
- 2 tbsp demerara sugar (optional)

1 Preheat the oven to 200°C/400°F/Gas Mark 6. Cut the rhubarb into 2.5-cm/1-inch lengths and place in a large saucepan.

2 Peel, core and slice the apples and add to the rhubarb, together with the grated orange rind and juice. Bring to the boil, lower the heat and simmer for 2–3 minutes until the fruit softens.

3 Add the cinnamon and sugar to taste and turn the mixture into an ovenproof dish, so it is not more than two-thirds full.

4 Sift the flour into a bowl and rub in the unsalted butter or margarine until the mixture resembles fine breadcrumbs (this can be done by hand or in a food processor). Stir in the sugar, followed by the nuts.

5 Spoon the crumble mixture evenly over the fruit in the dish and lightly smooth the top. Sprinkle with demerara sugar, if liked.

6 Cook in the preheated oven for 30–40 minutes until the topping is browned. Serve hot or cold.

Chapter 9
Baking

Introduction

There is nothing like the aroma of freshly baked bread, pastry, cakes and biscuits to stimulate the appetite. Baking these items for yourself is very satisfying, and the mouthwatering aromas will prove to be an irresistible temptation for your family and friends.

Making bread at home

Making your own bread does not have to be difficult – anyone can make delicious loaves and rolls with the minimum of effort. The key to making perfect bread is to use the right ingredients at the right temperature. Always use strong bread flour rather than ordinary flour: bread flour has a higher gluten content than ordinary flour, which increases the elasticity of the dough. You can use any of the different kinds of yeast, but each has a different method for breadmaking. You will also need to use the correct quantities: 15 g/½ oz fresh yeast or 1 tbsp dried yeast is enough to make 750 g/1 lb 10 oz strong bread flour rise. When you add water, make sure it is tepid because if it is too hot it will kill the yeast.

Fresh yeast
Crush this in a jug with a little warm water, then cover and leave it to stand until the surface starts to bubble.

Dried yeast
Sprinkle the dried yeast over a little warm water in a jug, then stir in a pinch of sugar. Cover and leave to stand until it froths.

Easy-blend dried yeast
Mix this yeast straight into the flour before the warm water is added.

Yeast

Key techniques for making dough

Making the perfect dough can be straightforward, but it is important to follow a certain procedure to achieve good results every time.

Knocking back

This process is also known as 'punching down'. After letting the dough rise for the first time for about an hour, simply punch your fist into the risen dough so that it collapses and releases the air. Then turn the dough out on to a floured work surface (some of it may need scraping out) and knead it for about 1 minute until it has lost its cold feel and has an even temperature.

Proving

This stage literally means proving that the yeast is still active. To do this, after knocking back the dough, divide and shape it as required (see below). Cover and leave it to rise for a second (but shorter) time, until the dough has doubled in size.

Baking and storing bread

The dough will keep, covered, in the refrigerator for up to a day before baking. To bake the bread, you will need a hot oven, so make sure you preheat it beforehand. Underbaked bread has a moist, doughlike consistency and flavour, so it is always better to overbake if necessary. To test if the bread is properly baked, remove it from the oven, turn it out of its tin, and use your knuckles to give it a sharp tap on the bottom. If it sounds hollow, the bread is done. It it does not, return it to the oven and bake for another 5 minutes or until the bread is properly baked. When it is done, remove from the oven and leave to cool on a wire rack. If you want a soft crust, cover the loaf with a clean tea towel while it is cooling. Freshly baked bread will keep, covered, for 2–3 days at room temperature, but no longer because it has no added preservatives. You can also keep it wrapped in the refrigerator for up to a week, or wrap it in a freezer bag and freeze it for up to a month.

Mixing

To mix the dough, sift the flour and salt into a mixing bowl. Make a well in the centre, then add the yeast. Pour in hand-hot water, then gradually pull in the flour from the edges and mix together, adding more hand-hot water as necessary in order to form a soft dough.

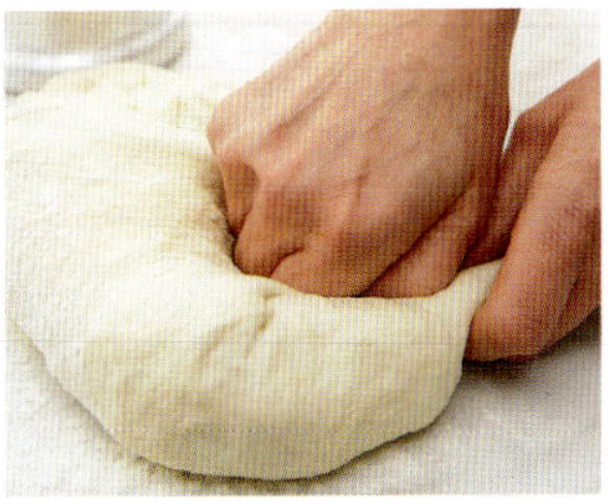

Kneading

This process is necessary in order to make the dough smooth and increase its elasticity. To knead the dough, push your hand into it, then stretch it away from you. Pick up the furthest end of the dough and pull it back to the top, then turn the dough 45° and repeat the kneading action away from you. Keep turning the dough 45° and repeating the kneading action. The kneading process usually takes around 5 minutes. To save time and effort, you could use a standing mixer or food processor with a dough hook to mix and knead the dough for you. Kneading will take about 3 minutes if you do it this way.

Rising

After the dough has been kneaded, place it in an oiled bowl, cover it with clingfilm and put it in a warm place, such as an airing cupboard. Leave it to rise to about double its original size.

Shaping

To shape the dough correctly for a loaf tin, use your hands to form the dough into an oval, then bring over the two short sides to the centre, turn the dough over and transfer, seam-side down, to a greased loaf tin. To make rolls, simply use your hands to roll even-sized pieces of the dough into balls, and then place them on a greased baking sheet.

Making pastry

Pastry is very versatile and lends a professional finish to a wide range of savoury and sweet dishes. Choose your pastry to match the occasion: shortcrust pastry for savoury or sweet pies, flans and tartlets; choux pastry for profiteroles and eclairs; paper-thin filo pastry for savoury pancake rolls or sweet apple strudel; or puff pastry for sausage rolls and a range of desserts.

Shortcrust pastry

This recipe will make enough pastry to line a 20-cm/8-inch flan tin.

175 g/6 oz plain flour, plus extra for dusting
90 g/3½ oz butter, diced
2–3 tbsp cold water

1.To make the pastry, sift the flour.
2. Use your fingertips to rub in the butter until the mixture resembles fine breadcrumbs. Gradually mix in enough water to make a soft dough.
3. Use your hands to shape the dough into a ball. Cover with clingfilm and refrigerate before use. When you are ready to use it, turn it out onto a lightly floured work surface.
4. Use a rolling pin to roll it out to the desired thickness.

Variation: To make a sweet shortcrust pastry, stir 1 tablespoon of caster sugar into the flour after sifting, and replace half the water with 2 beaten egg yolks.

1

2

3

4

Choux pastry

This quantity will make about 24 round choux buns.

185 ml/6½ fl oz water
75 g/2¾ oz butter
115 g/4 oz plain flour
½ tsp salt
½ tsp icing sugar
3 eggs

1. Preheat the oven to 200°C/400°F/Gas Mark 6. Pour the water into a saucepan and add the butter. Gently bring to the boil. Sift the flour and salt into a bowl, then mix in the sugar. In a separate bowl, beat the eggs.
2. When the butter is just beginning to boil, remove from the heat and stir in the flour mixture. Continue to stir until smooth, then return to the heat and stir until the mixture begins to pull away from the sides of the saucepan. Remove from the heat and gradually beat in the eggs until the mixture forms a thick, glossy paste.
3. Put 24 rounded spoonfuls of the mixture onto greased baking sheets and brush the tops with a little beaten egg. Bake in the preheated oven for 20 minutes, or until golden. Remove from the oven and cool.

Serving suggestion: Split the cooled buns in half horizontally and sandwich with whipped cream. You can also brush melted chocolate over the tops and leave to cool, or serve with a chocolate sauce.

Making cakes and biscuits

For cakes and biscuits there are four basic methods of mixing, as follows:

Creaming

This is a good method for making light sponge cakes. Simply beat the butter and sugar together until light, then beat in the eggs and fold in the flour. Use softened butter or margarine for this method.

All-in-one

This method saves time and effort when making light sponge cakes, and can be done manually or in a machine. Put all the ingredients into a mixing bowl and beat well until smooth. Alternatively, put the ingredients into a free-standing mixer or food processor and beat on slow speed for 2–3 minutes until the mixture is smooth.

Rubbing in

This method is ideal for scones and teabreads. Use your fingertips to rub the butter into the flour until it resembles fine breadcrumbs. Then mix in the sugar, egg and any other liquid ingredients. Stir in the flour from the sides of the bowl.

Melting

Use this method for moist cakes and biscuits. Melt the butter in a saucepan along with the sugar and any other dissolvable ingredients. Remove from the heat and allow to cool slightly. Meanwhile, sift the flour into a bowl and make a well in the centre. Beat together the eggs and milk and pour into the well, then add the egg mixture. Stir in the flour from the sides of the bowl.

Basic sponge mixture

This recipe will make enough for two 20-cm/8-inch greased and lined sandwich tins.

225 g/8 oz unsalted butter, softened, or soft margarine suitable for baking
225 g/8 oz caster sugar
4 eggs
225 g/8 oz self-raising flour, sifted
2 tsp baking powder
pinch of salt

1. Preheat the oven to 190°C/375°F/Gas Mark 5. Grease and line the sandwich tins. Put the butter or margarine in a large bowl, then add the sugar and use a wooden spoon to beat together until the mixture is smooth and light. Gradually beat in the eggs, making sure that the mixture stays smooth throughout.
2. In a separate bowl, sift together the flour, baking powder and salt, then fold into the egg mixture in a figure-of-eight movement. Divide the mixture between the sandwich tins and bake for about 25 minutes until golden and risen. Remove from the oven and leave to cool in the tins for about 5 minutes before turning out onto a wire rack to cool completely.

Variation: To make a chocolate-flavoured version of this sponge, replace 1 tablespoon of the self-raising flour with 1 tablespoon of cocoa powder.

Butter shortbread

This recipe makes 8 large pieces of shortbread or 16 smaller pieces.

125 g/4½ oz unsalted butter, softened, plus extra for greasing
175 g/6 oz plain flour
40 g/1½ oz rice flour
50 g/1¾ oz caster sugar, plus extra for sprinkling

1. Preheat the oven to 160°C/325°F/Gas Mark 3. Grease a 20-cm/8-inch loose-bottomed flan tin. Sift the plain flour and rice flour into a large mixing bowl.
2. In a separate bowl, cream together the butter and caster sugar, then stir in the sifted flours. Put the mixture into the prepared flan tin and smooth the surface. Lightly sprinkle over some caster sugar, then prick all over the surface using a fork. Using a sharp knife, score the surface into 8 wedges (or 16 smaller wedges, if preferred), then bake in the preheated oven for 30 minutes, or until lightly golden.
3. Remove the cooked shortbread from the oven and leave to cool in the tin for 5 minutes. Carefully slide the shortbread out of the tin, then use a sharp knife to cut along the score marks and divide the shortbread into wedges. Leave to cool on a wire rack, then serve immediately or store in an airtight container for up to a week.

Mixed Seed Bread

Makes 1 medium loaf

ingredients

- 375 g/13 oz strong white bread flour, plus extra for dusting
- 125 g/4½ oz rye flour
- 1½ tbsp skimmed milk powder
- 1½ tsp salt
- 1 tbsp light brown sugar
- 1 tsp easy-blend dried yeast
- 1½ tbsp sunflower oil, plus extra for greasing
- 2 tsp lemon juice
- 300 ml/10 fl oz hand-hot water
- 1 tsp caraway seeds
- ½ tsp poppy seeds
- ½ tsp sesame seeds

for the topping

- 1 egg white
- 1 tbsp water
- 1 tbsp sunflower seeds or pumpkin seeds

1 Place the flours, milk, salt, sugar and yeast in a large bowl. Pour in the oil and add the lemon juice and water. Stir in the seeds and mix well to make a smooth dough.

2 Turn the dough out onto a lightly floured work surface and knead for 10 minutes, or until the dough is smooth and elastic. Place the dough in an oiled bowl, cover with clingfilm and leave in a warm place to rise for 1 hour, or until it has doubled in size.

3 Oil a 900-g/2-lb loaf tin. Turn the dough out onto a lightly floured work surface and knead for 1 minute until smooth. Shape the dough the length of the tin and three times the width. Fold the dough into three lengthways and place it in the tin with the join underneath. Cover and leave in a warm place for 30 minutes until it has risen above the tin.

4 Preheat the oven to 220°C/425°F/Gas Mark 7. For the topping, lightly beat the egg white with the water to make a glaze. Just before baking, brush the glaze over the loaf, then gently press the sunflower seeds or pumpkin seeds all over the top.

5 Bake in the oven for 30 minutes, or until firm and golden brown. Test that the loaf is cooked by tapping it on the bottom – it should sound hollow. Transfer the loaf to a wire rack to cool completely before serving.

Bagels

Makes 12

ingredients

- 1 tbsp easy-blend dried yeast
- 2 tbsp sugar
- 3½ tbsp vegetable oil, plus extra for oiling
- 1 tsp salt
- 225 ml/8 fl oz warm water
- 425 g/15 oz plain flour, plus extra for dusting
- 1 egg, beaten
- 1 egg, beaten with ¼ tsp salt, for glazing
- poppy and sesame seeds, for sprinkling

for the filling

- smoked salmon
- cream cheese

1 Combine the yeast and half the sugar in a small bowl. Heat the remaining sugar, oil, salt and water in a small saucepan for 1–2 minutes, or until warm and the sugar has dissolved. Pour into the yeast mixture, cover with a tea towel and leave to stand for 5–7 minutes, or until the mixture begins to bubble. Put the flour into a food processor and, with the machine running, pour in the yeast mixture, then add the egg and process until a ball of dough forms. Add a little more flour if the dough is sticky – it should be smooth and elastic.

2 Lightly oil a large bowl and add the ball of dough, turning to coat on all sides to prevent a crust from forming. Cover with the tea towel and leave to rise in a warm place for 1½–2 hours, or until doubled in size. Turn out onto a lightly floured work surface. Knead lightly to deflate.

3 Divide the dough into 12 equal-sized pieces. Roll each into a rope about 18 cm/7 inches long and shape into a ring. Wet one end and press firmly to seal. Arrange on a floured baking tray, cover with the tea towel and leave to rise for 25 minutes, or until doubled in size.

4 Meanwhile, preheat the oven to 200°C/400°F/Gas Mark 6. Lightly oil 2 large baking trays. Bring a large saucepan of water to the boil. Working in batches, slide a few bagels into the water and cook for 1 minute. Remove with a slotted spoon and drain on paper towels. Arrange the bagels on the baking trays and carefully brush with the egg mixture. Sprinkle half with sesame seeds and the remainder with poppy seeds. Bake for 12–15 minutes, or until golden and shiny. Remove and place on a wire rack to cool slightly. Serve warm with smoked salmon and cream cheese.

Sourdough Bread

Makes 2 loaves

ingredients

- 450 g/1 lb wholemeal flour
- 4 tsp salt
- 350 ml/12 fl oz lukewarm water
- 2 tbsp black treacle
- 1 tbsp vegetable oil, plus extra for brushing
- plain flour, for dusting

for the sourdough starter

- 85 g/3 oz wholemeal flour
- 85 g/3 oz strong white bread flour
- 55 g/2 oz caster sugar
- 250 ml/8 fl oz milk

1 First, make the starter. Put the flours, sugar and milk into a non-metallic bowl and beat well with a fork. Cover with a damp tea towel and leave to stand at room temperature for 4–5 days, until the mixture is frothy and smells sour.

2 Sift the flour and half the salt together into a bowl and add the lukewarm water, treacle, vegetable oil and sourdough starter. Mix well with a wooden spoon until a dough begins to form, then knead with your hands until it leaves the side of the bowl. Turn out onto a lightly floured surface and knead for 10 minutes, until smooth and elastic.

3 Brush a bowl with oil. Form the dough into a ball, put it in the bowl and put the bowl into a plastic bag or cover with a damp tea towel. Leave to rise in a warm place for 2 hours, until the dough has doubled in volume.

4 Dust 2 baking sheets with flour. Mix the remaining salt with 4 tbsp of water in a bowl. Turn out the dough on to a lightly floured surface and knock back with your fist, then knead for a further 10 minutes. Halve the dough, shape each piece into an oval and place the loaves on the prepared baking sheets. Brush with the salt water glaze and leave to stand in a warm place, brushing frequently with the glaze, for 30 minutes.

5 Preheat the oven to 220°C/425°F/Gas Mark 7. Brush the loaves with the remaining glaze and bake for 30 minutes, until the crust is golden brown and they sound hollow when tapped on the base with your knuckles. If it is necessary to cook them for longer, lower the oven temperature to 190°C/375°F/Gas Mark 5. Transfer to wire racks to cool.

Crusty White Bread

Serves 4

ingredients

- 1 egg
- 1 egg yolk
- hand-hot water, as required
- 500 g/1 lb 2 oz strong white bread flour, plus extra for dusting
- 1½ tsp salt
- 2 tsp sugar
- 1 tsp easy-blend dried yeast
- 25 g /1 oz butter, diced
- sunflower oil, for greasing

1 Place the egg and egg yolk in a jug and beat lightly to mix. Add enough hand-hot water to make up to 300 ml/10 fl oz. Stir well.

2 Place the flour, salt, sugar and yeast in a large bowl. Add the butter and rub it in with your fingertips until the mixture resembles breadcrumbs. Make a well in the centre, add the egg mixture and work to a smooth dough.

3 Turn the dough out onto a lightly floured work surface and knead for 10 minutes, or until the dough is smooth and elastic. Place the dough in an oiled bowl, cover with clingfilm and leave in a warm place to rise for 1 hour, or until it has doubled in size.

4 Oil a loaf tin. Turn the dough out onto a lightly floured surface and knead for 1 minute until smooth. Shape the dough the length of the tin and three times the width. Fold the dough into three lengthways and place it in the tin with the join underneath. Cover and leave in a warm place for 30 minutes until it has risen above the tin.

5 Preheat the oven to 220°C/ 425°F/ Gas Mark 7. Bake in the oven for 30 minutes, or until firm and golden brown. Test that the loaf is cooked by tapping it on the bottom – it should sound hollow. Transfer to a wire rack to cool completely before serving.

Wholemeal Harvest Bread

Makes 1 small loaf

ingredients

- 225 g/8 oz strong wholemeal bread flour, plus extra for dusting
- 1 tbsp skimmed milk powder
- 1 tsp salt
- 2 tbsp soft brown sugar
- 1 tsp easy-blend dried yeast
- 1½ tbsp sunflower oil, plus extra for greasing
- 175 ml/6 fl oz hand-hot water

1 Place the flour, milk, salt, sugar and yeast in a large bowl. Pour in the oil and add the water, then mix well to make a smooth dough.

2 Turn the dough out onto a lightly floured work surface and knead for 10 minutes, or until the dough is smooth. Place the dough in an oiled bowl, cover with clingfilm and leave in a warm place to rise for 1 hour, or until it has doubled in size.

3 Oil a 900-g/2-lb loaf tin. Turn the dough out onto a lightly floured surface and knead for 1 minute until smooth. Shape the loaf the width of the tin and three times the length. Fold the dough into three lengthways and place it in the tin with the join underneath. Cover and leave in a warm place for 30 minutes until it has risen above the tin.

4 Preheat the oven to 220°C/425°F/Gas Mark 7. Bake in the oven for 30 minutes, or until firm and golden brown. Test that the loaf is cooked by tapping it on the bottom – it should sound hollow. Transfer to a wire rack to cool completely before serving.

Tomato & Cheese Tart

Serves 8–10

ingredients

- 125 g/4½ oz strong white flour
- 125 g/4½ oz self-raising flour
- 125 g/4½ oz chilled butter
- 1 egg yolk
- 4 tbsp cold water
- oil, for greasing
- salt
- rocket salad, to serve

for the filling

- 8–9 tomatoes, peeled, deseeded and cut in to eighths
- 150 g/5½ oz coarsely grated Emmenthal cheese
- 4 eggs
- 100 ml/3½ fl oz double cream
- 2 tbsp chopped fresh oregano or marjoram
- 1 tbsp chopped fresh chives
- salt and pepper

1 Sift the flours and salt into a bowl, then sift again to mix thoroughly. Dice the butter and work it into the flours, rubbing between your finger tips and thumb until the mixture resembles breadcrumbs. Beat together the egg yolk and water, and stir into the flour mixture with a fork. Once the dough starts to clump, knead very lightly to form a compact ball. Wrap in clingfilm and leave in the fridge for at least 30 minutes.

2 Preheat the oven to 160°C/325°F/ Gas Mark 3. Lightly grease a 28-cm/11-inch loose-based tart tin. Roll out the pastry very thinly and use to line the tin. Pass a rolling pin over the top of the tin to trim off surplus dough. Using the side of your forefinger, press the dough into the corner of the tin to raise it slightly above the rim. Line the pastry base with baking paper and weigh down with dried beans, making sure they go all the way to the edge. Bake blind for 15 minutes.

3 Arrange the tomato segments in the pastry case in concentric circles. Sprinkle the grated cheese evenly over the top. Beat the eggs lightly, then stir in the cream, oregano, chives and salt and pepper. Mix well, then pour into the pastry case. Return to the oven and bake for 20–25 minutes, until puffy and golden. Serve hot or warm with a rocket salad.

Leek & Onion Tartlets

Serves 6

ingredients

- butter, for greasing
- 225 g/8 oz ready-made shortcrust pastry
- plain flour, for dusting

for the filling

- 25 g/1 oz unsalted butter
- 1 onion, thinly sliced
- 450 g/1 lb leeks, thinly sliced
- 2 tsp chopped fresh thyme
- 55 g/2 oz Gruyère cheese, grated
- 3 eggs
- 300 ml/10 fl oz double cream
- salt and pepper

1 Lightly grease six 10-cm/4-inch tartlet tins with butter. Roll out the dough on a lightly floured work surface and stamp out 6 rounds with a 13-cm/5-inch cutter. Ease the dough into the tins, prick the bases and leave to chill for 30 minutes.

2 Preheat the oven to 190°C/ 375°F/ Gas Mark 5. Line the pastry cases with baking paper and baking beans, then place on a baking sheet and bake for 8 minutes. Remove the baking paper and beans and bake for a further 2 minutes. Transfer the tins to a wire rack to cool. Reduce the oven temperature to 180°C/350°F/Gas Mark 4.

3 Meanwhile, make the filling. Melt the butter in a large, heavy-based frying pan. Add the onion and cook, stirring constantly, for 5 minutes, or until softened. Add the leeks and thyme and cook, stirring, for 10 minutes, or until softened. Divide the leek mixture between the tartlet cases. Sprinkle with Gruyère cheese.

4 Lightly beat the eggs with the cream and season to taste with salt and pepper. Place the tartlet tins on a baking sheet and divide the egg mixture between them. Bake in the preheated oven for 15 minutes, or until the filling is set and golden brown. Transfer to a wire rack to cool slightly before removing from the tins and serving.

Mushroom & Spinach Puff Pastry

serves 4

ingredients

- 2 tbsp butter
- 1 red onion, halved and sliced
- 2 garlic cloves, crushed
- 225 g/8 oz open-cap mushrooms, sliced
- 175 g/6 oz baby spinach
- pinch of nutmeg
- 4 tbsp double cream
- 225 g/8 oz prepared puff pastry
- plain flour, for dusting
- 1 egg, beaten
- 2 tsp poppy seeds
- salt and pepper

1 Preheat the oven to 200°C/400°F/ Gas Mark 6. Melt the butter in a frying pan. Add the onion and garlic and sauté for 3–4 minutes until the onion has softened.

2 Add the mushrooms, spinach and nutmeg and cook for a further 2–3 minutes. Stir in the cream, mixing well. Season to taste with salt and pepper and remove the frying pan from the heat.

3 Roll the pastry out on a lightly floured surface and cut into four 15-cm/6-inch rounds. Spoon a quarter of the filling on to one half of each round and fold the pastry over to encase the filling. Press down to seal the edges of the pastry and brush with the beaten egg. Sprinkle with the poppy seeds.

4 Place the parcels on to a dampened baking tray and cook in the preheated oven for 20 minutes until they are risen and golden brown.

5 Transfer the parcels to serving plates and serve immediately.

Frosted Carrot Cake

Serves 16

ingredients

- 175 ml/6 fl oz sunflower oil, plus extra for greasing
- 175 g/6 oz light muscovado sugar
- 3 eggs, beaten
- 175 g/6 oz grated carrots
- 85 g/3 oz sultanas
- 55 g/2 oz walnut pieces
- grated rind of 1 orange
- 175 g/6 oz self-raising flour
- 1 tsp bicarbonate of soda
- 1 tsp ground cinnamon
- ½ tsp grated nutmeg
- strips of orange zest, to decorate

for the frosting

- 200 g/7 oz full-fat soft cheese
- 100 g/3½ oz icing sugar
- 2 tsp orange juice

1 Preheat the oven to 180°C/350°F/ Gas Mark 4. Grease and line the base of a 23-cm/9-inch square cake tin.

2 In a large bowl beat together the oil, muscovado sugar and eggs. Stir in the grated carrots, sultanas, walnuts and orange rind.

3 Sift together the flour, bicarbonate of soda, cinnamon and nutmeg, then stir evenly into the carrot mixture.

4 Spoon the mixture into the prepared cake tin and bake in the preheated oven for 40–45 minutes, until well risen and firm to the touch.

5 Remove the cake from the oven and set on a wire rack for 5 minutes. Turn out onto the wire rack to cool completely.

6 For the frosting, combine the soft cheese, icing sugar and orange juice in a bowl and beat until smooth. Spread over the top of the cake and swirl with a palette knife. Decorate with strips of orange zest and serve cut into squares.

Orange Flapjack Fingers

Makes 18

ingredients

- 175 g/6 oz butter, plus extra for greasing
- 150 g/5½ oz golden syrup
- 70 g/2½ oz Demerara sugar
- 200 g/7 oz medium rolled oats
- 70 g/2½ oz plain wholemeal flour
- 70 g/2½ oz raisins or sultanas
- finely grated rind of 1 large orange

1 Preheat the oven to 180°C/375°F/Gas Mark 4. Grease a shallow 25 x 20-cm/10 x 8-inch baking tin, then line the base and sides with baking paper.

2 Put the butter, golden syrup and sugar into a saucepan over a high heat and stir until the butter and syrup have melted and the sugar has dissolved, then bring to the boil without stirring.

3 Put the oats, flour, raisins and orange rind into a large, heatproof mixing bowl. Pour in the butter mixture and mix all the ingredients together. Tip the mixture into the tin and use the back of a wooden spoon to spread it evenly over the base of the tin and into the corners.

4 Put the tin in the oven and bake for 25–30 minutes until the flapjack mixture has set. Remove from the oven, place on a wire rack and leave to cool completely.

5 When cool, invert the tin onto a chopping board. Lift off the tin and peel off the paper. Using a serrated knife, cut the slab in half lengthways, then cut each half into 2.5-cm/1-inch thick fingers. These flapjacks will remain fresh for up to a week wrapped in clingfilm or stored in an airtight container.

Traditional Apple Pie

Serves 6

ingredients

- 750 g–1 kg/1 lb 10 oz–2 lb 4 oz cooking apples
- 125 g/4½ oz brown or white sugar, plus extra for sprinkling
- ½–1 tsp ground cinnamon
- 1–2 tbsp water

for the shortcrust pastry

- 350 g/12 oz plain flour, plus extra for dusting
- pinch of salt
- 85 g/3 oz butter
- 85 g/3 oz white vegetable fat
- about 6 tbsp cold water
- milk or beaten egg, to glaze

1 To make the pastry, sift the flour and salt into a large bowl. Add the butter and fat and rub it in with your fingertips until the mixture resembles fine breadcrumbs. Add enough water to mix to a dough. Wrap the dough in clingfilm and leave to chill for 30 minutes.

2 Preheat the oven to 220°C/425°F/Gas Mark 7. Roll out almost two-thirds of the pastry thinly on a lightly floured surface and use to line a deep pie plate or shallow pie tin measuring 20–23 cm/8–9 inches in diameter.

3 Peel, core and slice the apples, then mix them with the sugar and spice and pack into the pastry case; the filling can come up above the rim. If the apples are a dry variety add a little water to moisten.

4 Roll out the remaining pastry to form a lid. Dampen the edges of the pie rim with water and position the lid, pressing the edges together firmly. Trim and crimp the edges. Use the pastry trimmings to cut out leaves or other shapes to decorate the top of the pie. Dampen the shapes and attach. Glaze the top of the pie with milk or beaten egg, make 1–2 slits in the top to let the steam escape and put the pie on a baking sheet.

5 Bake in the oven for 20 minutes, then reduce the oven temperature to 180°C/350°F/Gas Mark 4 and cook for 30 minutes, or until the pastry is a light golden brown. Serve hot or cold, sprinkled with sugar.

Chocolate Chip Muffins

Makes 12

ingredients

- 100 g/3½ oz soft margarine
- 225 g/8 oz caster sugar
- 2 large eggs
- 150 ml/5 fl oz whole-milk natural yogurt
- 5 tbsp milk
- 275 g/9½ oz plain flour
- 1 tsp bicarbonate of soda
- 175 g/6 oz plain dark chocolate chips

1 Preheat the oven to 190°C/375°F/ Gas Mark 5. Line a 12-hole muffin tin with paper cases.

2 Place the margarine and sugar in a mixing bowl and beat with a wooden spoon until light and fluffy. Beat in the eggs, yogurt and milk until combined.

3 Sift the flour and bicarbonate of soda together and add to the mixture. Stir until just blended.

4 Stir in the chocolate chips, then spoon the mixture into the paper cases and bake in the preheated oven for 25 minutes, or until a fine skewer inserted into the centre comes out clean. Leave to cool in the tin for 5 minutes, then turn out onto a wire rack to cool completely before serving.

Crunchy Peanut Biscuits

Makes 20

ingredients

- 125 g/4½ oz butter, softened, plus extra for greasing
- 150 g/5½ oz chunky peanut butter
- 225 g/8 oz granulated sugar
- 1 egg, lightly beaten
- 150 g/5½ oz plain flour
- ½ tsp baking powder
- pinch of salt
- 75 g/2¾ oz unsalted natural peanuts, chopped

1 Lightly grease 2 baking trays. Beat the butter and peanut butter together in a large mixing bowl.

2 Gradually add the granulated sugar and beat together well. Add the egg to the mixture, a little at a time, until it is thoroughly combined.

3 Sift the flour, baking powder and salt into the peanut butter mixture. Add the peanuts and bring all of the ingredients together to form a soft dough.

4 Wrap the dough in clingfilm and leave to chill for 30 minutes.

5 Preheat the oven to 190°C/375°F/Gas Mark 5. Form the dough into 20 balls and place them on to the prepared baking trays about 5 cm/2 inches apart to allow for spreading. Flatten them slightly with your hand.

6 Bake in the preheated oven for 15 minutes, or until golden brown. Transfer the biscuits to a wire rack and leave to cool.

Strawberry Petits Choux

Makes 12

ingredients

for the filling and topping

- 2 tsp powdered gelatine
- 2 tbsp water
- 350 g/12 oz strawberries
- 225 g/8 oz ricotta cheese
- 1 tbsp caster sugar
- 2 tsp crème de fraises de bois
- icing sugar, for dusting

for the petits choux

- 100 g/3½ oz plain flour
- 2 tbsp cocoa powder
- pinch of salt
- 6 tbsp unsalted butter
- 225 ml/8 fl oz water
- 2 eggs, plus 1 egg white, beaten

1 Sprinkle the gelatine over the water in a heatproof bowl. Let it soften for 2 minutes. Place the bowl over a saucepan of simmering water and stir until the gelatine dissolves. Remove from the heat.

2 Place 225 g/8 oz of the strawberries in a blender with the ricotta, sugar and liqueur. Process until blended. Add the gelatine and process briefly. Transfer the mousse to a bowl, cover with clingfilm and chill for 1–1½ hours, until set.

3 Meanwhile, make the petits choux. Line a baking tray with baking paper. Sift together the flour, cocoa powder and salt. Put the butter and water into a heavy-based saucepan and heat gently until the butter has melted.

4 Preheat the oven to 220°C/425°F/Gas Mark 7. Remove the saucepan from the heat and add the flour, cocoa powder and salt all at once, stirring well until the mixture leaves the sides of the saucepan. Leave to cool slightly.

5 Gradually beat the eggs into the flour paste and continue beating until it is smooth and glossy. Drop 12 rounded tablespoonfuls of the mixture onto the prepared baking sheet and bake for 20–25 minutes, until puffed up and crisp.

6 Remove from the oven and make a slit in the side of each petit chou. Return to the oven for 5 minutes. Transfer to a wire rack.

7 Slice the remaining strawberries. Cut the petits choux in half, divide the mousse and strawberry slices among them, then replace the tops. Dust lightly with icing sugar and place in the refrigerator. Serve within 1½ hours.

Chocolate Brownies

Makes 12

ingredients

- butter, for greasing
- 55 g/2 oz unsweetened stoned dates, chopped
- 55 g/2 oz ready-to-eat dried prunes, chopped
- 6 tbsp unsweetened apple juice
- 4 medium eggs, beaten
- 300 g/10½ oz dark muscovado sugar
- 1 tsp vanilla extract
- 4 tbsp low-fat drinking chocolate powder, plus extra for dusting
- 2 tbsp cocoa powder
- 175 g/6 oz plain flour
- 55 g/2 oz plain chocolate chips

for the icing

- 125 g/4½ oz icing sugar
- 1–2 tsp water
- 1 tsp vanilla extract

1 Preheat the oven to 180°C/350°F/ Gas Mark 4. Grease and line an 18 x 28-cm/7 x 11-inch cake tin with baking paper. Place the dates and prunes in a small saucepan and add the apple juice. Bring to the boil, cover and simmer for 10 minutes until soft. Beat to form a smooth paste, then leave to cool.

2 Place the cooled fruit in a mixing bowl and stir in the eggs, sugar and vanilla essence. Sift in 4 tablespoons of drinking chocolate, the cocoa and the flour, and fold in along with the chocolate chips until well incorporated.

3 Spoon the mixture into the prepared tin and smooth over the top. Bake in the preheated oven for 25–30 minutes until firm to the touch or until a skewer inserted into the centre comes out clean. Cut into 12 bars and leave to cool in the tin for 10 minutes. Transfer to a wire rack to cool completely.

4 To make the icing, sift the sugar into a bowl and mix with enough water and the vanilla extract to form a soft, but not too runny, icing.

5 Drizzle the icing over the chocolate brownies and leave to set. Dust with the extra chocolate powder before serving.

GLOSSARY

THIS GLOSSARY IS NOT INTENDED TO BE EXHAUSTIVE BUT TO PROVIDE A CONCISE GUIDE TO KEY TERMS THAT MAY BE UNFAMILIAR TO A BEGINNER. SOME OF THE BASIC COOKING TECHNIQUES AND INGREDIENTS, INCLUDING SEVERAL OUTLINED EARLIER IN THIS BOOK, ARE LISTED HERE FOR EASE OF REFERENCE.

A

Agar agar Thickening and setting agent made from seaweed. A vegetarian alternative to gelatine.

Al dente Italian term, literally meaning 'at the teeth', indicating desired texture of cooked pasta, soft on the outside but still firm and not over-cooked inside.

Antipasto Italian term, literally meaning 'before pasta', denoting a hot or cold starter or 'hors d'oeuvre'.

Arborio rice Medium- to long-grain type of rice, from Northern Italy, that is ideal for risotto because it absorbs liquid while retaining a firm texture.

Arrowroot Starch extract of maranta root used to thicken sauces.

Aspic Clear jelly made from clarified meat, fish or vegetable stock mixed with gelatine. It is used to glaze or protect meat, fish and other foods or for savoury dishes set in a mould.

B

Bain-marie Method of cooking ingredients where they are placed in a dish, which is in turn placed in a shallow container of water and is gently heated in an oven or on a hob. This is used to melt ingredients, such as chocolate, without burning them.

Baking powder Raising agent used in baking cakes, biscuits and breads. It usually contains bicarbonate of soda, tartaric acid and dried starch or flour for absorbing moisture.

Balsamic vinegar Dark-brown vinegar from Italy, made from fermented, reduced white grape juice, and aged in wooden barrels.

Basmati rice Small but long-grained type of rice grown in the Himalayan foothills. It is a creamy yellow with a nutty flavour and aroma.

Basting Spooning or brushing food with melted fat or stock during cooking to add flavour and colour and to prevent the food from drying out.

Bay leaf Aromatic herb used for flavouring meat, casseroles and soups, often in a bouquet garni.

Béarnaise sauce French sauce made from reduced vinegar, white wine, tarragon, black peppercorns and shallots, finished with egg yolks and butter.

Béchamel sauce Basic French, smooth white sauce made from flour stirred into a mixture of milk and butter.

Beurre manié French term meaning 'kneaded butter', a mixture of flour and softened butter, used to thicken sauces.

Bisque Thick, rich soup, made with cream and usually shellfish.

Black butter Butter cooked over a low heat until dark brown and usually flavoured with vinegar or lemon juice, capers and parsley.

Black pepper Dried whole peppercorn, which is often crushed or ground to add flavour to food.

Blanching Technique of plunging food into boiling water then placing in cold water to stop the cooking process. This is used to loosen skins, or preserve colour and flavour.

Blind baking Partially cooking a pastry case before the filling is added. This involves cooking the pastry with a foil or paper lining and weighing down with cooking weights (such as baking beans). It avoids overcooking the pastry or making its base too moist when the filling is added.

Borsch or borscht Eastern European soup made with beetroot, cabbage and/or other vegetables and served hot or cold with soured cream.

Bouillabaisse Fish stew from southern France.

Bouquet garni Small group of herbs, usually parsley, bay leaf and thyme, tied together and used to flavour soups, casseroles and stocks in cooking, but removed before serving.

Brochette Cubes of meat or fish, and vegetables, cooked on a skewer.

Buttermilk Sour-tasting liquid remaining when milk has been churned to butter. It is often used in scones and soda breads.

C

Calvados Northern French dry spirit made from distilled cider and used to flavour meat dishes.

Canapés Small appetizers, often served with drinks.

Capers Sun-dried flower buds of a shrub from the Mediterranean and parts of Asia. They need to be rinsed to remove excess salt or brine, and are used to provide a piquant flavour to sauces or condiments, or as a garnish.

Caramelizing Heating sugar until it melts and turns brown, resetting as a hard glaze, or cooking chopped fruit or vegetables in water and sugar until they brown and glaze.

Cayenne pepper Ground spice with a hot flavour, made from the flesh and seeds of chilli pepper.

Chantilly cream Sweetened whipped double cream, often flavoured with vanilla, used as a topping for desserts, or folded into custards or cream for fillings.

Chiffonade Thin strips of shredded vegetables (usually sorrel or lettuce), used raw or lightly sautéed, often as a garnish.

Chilli Chilli peppers are small, come in many varieties and are characterized by their extremely hot seeds and flesh. Their potency can be reduced by removing their seeds, but this must be done carefully. It is important to avoid touching sensitive skin or eyes when handling chillies and to wash your hands thoroughly immediately afterwards.

Chinois Conical, fine-meshed sieve used to strain soups and sauces.

Choux pastry Light, double-cooked pastry used to make cakes and buns. It has a hard, crisp exterior and a hollow inside.

Clarified butter Unsalted butter heated slowly to evaporate the water content, and then strained to separate the milk solids. The clarified butter can then be used for cooking at higher temperatures than normal butter without burning.

Compote Dish of fruit, slowly cooked whole or in sugar.

Cornflour Fine, white, powdered starch extract of maize, used to thicken sauces. To avoid it forming lumps, the cornflour should be mixed with twice its weight in cold liquid before being added to the sauce, which should be continuously stirred until it boils.

Coulis Thick and smooth fruit or vegetable sauce. It may be served hot or cold.

Court-bouillon Spiced stock commonly used for cooking fish, seafood or vegetables.

Crème anglaise French term for rich custard cream, made with sugar, egg yolks and milk and flavoured with vanilla; it is served hot or cold with dessert.

Crème fraîche French term for a thickened, tangy-flavoured cream made from pasteurized cows' milk.

Croûtons Small cubes of grilled, toasted or fried bread, which are then drained and cooled. Used to garnish salads or soups.

Crudités Raw seasonal vegetables, sometimes sliced or grated, usually served as an appetizer with a dipping sauce.

Custard A smooth mixture of eggs and milk that can be used as the basis for a savoury or sweet sauce or dish.

D

Dariole Small, steep-sided cylindrical mould for shaping pastry, or the pastry cooked in it.

Daube French dish of red meat, vegetables and seasoning, slowly braised in a red wine stock, or meat, vegetables or fish cooked in a similar way.

Dauphinoise (à la) French term referring to the method of slowly baking in an oven with cream and garlic (such as potatoes).

Descaling Removing the scales from a fish by scraping the back of a knife along its surface, from the tail to the head.

Dropping consistency Required consistency of cake mix, where it reluctantly falls from the spoon.

E

Emulsifying Combining fats (for instance, butter or oil) and vinegar or citric juices together with a binding agent such as egg yolk.

Entrecôte French term, meaning 'between the ribs', referring to a tender beef joint, cut from the sirloin.

Escalope French term for very thin slice of meat or fish, often flattened for quick cooking.

Essence or Extract Concentrated extract or oil from foods such as fish, almonds, vanilla, coffee beans, or various plants, used to flavour foods.

F

Filo pastry Very thin layers of pastry dough, often used in Greek or Middle Eastern dishes, which dry out and cook very quickly.

Fines herbes French term referring to a mixture of chopped aromatic herbs, usually chervil, tarragon, parsley and chives, used to flavour dishes.

Florentine In the style of a dish from Florence, usually referring to dishes served on a bed of cooked spinach. It is also a small biscuit of dried fruit and nuts, usually coated in chocolate on one side.

Fond French term for stock.

French dressing Cold sauce, made from olive oil and wine vinegar, seasoned with herbs and salt and pepper, and used to dress salads.

Fricassée Stew made from lightly frying white meat, such as chicken, and then cooking it in a white sauce with vegetables.

Fritter Piece of meat, fish or vegetable coated in batter and deep-fried until crisp and cooked.

Fromage frais Fresh, soft, low-fat cheese made from pasteurized cow's milk.

G

Galangal Spice related to ginger and used in south-east Asian cooking for flavour.

Garam masala Mixture of dry-roasted, ground spices, including cumin, coriander and turmeric, mixed to form a paste, or added to a dish for flavour just before the end of cooking.

Gelatine Setting agent derived from the protein of animal bones, used to set sweet or savoury jellies or thicken soups. Agar agar is a vegetarian alternative, derived from red algae.

Ghee Type of clarified butter with a nutty, caramel-like flavour, created by simmering until the milk solids turn brown. It can be used for sautéing or frying at higher temperatures than normal butter without burning.

Gluten Flour protein, which gives dough elasticity and strength when mixed with water.

Granita Italian sorbet made from sweetened syrup flavoured with coffee or liqueur and often served as a refreshment.

Gratin Any dish topped with cheese or breadcrumbs, mixed with pieces of butter and heated until crisp and brown.

Gravy Sauce made from meat juices, mixed with a stock, wine or milk and thickened with flour. Also refers to the juices remaining in the pan after meat, fish or poultry has been cooked.

Griddle Flat, shallow, cast-iron pan, usually with ridges, for cooking food on a hob.

H

Harissa North African paste with a very hot flavour, made from chillies, garlic, cumin, coriander, mint and oil. It is usually served with cou scous, and is used to flavour soups and stews.

Herbes de Provence Mixture of herbs traditionally used in the Provence region of southern France, usually consisting of basil, bay, marjoram, oregano, parsley, rosemary, tarragon and thyme.

Hoisin sauce Thick, reddish-brown, sweet and spicy Chinese sauce, made from a mixture of soya beans, garlic, chilli peppers and spices, commonly used as a table condiment or flavouring.

Hollandaise Rich, creamy and smooth sauce made from egg yolks, butter and lemon juice, and usually served on vegetables, fish or egg dishes.

Horseradish Herb grown for its leaves (for salads) and root. The pungent and spicy root is peeled and grated, and used to flavour sauces.

I

Infusing Imbuing a liquid (usually hot or boiling) with the flavours of herbs, spices, tea or coffee, by leaving them to stand in the liquid.

J

Jambalaya Spicy Creole rice dish traditionally including ham, sausage, chillies and tomatoes, but can also consist of any kind of meat, poultry or shellfish.

Julienne Shredded or thinly cut vegetables or citrus zest, commonly used as a garnish.

Jus French term for 'juice', referring to fruit or vegetable extract, or juice from meat.

K

Kedgeree Traditional British breakfast dish, originally deriving from India, consisting of rice, flaked fish (usually smoked haddock) and hard-boiled eggs.

Kneading Stretching and mixing dough by hand or mechanically, to make it smoother, softer, more elastic and pliable. The movement helps the gluten strands in the dough to stretch and enables the dough to retain gas bubbles and rise when cooked.

L

Lardons Small chunks of fatty bacon or pork fat used to flavour dishes.

Lemon grass Root used in south-east Asian (especially Thai) cooking to impart a lemon flavour to sweet or savoury dishes.

Lyonnaise (à la) French term describing dishes including chopped onions. Lyonnaise sauce is made with sautéed onions and white wine and is then st rained. It is usually served with meat or poultry dishes.

M

Mace Pungent spice made from the outer membrane of nutmeg, used to flavour various sweet and savoury dishes.

Macerating Soaking fruit in a liquid, such as brandy, to soften and add flavour.

Madeleine Small, buttery sponge cake, made with sugar, flour, butter and eggs, usually flavoured with lemon or almonds.

Marinating Soaking food in a seasoned liquid mixture, or marinade (usually containing oil, lemon or wine, herbs and spices), to tenderize and add flavour.

Marinière (à la) French term meaning 'in the style of a mariner', referring to cooking shellfish, or other seafood, in white wine and herbs. It can also refer to a dish garnished with mussels.

Mascarpone Thick, creamy and soft Italian cheese used in savoury and sweet dishes.

Mayonnaise Thick, creamy dressing made from oil, egg yolks, vinegar or lemon juice, and seasoning.

Meringue Light, sweet dessert made by beating egg whites and sugar together stiffly and baking.

Meunière (à la) French term meaning 'in the style of a miller's wife', referring to the method of cooking where the food (usually fish) is coated in flour, then shallow-fried in butter.

Mille-feuille French term for 'a thousand leaves', referring to a dessert made from puff pastry, whipped cream, jam and fruit.

Miso Paste made from soya beans and used as a flavouring in Japanese cookery, including soups, sauces and dressings.

Molasses By-product of refining sugar, molasses is a thick, dark brown syrup with a slightly bitter flavour.

Mornay sauce Béchamel sauce with grated cheese (usually Gruyère or Parmesan) added, often served with fish, egg or vegetable dishes.

Mustard Plant that has seeds with a piquant taste; used in whole, ground or powdered form as a flavouring for seasonings, dressings, sauces and accompaniments.

N

Navarin French stew made from lamb or mutton, potatoes and other vegetables.

Noodles Thin pasta strips, made with flour and water, and egg or egg yolk.

O

Olive oil Rich oil extracted from pressed olives, used for shallow frying, dressings, marinades and baking. Extra virgin olive oil is the purest form of the oil, which is taken from the first pressing of the olives.

P

Pancetta Italian bacon cured with salt and spices and used to flavour pasta, rice, soup or salad dishes.

Panna cotta Italian term meaning 'cooked cream', referring to a cold dessert made from a set custard of cream and gelatine, often flavoured with vanilla or caramel.

Papillote (en) French term meaning 'in a parcel', referring to a method of cooking food in a folded parcel of greaseproof paper to protect it from the high heat of the oven and help it retain moisture and flavour.

Parboiling Boiling food until half-cooked, in preparation for adding to other ingredients with shorter cooking times or to tenderize the food before roasting (as with potatoes).

Parmesan Hard, dry cheese, made from skimmed cow's milk, with a rich, sharp taste and used grated, usually after cooking, to flavour a dish, especially pasta and sauces.

Passata Smooth Italian-style tomato sauce.

Pasta Italian for 'paste', referring to the dough made from durum-wheat semolina, water and sometimes egg. Pasta comes in a variety of shapes and sizes and is served with sauces or soups.

Pectin Natural gelling agent extracted from ripe fruit and vegetables, and used in making jams and jellies.

Pesto Italian term meaning 'pounded', referring to a green sauce made from a blend of pine nuts, fresh basil, Parmesan cheese, garlic and olive oil. It is most commonly served with pasta or as a dressing.

Pitta bread Middle-Eastern flat, hollow bread made from white flour or wholewheat flour. It is usually served with fillings or to accompany spicy dishes and various dips.

Polenta Italian cornmeal porridge, which can be eaten hot or, when cooled and firm, fried.

Prosciutto Italian term for a ham that has been seasoned, salt-cured and air dried, and served very thinly sliced, traditionally as an appetizer.

Puréeing Grinding or mashing fruit or vegetables to form a very smooth paste; this is done manually by pressing the food through a sieve, or mechanically in a food processor or blender.

Q

Quenelle Small dumpling made from seasoned, minced meat, fish, or ground vegetables, bound with eggs and usually poached in stock.

Quiche Open pastry flan or tart, usually filled with an egg and milk custard and savoury ingredients.

Quinoa Small, bead-like grain, very rich in protein and mild in taste, which is cooked and served like rice.

R

Ragoût Thick, well-seasoned French stew consisting of meat, poultry, fish or vegetables, flavoured with wine.

Ratatouille French vegetable stew consisting of aubergines, courgettes, tomatoes, onions, sweet peppers and garlic simmered in olive oil.

Reducing Boiling an uncovered liquid, such as stock, wine or sauce, quickly to reduce its volume by evaporation, thicken it and concentrate the flavours.

Relaxing Leaving pastry to 'rest' after rolling in order to prevent it from shrinking.

Ricotta Rich, creamy, smooth Italian cheese made from ewe's milk curd, used in many Italian dishes and as a stuffing for pasta.

Rissole Sweet or savoury round pastry, filled with chopped meat or fish, and breadcrumbs, and cooked by frying or baking.

Risotto Italian rice dish, made by gradually mixing hot stock and rice during cooking so that the rice absorbs the liquid. Traditionally, arborio rice is used because of its capacity to absorb liquid and retain a firm texture.

Rösti Swiss term meaning 'crisp and golden', referring to a flat, round pancake of shredded potato, shallow fried on both sides until crisp and brown.

Rouille French term meaning 'rust', referring to a hot, chilli-flavoured red sauce usually served as a garnish with fish or fish stews.

Roulade French term, referring to a sweet or savoury rolled dish. The savoury dish may be a slice of meat, poultry or fish rolled around a stuffing, while the sweet dish is usually a filled and rolled sponge.

Roux Mixture of flour and fat, slowly cooked over a low heat, and used as a base for soups and sauces to thicken them.

S

Saffron Pungent and aromatic spice, yellow in colour, and available in whole or powdered form, which is used for colouring and flavouring dishes. The spice is derived from the stigmas of the saffron crocus and is very expensive.

Salsa Spanish and Mexican term meaning 'sauce', and specifically referring to a spicy, hot-flavoured, thick relish made from chillies and fruit, and served cold.

Salt Sodium chloride crystals, used for seasoning and preserving food. It is available in various forms, including sea salt and rock salt, from which cooking and table salt are derived.

Samosa Indian triangle-shaped pastry, filled with spiced meat or vegetables, and deep-fried.

Satay Indonesian speciality, consisting of meat, fish or poultry cubes, grilled on a skewer, and usually served with a spicy sauce.

Shortcrust pastry Crumbly pastry usually used for sweet or savoury pies and tarts.

Shucking To remove the edible part of food from its outer casing, such as removing an oyster from its shell, using a small, thick-bladed knife.

Sirloin Premium cut of tender beef, from the back, available as fillet steaks or joints for roasting.

Slaking Mixing a thickening agent with a liquid.

Smoothie Thick, smooth and cold drink made from blending fruit or vegetables, often with liquids, such as water, milk or ice cream.

Sorbet Smooth, semi-frozen water ice mixed with fruit juice or liqueur, and sometimes egg white or gelatine, and commonly served as a dessert.

Soy sauce Sauce commonly used in Chinese and Japanese cooking, made from fermented and boiled soya beans. It is used to flavour sauces, soups, marinades, meat, fish and vegetables.

Stock Flavoured, strained liquid made by cooking meat, fish, poultry and vegetables, with seasoning, in water, used for flavouring sauces, soups, stews or braised dishes.

Sweating Method of cooking ingredients, usually vegetables, in a little fat, slowly over a low heat so that they cook in their own steam without browning.

T

Tabasco sauce Hot-flavoured, spicy sauce made from Tabasco chilli peppers, vinegar and salt, and used to add flavour to sauces, meat or cocktails.

Tapenade Thick French paste made from black olives, capers, anchovies, lemon juice, olive oil and herbs, used to flavour sauces, marinades, stews, pasta or meat.

Tarte Tatin French apple tart made in a shallow dish by covering butter, sugar and apples with a pastry topping and baking until the ingredients caramelize. The tart is served upside down.

Terrine Pâté cooked in a small, fat-lined, deep-sided dish (also called terrine), and usually made from pieces of fish or meat.

Timbale Dish cooked in a mould (also called timbale), consisting of layers, usually of rice and vegetables.

Tisane Infusion of herbs in boiling water, drunk hot.

Tofu This is made from the curd of the soya bean, pressed into firm cheese-like blocks. It is bland in flavour but rich in iron and protein. Commonly used in Asian dishes, it can be cooked in soups, stir-fries, casseroles or sauces. The flavour is improved by marinating.

Turmeric Spice derived from the root of a ginger-related plant, with a yellow colour and bitter taste, used in Asian cooking to add colour and flavour.

V

Vanilla Sweet and fragrant flavouring extracted from the dried pods and seeds of the vanilla orchid, and used to flavour sweet and savoury foods.

Vichyssoise Rich and creamy soup, served cold, made from potatoes, leeks and cream, and garnished with chopped chives.

Vinaigrette Cold sauce made from a mixture of vinegar, oil and seasoning, normally used as a dressing for leaf salads or other cold dishes.

W

White sauce Basic smooth sauce, also known as Béchamel, made from flour stirred into a mixture of milk and butter.

Y

Yeast Microscopic, live fungus that converts its food, through fermentation, into carbon dioxide and alcohol and is therefore used in bread-making to make dough rise, or in brewing to make alcohol.

Z

Zabaglione Italian frothy dessert made by whisking egg yolks, wine and sugar together, while heating gently, and is served slightly warm.

Zest Fragrant outer rind of citrus fruit, grated or shredded and used to add flavour or as a garnish or decoration for a dish.

INDEX